Also by Theodore Pelagidis

WELFARE STATE AND DEMOCRACY IN CRISIS (co-edited)

Understanding the Crisis in Greece

From Boom to Bust

Revised Edition

Michael Mitsopoulos
and
Theodore Pelagidis

palgrave
macmillan

First edition published 2011
Revised edition published 2012 by
PALGRAVE MACMILLAN

Palgrave Macmillan in the UK is an imprint of Macmillan Publishers Limited,
registered in England, company number 785998, of Houndmills, Basingstoke,
Hampshire RG21 6XS.

Palgrave Macmillan in the US is a division of St Martin's Press LLC,
175 Fifth Avenue, New York, NY 10010.

Palgrave Macmillan is the global academic imprint of the above companies
and has companies and representatives throughout the world.

Palgrave® and Macmillan® are registered trademarks in the United States,
the United Kingdom, Europe and other countries.

ISBN 978–1–137–00796–4   paperback

This book is printed on paper suitable for recycling and made from fully
managed and sustained forest sources. Logging, pulping and manufacturing
processes are expected to conform to the environmental regulations of the
country of origin.

A catalogue record for this book is available from the British Library.

A catalogue record for this book is available from the Library of Congress.

10   9   8   7   6   5   4   3   2   1
21 20 19 18 17 16 15 14 13 12

Printed and bound in Great Britain by
CPI Antony Rowe, Chippenham and Eastbourne

To Georgia and to our daughter Veronica
M. M.

To Elli
T. P.

Contents

List of Figures and Tables

Figures

Tables

Part I

1
Introduction

In December 2008, downtown Athens experienced three nights of street battles, arson and looting that became headlines in the international press. The pictures of these riots brought suddenly into the spotlight the reality of a Greece that struggles and seems increasingly deprived of any positive prospects in the aftermath of the recent financial crisis, at a time that the global economy seemed to gradually recover. This picture is in sharp contrast to the constant and high growth rates of a Greece that managed to join the eurozone a decade earlier. But a closer inspection of the fast growing Greek economy in the past 15 years and the failing economy that teeters on the edge of bankruptcy and freefall today reveals that what initially appears as a unique international paradox is, in the end – and once all the details have been carefully put together – simply a rather straightforward textbook case of modern economics and political economy. That is because Greece combined until a few years ago strong economic performance – that is, rapid GDP growth and strong productivity growth – with a very poor performance and pathologies on many other fronts. These failings range from a massive public debt, poor labor/product market institutions and low competitiveness to poor environmental protection, underperforming educational system and high levels of corruption. It is all these weaknesses that, when the global credit party ended, led Greece very close to technical default and to bankruptcy.

In this context the aggregate behavior of the macroeconomy and the individual behavior of the separate agents that form the aggregate macroeconomy can be explained by existing theories. At the same time, benchmarking exercises that compare data from Greece with data from other countries are delineating a setting that can reconcile all the stylized facts that initially may have appeared as deviations from the predictions of the standard tools of economic and political analysis.

3

We show in parallel how the case of Greece is unique: the factors that contributed to the strong economic performance of the past years have made the extraction of rents even more lucrative in this documented environment of weak institutions and weak governance. Thanks to the factors that had contributed to strong growth, the weakened institutions and the predatory behavior of aggressive rent-seeking groups had not led to the expected decline of the prosperity of the economy. Such decline could have reduced the ability of these groups to reward those that support them and to actively promote their goals with the help of plentiful resources.

The facts presented furthermore dispel any hopes that the country will automatically revert to the strong growth rates of the past. They also reveal that only a determined reform effort to address the weaknesses and failings that persisted all these years will successfully solve both the urgent problems faced currently by the economy (in particular, the public sector finances) and the significant challenges faced by a severely damaged society that must also deal with the rapidly deteriorating prospects of an already weak job market in an uncompetitive economy. By describing the details of this reality we are also able to present an overview of the problems that reform-minded politicians encounter in Greece today. As a result we can lay out the facts that can help determined politicians to formulate realistic and well-targeted reform strategies.

Crucially, we aim to provide a political economy explanation of how numerous "redistributive interest groups" use the weakness as well as the "closeness" of the Greek institutions in order to increase their rents. In particular, in Chapter 2 we argue that the numerous rent-seeking groups curtail competition in the product and services markets, increase red tape and administrative burdens and actively seek to establish opacity in all administrative and legal processes. We also argue that they do so in order to form an environment in which they will be able to increase the rents they extract. At the same time we demonstrate how these groups actively seek to ensure that the "rule of law" fails to such an extent that the society will not be able to hold them accountable for their actions. In Chapter 3 we document salient aspects of the Greek political system that – when compared with similar aspects of the political systems of other countries – strongly point to the reason for Greek politicians' inability to champion reforms and effectively confront the designs of these predatory interest groups. This analysis also shows how the broad design of the political system is related to the perpetuation of the current status quo. This status quo includes the failing of the "rule of law" and the Greek judiciary as described in Chapter 4 in a context of weak governance. The latter includes both the adoption of laws that do not serve the broader interests of society well and the functioning of an executive that is at the same time not held accountable and that rationally accepts the violation of existing laws, as described in Chapter 2.

In the second part of this book we proceed with a detailed presentation of a wide range of available evidence that includes the attributes of product markets, the business environment, the impact of the EU and EMU accession together with the deregulation of key markets in a given institutional and political setting. All these elements help to explain the paradox of past strong performances coupled with weak institutions that undermine the growth prospects of the country now that the impact of the drivers of the past performance have petered out. We move on to relate one aspect of Greece's institutional failings – namely, the unfavorable business environment and uneven playing-field created by the government intervention in the functioning of product markets. We consider the weak performance of the Greek labor market, the realities faced by salaried labor with respect to self-employment, the realities of the distribution of the tax burden in Greek society and how they relate to the fragile position of Greek public finances. The second part of this book also discusses the reality faced by Greek companies with regard to their tax burden, as well as their profitability and ability to compete on the global markets. We present data that documents the coexistence of, on the one hand, restrained profitability and high and increasing prices and, on the other hand, the low competitiveness of the economy and the high administrative burden imposed by the government. Putting gradually together the pieces of the puzzle allows us to proceed further and to put in context the challenges faced by the Greek financial system and certain stylized facts of the Greek pension system. It also enables us to document the relationship between the inability of the Greek government to control its expenditure and the current fiscal challenges faced by the country. Finally, we can see how the examples of reforms introduced in other countries that had experienced severe crises could help Greece today. We also present a more detailed analysis of the harmful impact that government regulations have on the market for freight transportation and of certain government policies that impose unnecessary burdens on the Greek private sector. Finally, an analysis of the potential effect of liberalizing shop opening hours, as well as of the arguments usually used against such initiatives, constitutes a good example of how policies that could benefit the wider public are not adopted in Greece as a result of insufficient documentation and a tendency to cater to the interests of organized groups.

2
Vikings in Greece: Rents, the Design of the Greek Political System and the Blockage of Reforms

2.1 Introduction

A detailed analysis of the Greek political system, which follows in Chapter 3, shows how that system hands over unchecked and unsupervised mandates to the winners of elections in an environment of weak institutions and in the presence of strong and "wealthy" special interest groups. At the same time, the slow and malleable proceedings of the judiciary ensure that any unlawful actions usually are not persecuted efficiently. This completes the design of a system in which reform-minded politicians, who threaten the status quo, are easily removed from the political scene. Those politicians who cooperate with the interest groups are rewarded not only with long-lasting political careers, but also with immunity from prosecution against almost any unlawful acts they may engage in, even if such acts are unrelated to their office and if their immunity violated basic human rights, as demonstrated for example by Application 24895/07 filed with the European Court of Human Rights and the subsequent condemnation of the Greek government's decision. The incentives formed by the details of the existing system also can explain other aspects of the Greek political system, including the undemocratic structure of the political parties and their tendency to accommodate and propagate the corrupt practices that are widespread throughout Greek society.

A comprehensive exposé is provided by Pelagidis in Pelagidis and Mitsopoulos (2006). Pelagidis analyzes the complex interactions between the various government branches, interest groups, voters and the media in the context of the weak Greek institutions. This allows us to understand why reforms are so difficult to implement in Greece today.

2.2 Description of the players of the game

These interactions exist, among others, between mandate holders, lawmakers, bureaucracy, mandate-issuing voters and interest groups, such as the media. These groups represent some of the key players in the reality of Greek politics and the Greek economy. Each of these groups plays a given role in this power game, which results in the defense of the status quo against any reforms. In this context, it is of foremost importance to show, prove and understand that the anomalies and rigidities of the various markets in Greece's economy, such as the labor and the product markets or the serious and unfair distortions of the tax system, all have roots in what we call "a closed society." Greece is a sum of semi-closed markets, the political market itself included, where corruption and nepotism prevail. In this context government intervention and regulation that limit competition in product markets and levy fees that benefit unrelated third parties are widespread. These activities create legal – in the sense that the law prescribes them – but often immoral and unethical rents – in the sense that they harm the broad interest of society to benefit specific interest groups. In addition they are looked upon favorably by the political establishment, powerful rent-seeking groups and a society that has been trained to be suspicious of free markets and to intuitively trust any leftist rhetoric that favors government interventions, even if it is not substantiated by solid arguments. So one has to look at the roots of the "paradoxes" that fuel departures from inefficiencies and that describe a country that is internationally known for its collapsing institutions and, at the same time, a country with, until recently, one of the highest growth rates in the eurozone. We thus proceed below to an analysis regarding:

1. The groups of special interests that defend the status quo and that seek and defend legal or illegal grabs, theft and rents.
2. The role of misinformation of the rational but uninformed voter in a system that shuns transparency.
3. The role of the media as information brokers that can play a crucial role in directing the dissatisfaction of the voters and that have the capacity to make voters understand the contribution of reforms. The media are themselves victims of blackmail from the constellation of interest groups.
4. The administrative insufficiency of the state as far as the establishment of the "rule of law" is concerned.
5. The failure of the mandate-holding politician as a lawmaker.

2.3 Powerful interest groups as rent-seeking "Vikings" in Greece

The alliances and the forces that defend the status quo in Greece are exceptionally strong. This observation, which is backed up by numerous anecdotal evidence from everyday life in Greece and, in the end, by the inability to promote effectively reforms, is the starting point of any analysis of the Greek realities today. In Greece there are numerous groups that act like the Vikings, in the sense that they grab anything they can while roaming freely through various aspects of social and economic activity. At the same time the existence of pockets of rent is widespread throughout the economy as a result of government regulations that aim specifically to create such pockets of rent by the obstruction of free competition, but also by the effective reduction of transparency and accountability in the management of public money in a way that allows the proliferation of pork-barreling. These pools of rent are claimed by the many small, but well placed and organized, groups that succeed to earn significant rents, and therefore have a strong motive to maintain the status quo and oppose any reforms that will lead to the removal of these pools of rent. These groups draw a significant advantage from their small size, as they do not contain free riders that could undermine their agenda or fail to contribute actively to their interests. These groups exhaust most of their available time and power in defending a comfortable income that does not require them to provide work that is commensurate in quality and effort to this income or, in some extreme cases, that requires to provide any work at all. These groups promote legislation that will favor them, and seek new opportunities that could increase their rents. In this effort, they rationally invest time and money to influence policy makers and the administration that will pass legislation to make their rents "legal" (in the sense that the law will dictate the rents' creation, levy them on unfortunate subjects – usually individuals who work for the private sector and entrepreneurs – and then distribute these rents with "socially objective criteria" to the established beneficiaries, that is themselves).

Unlike lobbyists, these groups do not enjoy a fixed and clear position in the system. However they usually consist of formations and alliances of smaller groups that occasionally merge unofficially and ad-hoc, whenever their interests are aligned in their search for new rents and/or their defense of existing rents. It is this peculiar attribute that allows them to enjoy, on the one hand, the benefits of small size and the absence of free riders, while on the other hand, have the clout that larger constellations of such groups can muster whenever any reforms must be resisted. These groups act within the society with a "hit and run" strategy, exactly like the first Vikings, whenever they spot a pool of rent, such as an uncompetitive market for example. They also form immediately loose alliances with other groups whenever any pool of rent is threatened by a reform, as they realize that the groups whose rent they defend today will also rush to support them as soon as their pool of rent is threatened by another reform-minded politician or a European Union legislation/directive. In this process, these groups fully take advantage of both the lack of checks in the system that would allow the interested general public to object to such a raid and the meticulously established lack of transparency. The absolute lack of separation of the executive and legislative branch in Greek politics is only one attribute that has been introduced in order to remove any checks and balances from the system. Further, the fact that not all court decisions are published and thus offered to the public's scrutiny, together with the fact that the minutes of the committees of the parliament are also not published, are only basic examples of how the lack of transparency has been effectively and meticulously established in Greece. The lack of transparency is crucial to support the argument that the legislative initiatives that so blatantly favor specific groups are in place to protect the interests of the general public, which would, supposedly, suffer greatly in the case of a "neoliberal" onslaught on their basic subsistence. Transparency would reveal the sums that these groups collect without any effort or professional merit and how these sums burden the general public in order to provide an effortless and comfortable living to the members of the fortunate interest groups.

The acquisition of these rents takes any convenient form. It can be legal as long as legislation, which is passed effectively unchecked, creates a legal rent or shuns competition in a market and allocates privileged access to this market to the beneficiary interest group. And it can be illegal, in which case it often also takes the form of corruption. But it should be noted that thanks to the, again, meticulous undermining of the rule of law, the interest groups deem that illegal rents are broadly as attractive as the legal rents. In these cases of illegal activity the rent is obtained through suffocating blackmailing of the lawmakers and the executive, and blunt horse-trading with the administration, in the sense of Tullock (2005): it is taken as a given that nobody will ever report the breaking of the law and in the rare case that this happens no punishment or remedy will be enforced in any effective way.

2.4   Rationally ignorant and misinformed voters who are afraid of reform

The expression of the voice of a voter in a system that favors public debate and the incorporation of different preferences that are voiced by various participants in the debate is shunned by the Greek political system that privileges the lack of both transparency and accountability of the mandate holders in the executive and legislative branches of government. In the Greek system the maintenance of the status quo is secured as long as mandate holders are held accountable for their actions only by the strategically placed interest groups that blackmail and unofficially control elected parties, and not by the public. This control is necessary to maintain the status quo because in Greece mandate holders can promote any legislative and executive initiative without any checks from a body that represents truthfully the interests of the general public. This means that in theory it would be very easy to pass any reform and, after passing such reform, to impose legislation that reintroduces sufficient checks and balances. The only thing that guarantees that this does not happen is the entanglement of the politicians in a powerful web of special interests that threatens to end their political careers as soon as there is any indication that they favor such reforms. As a result these groups successfully create rents and ensure that the legislator adopts laws and practices that allocate these rents to the groups, at the static and dynamic loss of the general public and of outsiders who are not placed in any of these powerful groups. The losers are usually large but unorganized groups like the unemployed, low-wage earners, consumers, honest taxpayers, parents of schoolchildren and, last but not least, entrepreneurs and private sector employees who simply want to do their job well and honestly. Since lack of transparency is one of the necessary preconditions to the transfer of these rents to the beneficiaries – that is the interest groups – there is also an effort to suppress the publication of the problems faced by the general public as a result of these activities. This is especially true of the significant level of income inequality that is a result of these large transfers to so many privileged groups while society as a whole does not reap the benefits of a well working state that promotes social coherence. On certain occasions these efforts to suppress the publication of these problems and privileges becomes almost ridiculous. For example, in the past employees of the Greek parliament took over the parking spaces of journalists who are accredited to the Greek parliament because these employees thought that these journalists were responsible for the coverage that the privileges, such as the fifteenth and sixteenth salary these employees receive during any fiscal year, received in the press.

Another important ingredient of the current status quo is the fact that in Greece almost everyone participates, more or less willingly, in the shadow economy. Simple transactions, like buying a plot of land, usually entail payments of undeclared sums. This comes as a result of the very high taxes and obligatory payments to third parties and the administratively set minimum values for the taxation of property. Very often Greeks are also, de facto, forced to break the law because laws are either impossible to adhere to or have already been infringed. For example, most apartments built in the past 15 years exceed the size specified in their permit. This is because agencies that should ensure that new buildings do not exceed their legal size are corrupt. This means that anyone who desired to purchase a relatively new apartment was in effect breaking the law by buying an apartment that does not conform to its building permit, and according to recent laws has to pay a fine for this. Even other simple economic acts, such as the purchase of services from a plumber or even a doctor, often entail undeclared sums of money. The chances that a trusted plumber or doctor will provide a receipt is often low, which makes the exchange of undeclared sums of money for services provided less of an option and more of a necessity. As a result most Greeks break the law at least occasionally, which means that they are at ease with the notion of unlawful behavior. So when the time comes to exchange favors, in the sense that they will cover for the unlawful activity of someone else, they usually have a favor to ask in return. Or at least, they will have committed some unlawful act themselves at some point of time and as a result they will be afraid to come forward to denounce the illegal acts of others, even if these are much more serious than the one they have engaged in themselves. This widespread breaking of laws, even if it is minor for the majority of Greeks, is an important ingredient of the widespread resistance to reform in Greek society not only because it entrenches the perception of lawlessness and encourages further engagement in unlawful activity according to Keizer et al. (2008) and Kelling and Coles (1997). More importantly, most Greeks, when faced with a determined reformer, will quickly identify the loss they stand to incur should the rule of law suddenly apply. They find it much more difficult to relate to the promises of increased competitiveness, increased job opportunities and improvements in the quality of governance that seem more distant and uncertain, in the sense analyzed by Fernandez and Rodrik (1991).

This situation means that a resolute reform in Greece, which would inevitably include the strengthening of the rule of law, would translate into very tangible little daily personal losses for almost all Greeks. These losses will occur in a context in which the notion of "liberty" has been subject to extensive and abusive rhetoric, in the sense described by Hayek (1960). This rhetoric dismisses any rule of law as a limitation to the freedom of the individual to "do what it wants," including both the abovementioned daily small illegal acts that Greeks are almost forced to engage in and have grown accustomed to, but also acts that are socially more damaging and that may range from tax evasion and traffic violations up to pollution and sometimes even more sinister and violent acts that harm foreign property and put the lives and livelihood of others at risk. These costs are very visible; at the same time Greeks are unable at this point to visualize how they could benefit personally first, and collectively as a secondary effect, from a determined reform effort. The importance of this point is highlighted by the fact that, according to Schonhardt-Bailey (2006), the extent to which a large part of English society perceived that they would benefit from free trade, in one way or another, was one of the crucial elements that helped repeal the Corn Laws. For this to happen, the emerging English middle class had to understand how this new environment would allow them to better pursue their own aims of personal improvement. Hayek (1960), indirectly, suggests a number of reasons which make such a development much more difficult in modern Greece. One reason is that, as a result of the prevailing rhetoric, the notion of individual responsibility is largely diminished in modern Greece while almost all responsibility is delegated to the vague concept of the "state." In a setting of generalized government intervention, an ever increasing portion of the Greek population seems convinced that it has no personal responsibility and that the state has to provide for everything and to solve all the problems of the individuals that, we remind our readers, have a right to unlimited personal liberty and no moral obligation to adhere to the existing laws. Furthermore these individuals are convinced that they have no obligation to improve themselves and their lives, or to do this in a way that will benefit society too. These convictions are not totally unjustified. Since individual economic initiatives such as entrepreneurial activity are so severely restricted by government interventions and by obstacles introduced by the numerous government-sponsored interest groups, individuals have rationally formed over time a conviction that they cannot take initiatives to improve their lot themselves. They rationally turn to the omnipresent state, which determines everything and without whose consent nothing can happen, to take any initiative in spite of the failings of this state and its proven inability to solve these problems.

Individuals furthermore are justified to fear the alternative of an open society with competitive markets as they lack a good education. In other words they lack the main perquisite to take advantage of the opportunities such a setting provides and to fend off the threats that such an open and competitive environment will pose for them. We have analyzed extensively the failings of the Greek education system in Pelagidis and Mitsopoulos (2006), Mitsopoulos and Pelagidis (2007, 2008). These works have shown that these shortcomings are directly related to the prevailing equilibrium of closeness and the rent-seeking nature of the Greek economy and society. Greeks are therefore justified to fear a society that, according to Hayek (1960), distributes rewards according to merit; they seem to feel more secure in the current environment in which the state distributes rewards not according to merit, but in a rather haphazard way depending on participation in interest groups, affiliations with the political establishment and other criteria that may be favored at any particular point in time. The fact that even if the current equilibrium in the Greek educational system would change along with the current equilibrium society is still propagating, the advantages would become clear to the majority of Greeks, and especially the less privileged ones, only after a significant delay of time. Surely this does not help the majority of Greeks to visualize how they could gain themselves, or through their children, from reform.

These observations have to be complemented by the fact that voters are generally rationally not well informed, as described by Caplan (2007). In Greece, in particular, they are not able to maximize their welfare when faced with a choice of political propositions by candidates to executive and legislative positions, even if the voting public seek to maximize their welfare in any way the political system allows them to do in the sense described by Rowley (1988). This follows from, among other things, the complexity and opacity of the horse-trading game in Greek politics and the interactions of the citizen with the administration. These raise the cost of being well informed and ultimately lead to a bounded rationality of the voters, itself resulting from a lack of information that is, rationally, not acquired because of their high cost of doing so. It also results from the fact that casting a simple vote that allocates both legislative and executive power to an elected individual who essentially governs unchecked until the next elections does not allow voters to express their varying preferences regarding the maximization of their welfare in a more complex way. Instead they cast a vote on a broad bundle of propositions that does not offer the possibility to express separate opinions. Consequently, the voters do not engage in a costly, and futile, process to inform themselves.

2.5   The role of the media as an obstacle to reform

In this context the media, which are operating in an opaque and unchecked legal and institutional framework, actively engage in a game of misinforming the voters. Effectively, the media take advantage of the high cost of documenting and publicizing any misinformation; they trade their ability to guide the opinion of the uninformed public for favors from the executive, legislative and administrative powers. Given that this ability to form the opinion of voters could also be used to inform the public about the necessity and the benefits of effective reforms, the participation of the media in the constellation of interest groups that interact with the branches of government emerges as a crucial aspect of the inability of the Greek society of promote these reforms.

In the hypothetical case of *Coase Theorem*, where it would be possible to inform voters without any cost or intermediary, the media would not exist. In the real world the media gain significantly value as they contact and inform the voter. According to Tullock (1993), the role of the media is especially critical in the effort of politicians to inform (or misinform) the voter groups that they target. As a result the level of competition in the media market is crucial. Where the players in the media market are few, as is the case in dictatorships, this level of competition is largely reduced, even if the modern technology makes it more difficult to establish such media monopolies.

In modern democracies the level of competition in the media is ensured by the existence of groups with different interests and the low cost of conveying information. In such a context the decision of a politician to misinform the voters is more likely to backfire, as the voters are better informed and may more easily understand the effort to manipulate them. This is especially true if the politician attempts to misinform the voters about privileges he is about to allocate to an interest group at the expense of the interest of the general public. On the other hand, when the general public is not well informed and the media is cooperating with the effort to misinform the public and the voters, then the ability of the politicians to yield to the pressures of the interest groups increases. In the case of modern Greece the design of the political system favors the emergence of uninformed voters; the systematic removal of accountability and transparency from the activities of the legislature, the executive but also the judiciary strengthen the power of the media to an unprecedented extent. As a result it comes as no surprise that the influence of these interest groups on the political establishment has led to the entanglement of the media in a weak and distortive framework that ensures that the media groups are themselves victims of blackmail from the political system and, indirectly, from the interest groups. The media are forced to cooperate with the interest groups because of the deliberate existence of a vague legal framework that condemns the media to effectively operate illegally and the dependence, by law, of their revenue on undeclared remunerations, as well as declared revenue that is allocated, unchecked and in non-transparent ways, by the administration. Therefore the media emerge as a critical obstacle to reforms, instead of using their potential to inform the public about the necessity and benefits of reform. Their role is becoming especially critical given the omnipotence of the merged executive and legislative powers and given the lack of checks and transparency in the activities of the government and administration: the media are the essential tool that will secure the end of the career of any politician who wants to introduce reforms that threaten the various pools of rent that the interest groups benefit from.

2.6   The administration as a prize for the interest groups

The government and the administration are supposed to have the monopoly on setting the rules to form and validate contracts between the agents of society; these contracts are agreed on between the relevant parties in the framework of free and competitive markets, according to the traditional neoclassical approach. The state, according to the Chicago School and public choice are used to maximize the income and serve the interests of the most powerful groups. According to this view, the state and its mechanisms are aligned to serve the interests of each government and the broad group of private individuals that acts within its context in order to maximize its interests. It is possible that the state is simply the sum of individual bureaucrats who aim to serve their own interests, as demonstrated by Niskanen (1971), and who happen to have a strong bargaining position against legislators. These individuals also take advantage on the information they have on the implementation of public policies. According to the "institutional economists," like North, and the theory of property rights, the operation of the state enhances the security of property rights and, as a result, economic development through the reduction of transaction costs described in North (1986).

According to this approach the state, having the monopoly to set property rights, ensures that the welfare of society is maximized as this will lead to the maximization of the state's own revenues.

In Greece all these descriptions can be applied to an administration that was, in theory, established to help the arbitration of differences among individuals, to implement public policies, to rectify market failures when they occur, to reduce the transaction costs of the individuals that form the society and to enhance social coherence. This administration, which has interests of its own according to the description by Niskanen, maximizes these interests within the framework of existing laws and often also in the context of the public policies that the government promotes. It is this separation of the interests of the politician and the administrator that allows the latter to have different interests that he wants to promote. In countries like Greece the administration is not Weberian and powerful, but rather sprawling and both powerful, because of the lack of checks and transparency, and weak, because of the inability to implement policies in an environment of contradictory and vague rules paired with unorganized and badly trained enforcers. This bureaucracy is easily penetrated by the various interest groups. These groups have no trouble converting members of the administration to their cause since the abuse of the public office will generally be lucrative and go unpunished. This behavior is rational both for the interest groups and for the bureaucrats; the opportunities – in terms of extra-legal privileges, undeclared income and other legal or illegal benefits – that this behavior offers to the members of the bureaucracy that are recruited by these groups are one of the reasons why public sector employment is so desirable in Greece.

As a result the bureaucracy in Greece has evolved to be closer to the descriptions of Niskanen and the Chicago School. This evolution suits the rent-seeking groups that hire the members of the administration to align their interests. This is to the detriment of the neoclassical description of the state as a guarantor of the rules of the game and as an establisher of more effective institutions and secure property rights, similar to the description of North (1986) and Rowley (1988).

2.7   The failure of the mandate holders

In the context of the Greek political system, where the interests of the elected individuals are not aligned with those of the voters (as a result of both the way the mandates are allocated and the lack of any checks after the mandates have been issued), the agency problem emerges as very important. The mandate holders operate in an environment of weak institutions which does not incorporate open policy debates and the varying interests and opinions that any society harbors. Furthermore, the fact that these individuals are essentially unchecked in a framework that effectively suppresses transparency further enhances the differentiation of the interests of the misinformed voters from the interests of the mandate holders. Acting rationally in this context, these mandate holders aim for re-election by choosing to cooperate with the interest groups and the media they control. They also shun reforms that would benefit society as a whole. This is because such reforms would trigger the severe punishment from the interest groups and the media, which would aim to end their political careers by mustering with great speed an alliance to that purpose. The only defense against such an attack would be strong institutions that would curtail such a punishment, which often is itself unlawful, and transparency to enable voters to be informed about the true intentions of both the reform-minded politician and the resisting interest groups which constantly use their propaganda mechanisms to present their often obscene privileges as socially beneficial.

As long as any single reform-minded politician faces this orchestrated and powerful reaction, it will remain unlikely that any will choose to take the gamble to implement reforms – even though in Greece the executive power and legislature are effectively joined. Furthermore, as long as the political system offers no opportunities both to voice disagreements and to incorporate these in the official process that shapes policies, there is little chance that politicians will promote reforms through an open debate that will incorporate the true interests of society. This reality may indeed be also correlated by the fact that, as we will show in Chapter 5, the average family used to pay no income tax and only a very small proportion of the population used to pay the vast majority of income taxes; this formed a much more progressive tax system than those of Germany or France for example. Since the average voter is not a taxpayer, the incentive for politicians to misuse tax funds appears to be largely increasing, especially in the abovementioned context of the widespread acceptance of illegal conducts. In this environment, and from a political perspective, it seems reasonable to promote the design of a tax structure that puts most of the burden on a small number of high-income earners and to exempt from taxes, or accept tax evasion, for all but the highest incomes that originate with those unconnected with the political establishment and interest groups private sector professionals. Figures 2.1 and 2.2 show how the distribution

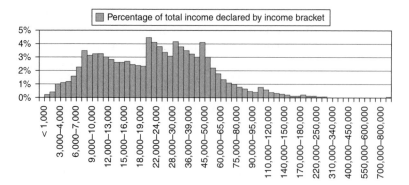

Figure 2.1   Total income declared by income bracket

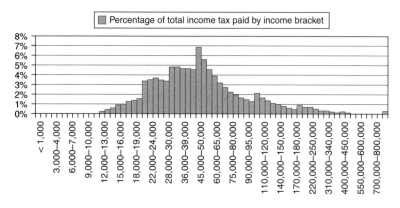

Figure 2.2   Total income tax paid by income bracket

of declared incomes was still in 2007 unusually flat in the middle and how the bulk of the income tax is paid by the higher and upper-income brackets, which comprise a smaller number of families and therefore voters. The behavior of the policymakers was thus not driven by their intention to ensure a socially just sharing of the tax burden, but rather by a blunt calculation that a policy that levies most of the income taxes on few families that are predominantly employed in the private sector, while such policy exempts more than half the population from any personal income tax, will yield, on a net basis, tangible benefits for elected individuals at the ballot box. Their rational motives and a choice between political survival and the end of their political careers are further explained by the consideration of the fate of a politician who will try to enforce income taxes on this majority of the voting population that now is not subject to any personal income tax. In Greece such politicians have been relegated to the role of simple intermediaries and brokers between the voting (and tax paying) public and the interest groups; they are now unable and unwilling to act on altruistic motives and ideology, contrary to what the Founding Fathers of the U.S. did.

The current design of the political system encourages the lack of expert support to lawmakers. This both hampers the enactment of good laws and facilitates the adoption of laws that favor interest groups. As a result the administration does not have the capacity to produce legislation that is adequate in the context of a global and competitive world market and that forces economic activity. Instead the administration is stuck in a mud of vague, contradictory and often irrational legislation that pushes up administrative costs, encourages the violation of these irrational laws, creates rents and provides the members of the administration with the ability to blackmail those who are economically active by issuing illegal remunerations and granting favors. This process can only be described as a failure of the legislature that results in high administrative costs. Any business initiative in Greece requires excessive time and costs, both legal and illegal. These costs are the revenue of the interest groups, which will of course defend them with all their powers. Meanwhile entrepreneurs that consider to incorporate these costs in their sale prices are quickly labeled by the media and the majority of the politicians as black-marketers and as guilty of "profit seeking."

The widespread corruption in Greece is, according to Transparency International, more comparable to the situation of a developing country than that observed in other members of the Organization for Economic Cooperation and Development (OECD) and the eurozone. Accordingly, public opinion toward market-oriented reforms may well be muted. Alesina and Angeletos (2005) argue that entrenched beliefs regarding redistribution may lead to increased corruption and further demands for redistribution. In an environment like that of Greece, corruption will be attributed by the voting public to the failings of markets. This will lead to demands for further government intervention to limit corruption. The reaction of the wider public in a society in which redistribution and corruption, rather than honest and talented work, often secure personal wealth is compatible with the general attitude people seem to have when they perceive that some of their peers have acquired excessive privileges in a way that is considered to be unfair. The existence of such a natural reaction is documented by studies like the one of Fehr and Gaechter (2000). They document the negative feelings that are provoked when people observe free riders, as well as their willingness to expend some of their own resources to punish the free riders and reduce their prevalence. Other works, like Zizzo and Oswald (2001), also show that humans will expend resources to harm peers that are perceived to have benefited excessively and in unjust ways. Such a process may have significant dynamic implications on an economy, as shown by Mitsopoulos (2009). It can also explain the spite with which entrepreneurial initiatives are often attacked in Greece.

In countries like Greece the vague notion prevails that individual effort and entrepreneurial activity do not create new wealth, but rather that they redistribute existing wealth and thus take it away from the public unjustly. This conviction that the market economy leads to the socially unjust hoarding of wealth is then easily taken advantage of by the well organized interest groups that, as already mentioned, describe the government interventions that provide them with very concrete privileges as policies aiming to check profiteering in markets that cannot be trusted by society. Di Tella and McCullock (2007) show how the animosity toward the market economy in many developing countries can explain their inclination toward leftist political positions, something that is largely applicable to Greece. In a context of widespread corruption, they argue, voters become suspicious of the market economy and prefer government regulations that will check the unjust concentration of wealth as attributed by the market economy. In doing so voters ask for more government intervention in markets. Such intervention limits competition and increases administrative burdens; it has also been found by work that is included in Rose-Ackermann (2006) to lead to increased and more widespread corruption.

2.8   Conclusion

The preceding analysis shows that the current situation calls for a group of reform-minded politicians that will not yield to the pressures of the interest groups and that will have sufficient knowledge to use the significant powers of the government, even though the administration is a weak tool to implement policies. These reformers will have to significantly change the "rules of the game" by setting a legislative framework for free and competitive markets across the board. Then they will have to test the depth of their democratic convictions, as they will have to dismiss the opportunity to abuse the unchecked powers that their mandate vests on them; they will also have to change the constitution, as well as the rules of the parliament, in order to introduce a sufficient separation of the executive and legislative powers. These reformers will have to do this in a way that will allow both the increase of the ability to voice disagreements within the official political process and to ensure that the government will be able to govern "at the end of the day." Most importantly, this effort must also be complemented by the establishment of sufficient checks and balances and the setting of a legal basis for the widespread development of transparency and accountability at all the levels of government and administration in order to effectively limit their own powers. The pressure that the current design of the system puts on the government and administration to take all the decisions should also be reduced. Last but not least, wider reform will be needed in the critical domains of justice and education.

The rest of this book aims to describe a bundle of measures that could overcome the current obstacles and yield tangible results for the whole of the Greek society – both quickly and in a way that will start a chain of events that will reposition the Greek society from its current equilibrium between optimal individual lawlessness and weak institutions and qualitatively weak laws to a new equilibrium, in which institutions and individuals will cooperate in an environment of strong institutions and laws that serve the general public interest. Such "relocation," in the sense of Cooper and John (1998), would entail changing the daily activities of the members of Greek society from rent-seeking in closed markets to activities that create new wealth in open and competitive markets, as described for education by Mitsopoulos and Pelagidis (2007). Yet while we can attempt to suggest appropriate initiatives as the first steps of a path that could unravel such a process, we cannot suggest how to overcome the more deeply rooted mistrust of free markets that currently prevails in Greece. Schonhardt-Bailey (2006) evokes the extent of the preparatory work – that is, the appropriate shift in interests and the fermentation of political ideas – that was required to repeal the Corn Laws in England. We can only suspect that the change in policies that is required to deal with the problems Greece faces today would most likely require a similarly favorable coming together of events and coincidences. While our purpose is not to create these favorable circumstances, we aim to provide a map of the obstacles at hand and the actions that would be most appropriate should such an auspicious setting emerge. Furthermore we can provide facts and arguments that can strengthen the conviction that a favorable result can be achieved by those willing to take the initiative to guide the country toward this new, better, equilibrium – regardless of the apparently prohibitive personal costs they will have to pay. The absolute prerequisite for the success of any reform effort is knowing both how the obstacles to reform emerge in modern Greece, as well as where reforms would provide the "most growth bang for the reform buck," and how these reforms have to be worked out in their details in order to yield these results. For this reason we have elected to put the emphasis in the book on the incentives structure built into the Greek political system, the shortcomings of the Greek justice system and the implications that the extensive government intervention in product markets has both for employment and public finances and the realities faced by Greek companies. The emphasis on these subjects does not mean that other areas, such as education, public health and spatial planning, among many others, are not important. Instead it reflects our belief that the reform of the selected issues are a prerequisite for the success of reform in all other issues, while any effort to reform these other areas without first reforming the issues highlighted will probably be short-lived and unable to withstand the test of time. In late 2011 the conditionality program that had been agreed between Greece and the EC/ECB/IMF as part of the bilateral financial assistance towards Greece following the Council agreement of May 2010 was completing its second year of implementation. The experience of these, almost, two years of implementation as well as the events that led to agreements of the Euro Area heads of state on July and, subsequently, October 2011, appear to reaffirm this belief.

References

Alesina, A. and G. M. Angeletos (2005), "Corruption, Inequality and Fairness." *Journal of Monetary Economics*, 52(7): 1227–44.

Caplan, B. (2007), *The Myth of the Rational Voter*. Princeton: Princeton University Press.

Cooper, R. and A. John (1988), "Coordinating Coordination Failures in Keynesian Models." *Quarterly Journal of Economics*, 103(3): 441–463.

Fehr, E. and S. Gaechter (2000), "Cooperation and Punishment in Public Goods Experiments." *American Economic Review*, 90(4): 980–94.

Hayek, F. A. (1960), *The Constitution of Liberty*. Chicago: University of Chicago Press.

Keizer, K., L. Lindenberg and L. Steg (2008), "The Spreading of Disorder." *Science*. OI: 10.1126/science.1161405.

Kelling, G. L. and C. M. Coles (1997), *Fixing Broken Windows: Restoring Order and Reducing Crime in Our Communities*. New York: Touchstone.

Mitsopoulos, M. (2009), "Envy, Institutions and Growth." *Bulletin of Economic Research* 61(3): 201–22.

Mitsopoulos, M. and T. Pelagidis (2008), "Comparing the Administrative and Financial Autonomy of Higher Education Institutions in 7 EU Countries." *Intereconomics: Review of European Economic Policy*, 43(5): 282–288.

Mitsopoulos, M. and T. Pelagidis (2007), "Rent Seeking and Ex Post Acceptance of Reforms in Higher Education." *The Journal of Economic Policy Reform*, 10(3): 177–92.

Niskanen, W. (1971), *Bureaucracy and Representative Government*. Chicago and New York: Aldine-Athortan.

North, D. (1986), "The New Institutional Economics." *Journal of Institutional and Theoretical Economics*, 1(142): 230–237.

Pelagidis, T. and M. Mitsopoulos (2006), *An Analysis of the Greek Economy: Rent Seeking and Reforms*. Athens: Papazissis Publishers.

Rose-Ackerman, S. (ed.) (2006), *International Handbook on the Economics of Corruption*. New Haven: Yale UP.

Rowley, C. (1988), "Rent-Seeking Versus DUP Profit-Seeking Activities," in C. Rowley (ed.), *The Political Economy of Rent-Seeking*. Boston: Kluwer.

Schonhardt-Bailey, C. (2006), *From the Corn Laws to Free Trade. Interests, Ideas, and Institutions in Historical Perspective*. Cambridge, MA: MIT Press.

di Tella, R. and R. McCullock (2007), "Why Doesn't Capitalism Flow to Poor Countries?" *NBER WP* 13164.

Tullock, G. (2005), *Public Goods, Redistribution and Rent Seeking*. Cheltenham: E. Elgar.

Tullock, G. (1993), *Rent Seeking*. Cheltenham: E. Elgar.

Zizzo, J. D. and A. Oswald (2001), "Are People Willing to Pay to Reduce Other's Income?" Warwick University Manuscript.

3
Corruption, Policy Inadequacy and the Greek Constitution

3.1 Introduction

Both corruption and the way individual preferences are transformed into collective policy choices by democracies have received widespread attention in the literature. The literature has investigated in great detail how the design of political systems and the incentives, that affect both individuals and officials, determine their behavior toward corruption and democratic policy choice, and the ultimate outcome for both individuals and society as a whole. This work has placed, in addition, great emphasis on the significance accountability has. At the same time seminal work has strived to understand how the structure of these policital systems affects the ability of the different political systems to aggregate and effectively enforce the policies that are preferred by society.

The presentation of the challenges and conclusions that emerge from this work suggests that the attributes of a political system that encourage both accountability and the ability to effectively enforce the aggregated preferences of the society can coincide with the features of a system that promotes choices that tend to be closer to the individual preferences of a larger part of the population. Also, when policy choices are such that there is a significant discrepancy between the individual preference of many members of society and the policy decision that is made, the cost of compliance increases for a larger part of the population. As a result, it appears plausible that a political system that promotes accountability can also promote collective policy choices that the individual members of society will find less onerous to abide to, and therefore will not try as hard to avoid complying with. Since corruption is one of the most common manifestation of the way agents avoid compliance with policy decisions, it seems reasonable to argue that in the cases where both these attributes coincide, the incentives to engage in corruption are weaker – not only because of the influence of increased accountability, but also because of the diminished incentive to avoid compliance.

Given the prevalence of corruption as well as a record of policy decisions that seem to disregard the interests of a wider range of members of society, building on this analysis seems relevant in the case of Greece. The aim of this Chapter is to examine in greater detail how and when the attributes that are assigned by the literature to political systems that enhance accountability actually coincide with the attributes of systems that lead to policy decisions that are closer to the preferences of large numbers of citizens, and that reduce the incentives for the minorities these citizens form to either illegally seek exception from these policy decisions or to take advantage of the reduced accountability of the system to ensure legal (but unethical) exceptions and privileges for themselves. We then compare the Greek constitution both with the findings of our analysis and with the attributes of the constitution of a number of other countries. We thus aspire to identify attributes of the broad design of the Greek political mechanics that may be related first, to the inability of the political system to withstand pressure from organized groups and second, to the policy failings that have been described in the previous Chapters. An investigation into the attributes that lead to the formation of stable governments needs to be included in this analysis. The reason is that it emerges that the attributes of political systems that lead to the desired outcomes regarding accountability and the congruence of policy decisions with the preferences of many citizens are likely to reduce the stability of governments – unless the political system has certain carefully designed properties and details. Furthermore, the experience of unstable governments in the period that predated the dictatorship of 1967–74 in Greece largely influenced the design of the core of its current constitution. Therefore this experience should be taken into account in our analysis.

Our first step in this Chapter is to give an overview of the relevant literature that also provides the necessary starting point to investigate the relationship mentioned above between policy decisions and corruption. Then in section 3.3 we examine briefly what motivates agents to engage in activities that we have defined as corruption. In section 3.4 we revisit seminal work that allows us to describe the challenge that democracies face when they have to balance, on the one hand, the need to provide society with a government that is able to govern, and, on the other hand, take into account the preferences and rights of minorities. We then examine in section 3.5 the role of these minorities in a democracy. We also see how they are both potential corruptors and those who will first take the initiative to defend the democracy, if it is threatened by some encroaching power. At this stage we can now observe how the same attributes of democracies that lead to decisions that reflect the preferences of a large spectrum of minorities can also create an environment that is not favorable to the emergence of corruption. In the closing section we look at the attributes of a number of select constitutions to see how they manage to secure, on the one hand, strong governments and, on the other hand, the protection of minority rights in a democratic setting. We can subsequently use both the theoretical background of the previous sections and the attributes of a number of the constitutions examined to put in perspective certain salient attributes of the Greek constitution. We also link these elements with the inability of Greece to promote a decisive reform agenda that would allow the country to overcome the obstacles that now seem to endanger gravely its prospects and, at the same time, to fend off corruption. Before concluding we suggest basic principles for a constitutional amendment in Greece in order to eliminate in the future a number of characteristics that may well be significantly related to the country's current troubles and difficulties.

3.2   Literature survey

The relationship between accountability in the political system and corruption has received significant attention in the literature. Persson et al. (1997) emphasize the moral hazard that arises when the electorate hands over powers to officials, and present a theoretical model that examines conditions under which the separation of powers can help voters to keep the elected officials more accountable. This therefore reduces the temptation to abuse their office. Lederman et al. (2005) examine the determining elements of corruption, paying particular attention to political institutions that increase political accountability. Using a novel panel dataset, they show that the role of political institutions is indeed very important. According to the way they approach the problem of corruption, political mechanisms that promote accountability, either by encouraging the punishment of corrupt officials or by reducing the informational problem related to government activities, tend to reduce the incidence of corruption. Persson et al. (1997) also make the same suggestion. They argue that this also holds true for institutions that foster a competitive environment in the provision of public services, and that do not allow the emergence of cases like the theoretical monopolist suggested by Laffont and Meleu (2001). Lederman et al. (2005)

explicitly state that the checks and balances across the different branches of government, when paired with a separation of powers, largely determine both the degree of accountability that is built in the political system, and the prevalence of corruption. Lederman et al. come to the general conclusion that reducing accountability seems to be strongly correlated with the indexes of corruption in their sample.

Of course, the issue of accountability has been put on the center stage before in seminal contributions like Madison (1788c) and de Montesquieu (1748). At the time this issue was approached in relation to the general ability of the electorate to control the moral hazard problem that arises in all indirect democracies, rather than in the context of a focused study of corruption. In addition, such general worries about the accountability of officials apparently have been an issue even before the time of Madison and de Montesquieu. For example, Sakellariou (2007) describes how the Athenian democracy ensured the accountability of public officials without the deliberate separation of powers and the checks and balances encountered in modern indirect democracies. Similar measures that introduce accountability were even present in the system of Sparta, otherwise not considered as democratic, as described by Panagopoulos (1996). These considerations persisted as democracy was tested, as a concept, on a much larger scale. Lintott (1999) describes how such checks and balances prevailed for most of the time during which the Roman Republic prospered, even though they where often the result of customs and practice rather than of written law or a deliberate design that we would identify today as a constitution.

Besides the issue of accountability, the question arises of how closely the decisions made by the government resemble the true preferences of the electorate and society as a whole. Blais and Bodet (2006) directly raise the question of whether proportional representation fosters a closer link between the views of citizens and the positions of the government. In particular, Blais and Bodet argue that proportional electoral systems produce a legislature whose overall positions are more congruent with the general views of the voters, and lead to the presence of more parties in the government. They also argue that in the proportional electoral systems the need to govern ultimately forces these numerous parties to cooperate in coalition governments. As a result the final policy decisions that are made are once again close to the preferences of the median voter as happens in less proportional systems. Works like Persson et al. (2003) argue that countries that adopt proportional systems usually suffer from a higher level of corruption. This result is apparently verified with different data in numerous countries by the quantitative approaches of other researchers such as Treisman (2007), Kunicova and Rose-Ackerman (2005), and Gerring and Thacker (2004). This evidence seems to refute the proposal of Lijphart (1999), based on a sample of numerous elections in 36 democracies, that consensus democracies should be less corrupt.

The findings from this recent research appears so intriguing for the very reason that the proposal of Lijphart (1999) seems so intuitive in its conception and formulation. This is reflected in statements like that of Persson and Tabellini (2003), who argue that a political system that has desirable attributes – such as accountability – and which makes decisions that reflect the preferences of a majority of the citizenry should be less corrupt. Yet it is also true that the existing research, in spite of the statement of some general principles – including the classification of political systems and some tentative conclusions – has not yet succeeded in securing a consensus on the relationship between the design of political systems and the emergence of corruption. The lack of such a consensus appears to be related to the comments made by Persson et al. (2003), Kunicova and Rose-Ackermann (2005), and Persson and Tabellini (2003), among others, that a vast number of smaller details in the design of political systems can have a critical influence on the workings of the interdependent parts of a political system and, of course, corruption and the quality of democracy. As Persson and Tabellini (2006) note, "the devil is in the details." This is in line with both the observations made by Kunicova and Rose-Ackerman (2005), Gerring and Thacker (2004), and Alt and Lassen (2008). The last two demonstrate the need for high quality data and a careful econometric approach when dealing with corruption. The comment is further supported by observations such as those of Persson and Tabellini (2003), for example, who note that their conclusion regarding the relationship between corruption and proportionality is largely drawn from the prevalence of party lists and proportional systems, and the positive relationship party lists seem to have with corruption.

The challenges that any researcher who attempts to investigate the implications of such details faces are very significant. In reality, it is not even clear how we can, and must, classify political systems according to the basic attributes of their design and their smaller details. This seems to be especially true in the case of countries where a number of smaller details seem to affect crucially the way in which the democracy operates on an daily basis. This can be true even in the case of countries which, at first glance, seem easy to classify, like the US. Indeed, some smaller details of the design of the US constitution are often considered as very important as, for example, is done by *The Economist* (2010).

For example, systems that promote the decisions of a majority, whether absolute or relative, are often classified as presidential, on the basis of the process through which presidents are elected. For these systems the problem that usually arises concerns the incorporation in the political process of the preferences of the various minorities, since the mandate to rule is issued through a simple majority, which usually leads to the formation of strong governments. On the other hand, parliamentary systems are often classified as proportional on the basis of the electoral process that allocates seats in the parliament. Such systems may be able to incorporate the preferences of minorities. This initially seems to lead to a design in which decisions are made to minimize the number of those who are very dissatisfied with the policies that are adopted, as is described by Colomer (2001). But, as has already been mentioned, such a system may easily lead to the emergence of situations in which making decisions is almost impossible at the end of the day, thus leading to an inability to govern. This inability in turn threatens the effectiveness of government and its ability to enforce the laws that have been adopted by the democracy. Such a situation of course can also encourage the proliferation of corruption because an inability to enforce existing laws or to implement policies consistently undermines the ability of the government to supervise its employees. Yet often these broad observations are not true: smaller details of the design may completely alter the reality that corresponds to the broad design of a system. The fact that smaller details may have such important implications means that it is finally often impossible to classify the various political systems in a truly compatible way.

These difficulties, which are associated with the classification and subsequent analysis of political systems, suggest an intriguing possibility that the assertion of Lijphart (1999) may be finally valid, but under certain caveats. A theoretical setting that could assist the formulation of such caveats is presented by Mitsopoulos and Pelagidis (2009). These authors suggest a possible broad reconciliation between the assertion of Lijphart (1999) and the empirical findings of the research that has been made available so far. Lijphart's (1994) investigation shows how different combinations of basic building blocks of political systems can yield comparable outcomes regarding the basic attributes of a political system, like proportionality. But while other possible combinations clearly may exist, it appears that – at least in the setting of this theoretical approach – some information regarding the possible divergence among the proposal of Lijphart and the findings of other researchers may be identified. This in particular relates to the design of a system that both takes advantage of proportionality in a given structure to ensure a better incorporation of the preferences of society in the policies that are adopted and implemented, and introduces a satisfactory level of accountability for public officials. And, of course, all these characteristics should be combined in a system that will make it possible for the government to govern at the end of the day, as Madison firmly recommends.

It seems worthwhile to try and overcome the inherent weakness of proportional representation by carefully designing the details of the system. Empirical evidence presented by Norris (1997) suggests that systems that are based on proportional representation lead to a higher degree of satisfaction among the citizenry as well as increased congruence with the preferences of the electorate, as argued by Huber and Bingham (1994). Lijphart (1999) also suggests that the incorporation of the voice of minorities in the political process leads to a higher level of satisfaction with the quality of democracy. More recent work, including that of Wagner et al. (2009), who use for the first time panel data regarding satisfaction with democracy, find that the rule of law, low corruption, and checks and balances – rather than proportional representation – lead to greater satisfaction with democracy. Yet the most recent empirical work does not necessarily contradict this older work in so far that systems with sufficient proportional representation coincide with systems in which the rule of law prevails, checks and balances are effectively built in the system and corruption is low, as a result of the previously listed attributes. All this evidence suggests that the choice of strong and stable governments, in the sense described by Sartori (1997), which only require a low threshold of majority to win a strong mandate, are not the best possible solution to devise a democratic system. This is especially true given that the design of political systems that combine proportional representation with the election of a strong and stable government seems to be possible – as long as a minimum level of care is given to the design of the details of the system. The design of a system that incorporates minorities in a way that will empower them to defend their rights will of course have tangible effects only if the government is also strong – that is, when the political system maintains also the ability to design and to implement policies in an effective and systematic way.

3.3 Mandate holders and their motive to get corrupted

As a first step of the investigatation into the relationship between the policy decisions society takes and corruption, we need to describe the nature of the incentives that members of society are offered, both as individuals who try to comply with the policy decisions made by their government and as officials who adopt and implement these policy decisions in the name of society.

Officials who receive a mandate from the people to form laws, to enforce these laws and to manage the daily affairs of the country according to these laws may be tempted to endogenize the utility from holding office, or part of it, as argued for by Persson et al. (1997). The official, as a rational private agent, values resources and other benefits that public office offers, if he can divert them for personal use. The official, as a rational individual – like the judges of Posner (1993), the bureaucrats of Niskanen (1994) and as described in Colomer (2001, 2005b) and Madison (1788h) – now responds to the incentives and disincentives that are pertinent to him, given of course the parameters that determine his powers and the potential ability to increase his utility by abusing them. Given this set of incentives, the question is in what circumstances the official becomes more susceptible to adopt practices that lead to the advancement of his personal interests, to the detriment of the interests of society, which he should promote under his mandate. Personal interests can of course include both the interests of individuals or groups of individuals who may participate either in interest groups or legal private sector entities like corporations. Such an abuse of power has an increased significance for society given that the behavior of the public official affects the lives of many other private agents. One reasonably expects that such practices, which are usually called corrupt practices in definitions such as those of Svensson (2005), become more widespread when the mandate holders are encouraged to adopt them after rational consideration – that is, when the gain of adopting such practices is significant and when the cost, or the probability that the cost will have to be paid, are small.

For the officials, these incentives are largely shaped by the nature and the extent of the powers that the mandate vests on the official. In turn both elements are determined by the process and procedures through which the official receives, retains and exercises this mandate or, according to Lederman et al. (2005), "the political macrostructure." Even if one finds other factors that shape the set of incentives and disincentives that the official faces, in the end these factors can be seen as mere elements of the primary factors, which essentially determine the form of government, and the electoral rules described by Persson and Tabellini (2003).

As far as the mandate givers are concerned, the presence of a positive number of members of society who will find it profitable to gain from an exception to the general rules and laws that society has adopted is certain at any point of time because general rules and laws can never be optimal for every single member of society. Therefore, there will always exist some private agents who are willing to try to corrupt an official. As a result the necessary condition for the emergence of corruption is the willingness of the mandate holders to get corrupted, rather than the willingness of the private agents to corrupt. The incentives for both individuals and officials to engage in corruption are therefore enhanced when both these factors encourage it simultaneously – that is a) when the mandate holders are not monitored effectively and b) when many individual agents find that the policy decisions that have been made by the officials are very different from their preferences, making compliance with these decisions very difficult and encouraging a rational attempt to corrupt an official.

3.4   Democracy: The strength of the government, minorities and the separation of powers

Seminal work by de Montesquieu, de Tocqueville and Madison, which is often supported by empirical experience, warns against the dangers of unifying the executive and the legislative powers in one ruling body that will have the ability to both set the rules of the game and, at the same time, run the daily affairs of the society according to these rules. One of the great dangers to society in this case is that the said society will experience what de Tocqueville (1835) describes as the "tyranny of the majority" – an argument that seems to be supported by the literature, like Wagner et al. (2009) and Lijphart (1999), that investigates the perceptions of those that belong to minorities within the political party that fails to win an election. Unfortunately, it is widely recognized that a system in which it is not likely that some significant minority will have to suffer the "tyranny of the majority" – like a system with proportional representation, which allows such minorities to participate in the political process might ensure – usually is also a political system that will easily permit any powerful minority to undermine the ability of the government to effectively take and enforce decisions, especially in the case of testing events.

Regarding the strength of the government, it has to be stressed that the effective balancing of the powers in the American system was influenced by the reluctance of the states to hand over too many of their powers to the federal government, as is described by Madison (1788a, 1788h). But in spite of these considerations one should not underestimate the conscious effort of the framers of the constitution to deliberately design a democracy that will be able to take "a decision, even if it is not perfect," as Madison notes. At the same time that democracy will limit any potential abuse of power from the mandate holders, through the separation of powers, and effectively protect the rights of the various minorities. Madison (1788c), who adopts at this point the realistic suggestions of de Montesquieu (1748), stresses that the separation of powers in a democratic government needs not be absolute, but needs to be sufficient, so that it effectively discourages the excessive concentration of the various powers in the same hands. He argues in Madison (1788e) that it is possible to design an intermediate solution that will balance the extremes of the absolute separation of powers and the promotion of the will of the majority with a government that is strong enough to govern. In particular, Madison (1788f) suggests that the mandate should both allow the officials to exercise their authority to a sufficient, but not unlimited, degree within their field of responsibility and at the same time empower them to fight off any undue encroachments on their powers by the officials that have received another mandate. Finally, Madison suggests that each power should face limits to its authority to deter it from usurping the responsibilities of the other powers. At the same time it should be strong enough to fight off any attempt to take over its own mandate. But between these extremes, it should have enough leeway to fulfill its mandate every day and so to effectively govern the country. These concerns seem to apply especially to the legislature. De Montesquieu (1748) recommends that the executive should not participate in the preparation of laws, but that it should retain both the right of first refusal and the ability to return extreme legislative initiatives back the legislature. He further suggests that such a power will be meaningful only if subsequently the legislature has to re-approve the contested text with an increased majority before it can pass the new law – in spite of the first refusal of the executive.

The mechanism for checks and balances, which minimizes the event of the "tyranny of the majority" and is described in this seminal work, offers certain attributes that outline a political system of increased accountability, in which it would be more difficult for any official to engage in activities that promote his selfish interest over the interest of society through the abuse of his mandate. On the other hand the introduction of such accountability will not stand in the way of a government that is able to govern; it will also not undermine the ability of the officials to effectively complete the tasks needed to fulfill their mandate, as long as the officials do not pass some threshold of abuse of their office. Up to that point they retain sufficient freedom to act. The US constitution shows that such a mechanism of accountability can be introduced through a separation of powers, which itself leads to the presence of more than one mandate holder with sufficient powers to enforce this accountability. Following this example, any system that features increased proportionality, and therefore more opportunities for different minority opinions to be incorporated in the process of government, could lead to such a system in a convenient way. Yet any such system will still require the establishment of the threshold that marks the freedom of officials to act and the reaction of those to whom the officials are accountable. The difficulty of combining the strength of the government with sufficient accountability will remain a challenge in any system that incorporates minorities in the process of governing. Even though other practical solutions may be available, there exists one intuitive alternative, which in addition can lead, if designed properly, to a satisfactory separation of powers. This solution includes the selection of a definitive winner for the executive branch of government. The executive power needs this certainty because it has to take care of the daily affairs of government and obtains it through a system of plurality. Conversely the legislative branch of government, which does not have to take care of the daily and pressing needs of the management of society, is selected through a proportional system that allows the incorporation of different minorities in the political process. The analysis of separate constitutions in section 3.6 shows the extent to which the successful establishment of this limit does not depend only on the main characteristics of the design of the system, but also on its details. If the threshold is not successfully put in place, it indeed seems that, even if an initial separation of powers is achieved, it is unlikely to withstand the test of time, as suggested by Madison but also more recently by Colomer (2005b).

3.5 Minorities: Potential corruptors and protectors of democracy

By definition minorities that are formed by individuals who have relatively similar preferences rarely will have exactly the same interests as any given majority, which is actually the sum of many minorities. The existence of minorities, whether outside a given majority or even within it, is therefore certain in any society, as also stressed by Madison (1788f). The existence of some minorities that would prefer to be exempted from the scope of the applicable rules and laws is similarly certain.

If a system considers a weighted average of the preferences of a sufficient number of different minorities, then it becomes more likely that the decisions will reflect well the preferences of a large spectrum of voters, as Persson and Tabellini (2003) state and as is the case in systems with proportional representation according to Blais and Bodet (2006). If this is not the case, it becomes more likely that some minorities will have preferences that differ significantly from the policy choice that is adopted by the majority, especially if these preferences differ significantly from the preferences of the median voter, which are promoted in a non-proportional system. Madison (1788f) suggests that each mandate has to be subdivided into a sufficient number of smaller mandates, which will each represent a majority that is formed by a different combination of minorities. That way the number of minorities that will be represented in the government increases and, as long as the holders of the different mandates can resist undue encroachments by other mandate holders, it becomes less likely that a decision will be taken by a majority that is unreasonably onerous for any given minority. Such a system has a better chance of satisfying the preferences of different minorities because the decisions of the majority are essentially separate weighted decisions on many issues that collectively form the aggregate decisions of society, and are not simply the decision of a given majority that bundles together many separate decisions in a way that will be merely acceptable to a certain majority in a given election, as explained by Colomer (2001).

When decisions are taken in such a way, the number of minorities that have a strong incentive to serve their best interest by seeking an exemption from the enforcement of the decision, and their willingness to do so, decreases. At the same time, and as a positive side effect, their incentive to participate in the political process increases and their motive to abstain from the political system is reduced. Madison (1788b) also describes the role of alarmed states that are participating in the political process and act as whistleblowers when they detect a federal encroachment. His description is very dramatic and essentially puts the alarmed minorities at the center of the system's defensive mechanisms.

The reasons for minorities to seek special treatment from the officials is only one part of the set of incentives and disincentives that determine the emergence of corruption. This is because the system also performs effective checks that are performed by the system to see if such special treatment is provided, as mentioned in Persson et al. (1997). When each power is sufficiently monitored by another power, the effort of any given power to offer such special treatment to a requesting minority can be located and intercepted by the controlling power. The eagerness of the other power to control is ensured, assuming that it exists in the first place, by the fact that the majority that gave it the mandate is not formed by the same combination of minorities as the majority that gave the mandate to the corruptible official. Therefore, having different combinations of minorities forming different majorities that give mandates to different powers, and that then check on each other, not only ensures that the choices that are accepted by the different majorities respect to a larger degree the legitimate interests of many different minorities, but it also ensures that the checks and balances are manned by minorities that will actively defend themselves against any effort of encroachment that is initiated by a separate power. This is precisely the mechanism that Madison suggests will combine the introduction of sufficient checks on the three separate powers with the protection of the rights of the minorities that form society. It is identical to the mechanism that Colomer (2001) describes whereby decisions are made after weighing the interests of separate minorities.

The preceding analysis allows us now to describe different political systems according to the attributes that we have mentioned. On the one hand we have systems that are based on separate powers, that introduce effective checks on these powers and that ensure that the decisions of any majority have incorporated, to a sufficient degree, the legitimate interests of different minorities. Such systems will, in the end, adopt decisions that do not lead to very dissatisfied minorities. Therefore not many minorities will seek exemption, institutional or not, from the decisions approved by a majority. These systems will also have the ability and the will to check effectively on those officials that are tempted by corruption. On the other hand, we have systems with an insufficient separation of powers. There the choices of the majority are adopted, but as long as the bundle of decisions that has to be decided on receives a majority, the rights of minorities are not particularly respected – neither during the preparation of the proposals nor during their adoption. The motive for any very dissatisfied minority to seek an exemption increases, as do the chances that this exemption will go undetected as there are no separate centers of power. In addition, the branches of power are not staffed with officials who represent interests that are offended by any exemption, and who can check on the mandate holder that is about to yield to the corrupt proposals. Still, the latter systems seem to have one significant advantage over the first ones. Making decisions is much easier in such plurality systems, especially when only a small, or relative, majority is needed to secure the mandate and decision-making processes are not slowed down by the objections of different minorities. The fact that minorities can hold majorities hostage, and make it effectively impossible to govern society, is a weak point of any system that protects minority rights. The consequences that this entails may easily overshadow all its other advantages.

As effectively dealing with this problem has no general solution, and largely depends on the details of the system, as we have seen, means that all aspects of the system have to be examined and taken into account. Persson and Tabellini (2003), for example, demonstrate the importance factors like the use, or not, of party lists, the size of electoral districts and the use of plurality rules to elect candidates have on corruption. Among others, Colomer (2008, 2011) suggests further details that may turn out to be decisive, notwithstanding the size of a democracy, while Massicotte and Blais (1997) suggest how to combine the desirable attributes of both proportional representation and the stability of plurality in a working system. In spite of the wide array of details that need to be taken into account, an intuitive proposition that remains throughout this work is that the executive branch of government should receive a clear mandate, even by a reduced majority, while the legislative process – which does not face the pressures of the daily management of the affairs of society – seems better suited to incorporate a more proportional representation.

3.6 The practice of creating strong governments with sufficient separation of powers

Given these theoretical considerations, we now consider how the details of the different systems can determine the way the political system actually succeeds in both governing democratically and respecting minority rights. Following our analysis so far, we can summarize the descriptions of the alternative systems as, on the one hand, "systems of majority rule, with effective checks and respectful of minority rights, but where the ability to govern needs to be ensured by sophisticated design" and, on the other hand, "despotic and corrupt, but strong governments." Effectively, all existing democracies try to combine the need to create a government that will be able to govern with the need to maintain a sufficient ability to translate the preferences of the electorate into policy decisions. The purpose of the following description is to highlight details of the systems of different countries that affect decisively both their proportionality and their ability to maintain political stability. Our brief analysis indeed seems to verify that among the general attributes that are usually the basis for the classification of political systems, the systems in different countries also feature smaller elements that crucially affect the way they work. In most cases both the main characteristics and the smaller, but crucial, details were introduced according a rationale that depended heavily on the political circumstances of the time. Still, they determine both the extent to which the political systems are able to cater to the needs of society and the extent to which the governments they form are stable.

A good example to start with is the French system. The French constitution foresees, in theory, the separation of powers and also holds the mandate holders accountable to the people. The legislature is formed by the National Assembly, which has effectively the power to legislate and which is elected directly by the people every five years, and the Senate, which is elected by elected local officials and which does not have decisive legislative powers. The members of the Senate are elected for six years, but half the members of the Senate stand reelections every three years. The legislature has the initiative to propose new laws, and it can control the executive through inquiries and by appointing investigative committees. The executive is shared between the president and the prime minister, since the prime minister is proposed by the president from among the members of the party that has the majority in the National Assembly. The National Assembly has then to give the president, and his government, a vote of confidence. On the other hand, the president, who is elected as the result of separate elections, has the power to dissolve the National Assembly and to call new elections for the National Assembly, regardless of any objection that the prime minister or the National Assembly may have. In addition, it is rumored that presidents often ask prime ministers, before he proposes them for the office, to hand in an open letter of resignation. The president must sign laws before they take effect, but he has the ability to send laws back to the legislature for further deliberation if the prime minister, who – we remind – often has signed already his resignation letter and handed it to the president, agrees with him. But once the law is presented again to the president after the National Assembly has passed it with a simple majority, as it had done the first time around, the president must sign it. In practice, the president often selects the ministers himself, even though the prime minister formally presents his selection of ministers to the National Assembly. This is a normal result stemming from the power of the president to dissolve the National Assembly; this near-prerogative is almost certain when both the president and the prime minister belong to the same political party. Finally, one should add that in France the ministers can propose laws and, as long as the party they belong to has the majority in the National Assembly, these laws are usually passed.

From this brief description we observe that the French system has a very peculiar attribute. Even though the president and the main legislative body, the National Assembly, receive their mandate through separate direct elections – something that creates favorable initial conditions to achieve a sufficient separation of the legislative and executive powers – the other features of the political mechanism cancel out this advantage. This is because, in spite of the fact that France is a presidential democracy, the executive needs to receive a vote of confidence from the legislature and the president, who selects the head of the executive, can at any point dissolve the body that issues the vote of confidence to the executive.

As a result the "checks and balances" that are built into the system are weak. The ability of the president, or even the Senate, to obstruct the legislative initiatives that the National Assembly takes are negligible. In the US, for example, after a presidential veto the legislature needs an increased majority to pass the contested law. In France the daily business of the National Assembly goes essentially unchecked, but there always exists a larger threat that the mandate that the National Assembly has received from the people may be arbitrarily revoked by the president. This design creates severe practical problems whenever the majority in the National Assembly does not belong to the same political party as the president. The fact that this combination, where the president had to select a prime minister from the opposition and accept the legislative choices of the opposition, did often not work well meant that the ability of the government to govern effectively was severely reduced.

The solution to the problem is awkward, and affirmed the prophecy of de Montesqieu "that all will be lost." Following a recent amendment of the French constitution, the president now holds his office for five years, instead of seven, and the elections for the president and the National Assembly take place close together. Thus the chances that such a "cohabitation" will occur are drastically reduced. That is, the measures envisaged by the constitution to enable the government to govern have effectively reduced the separation of the legislative and executive power by making sure that both mandates are handed over by a majority that is as similar as possible. The solution that was adopted to solve the problem of the insufficient strength of the government did not aim to fine-tune the checks and balances of the system by, for example, replacing the ability of the president to dissolve the National Assembly, or the requirement that he selects the prime minister among the members of the party that has the majority in the legislature, with a requirement that the laws he refuses to sign must receive, say, an increased majority in the National Assembly or the Senate. Instead it was a solution that completely canceled out the inherent advantage that the two separate elections give to the system, and that aimed to maximize the coincidence of the majorities that hand over the mandate of both the legislative and executive power.

The solution adopted in the US constitution is different. First, we note that the legislature itself is split into two distinct bodies, and that each has substantial legislative powers and receives its mandates through elections that do not overlap, which means that the two bodies differ quite substantially in the interests they represent. One should remember that the creation of the two legislative bodies that form the congress was a point of friction before the US constitution was adopted because the laws the congress passes take precedence over the laws of the individual states. Wilentz (2006) describes how the opponents to the constitution wondered if such a strong legislative power would lead to abuses, like the ones described in Madison (1788b), that would harm individual states – a doubt that is legitimate to some extent as even Madison (1788d) accepted that an unchecked legislature can easily usurp all other powers. These concerns, which where stressed not only as reasonable doubts but also because of the rational reluctance of the state legislatures to yield a significant part of their powers to a federal legislature, led to the particular design of the US legislature. The existence of two separate bodies that represent, the first, the population proportionally and, the second, each state as a separate entity, and the need to secure the agreement of both these bodies, which are formed as a result of separate elections, means that the majorities that are needed to make a decision represent the balanced interests of a sufficient number of separate minorities. It follows therefore, mainly as a result of the necessity to solve problems particular to a federal system, that this system secures – to an unusually large extent – the representation of different combinations of minorities in the legislative process.

While one part of the congress is replaced in relatively short periods of time, the executive receives a distinct four-year mandate following a general election. This election may coincide with the elections for the one-third of the members of the congress, but the fact that half way through the presidential term the congress changes again ensures that the mandate that the executive receives differs sufficiently from the mandate the legislature receives. In addition, the representation in the legislature is largely proportional, while the mandate of the executive is handed over by a relative majority. This ensures that the executive will receive after the elections a mandate that is strong and that will allow it to govern. The constitution in the US gives the executive no power to take legislative initiatives, even though the president can repeal laws that are presented to him by the legislature. Still, following a first veto of the executive, the legislature has the last word – although it needs an increased majority to override the presidential veto. Therefore, in extreme cases, the legislature will be able to enforce its will, but the head of the executive has the ability to influence indirectly laws he, and his party, disagree with. Comparing with the French system, we see that in the US the legislature needs an increased majority to enforce its will after the first refusal of the president to sign a law, but at the same time the executive does not have the power to dissolve the legislature. The design of the American system is deliberate; Madison stresses that if the executive has the power to put an absolute veto to the will of the legislature, and the power to dissolve the legislature is such an extreme power, that power will not work as a deterrent to smaller disagreements, and it will in fact allow larger disagreements to appear. This can lead to large crises, where putting such a strong power in the hands of one of the two disagreeing parties may not lead to satisfactory results.

With regard to the ability of the legislature to check the executive, the legislature in the US can impeach individually the president, or another member of the executive, but the process is complex since it requires first a proposal by the House of Representatives and then the agreement of the Senate. This design, which requires two separate bodies to agree before the mandate holder of another power is removed from office, is also adopted in the case of the judiciary and described by de Tocqueville (1835) in the Chapter on the tyranny of the majority. Again, this check is different from the check encountered in most parliamentary systems, where the simple majority of the legislature can withdraw its vote of confidence to the whole executive – something that rarely happens as long as the executive and the legislature belong to the same political party, but that can present a severe threat to the stability of the government (if it enjoys a marginal majority) and is susceptible to manipulation by small but unscrupulous minorities. The need to secure a strong government is complemented in the US constitution by the fact that the president can appoint the members of his cabinet without a (revocable) vote of confidence from the legislature. Instead the appointment is made through a nomination process that requires a simple majority in the congress. The need of the consent of the legislative body to appoint a number of other officials, including judges and ambassadors, is not always as straightforward. Cases where candidates were withdrawn, or at least were thoroughly interviewed by the legislative body, are more common.

We can see how the US system is designed to elect democratically two separate legislative bodies and an executive, so that each power is exercised separately, but at the same time each can enforce its will on the other in the case of an extreme crisis. The executive is elected with a simple majority, which secures a strong mandate and a strong government. By contrast the legislature, which does not run the daily affairs and therefore needs not be so strong, represents the will of the people in a more proportional way that also maximizes the combinations of minorities that form the majorities that will make the decisions.

The fact that the American system has worked so well for the past 200 years – a period that includes significant crises and a civil war – is possibly not only the result of all these deliberate designs, but also the result of a relatively obscure rule of the legislature. Before a new law is sent to the president, the incentives to reach a consensus between the many minorities that are needed to form a majority are increased by the rule of the Senate that allows the speaker to insist on the physical presence of the senators for an unlimited period of time before the beginning of the voting process. Only when three-fifths of the senators ask him to stop will he be forced to stop talking. Crude as it may seem, this mechanism, which physically wears out the members of the legislature, seems to be quite an effective mechanism that forces lawmakers to seek out consensual solutions, which – incidentally – are also less likely to be vetoed by the president. The filibuster minimizes deadlocks in the production of laws, in spite of the proportional representation of many minorities in the legislative body. Evidently, this system has so far made sure that the separate executive and the two legislative bodies do engage with each other in the bargaining processes described by Cooter (2000). De Tocqueville mentions that the speed at which the American system replaces laws implies that the laws lack a desired stability. But this also shows that the system is able to govern, and even de Tocqueville agrees that the fast pace at which the US legislature works ensures that the laws that are in force generally are not outdated, and that they serve well the current interests of the country.

The significance of the details of the design of the US constitution should not be overlooked, in spite of the merits that the basic design seems to have. As Colomer (2008) mentions, some elements of the American system have been copied in the constitutions of other (mainly Latin American) countries. Failing to organize these elements in a well functioning entity and failing to copy a number of essential elements, these countries ended up with political systems that were unable to replicate the successes of the US system.

Looking at the Austrian constitution, which is described by Neisser et al. (2006), we see again that the existence of different elections for the executive and the legislature is not taken advantage of, and that the separation of the two powers is reduced because the executive has to gain the support of the National Council, which is the body that effectively yields the legislative power. Austria, which is a federal country, has some similarities with the French system, even though France is not a federal state. Both countries have separate elections for the legislature and the executive, but then require the executive to secure the support of the legislative body. Also both systems have a bicameral legislature in which one chamber (the one that receives its mandate from a direct election) has significantly more power than the other (which receives its mandate from officials, in the case of France, and local governments, in the case of Austria).

The German system, on the other hand, manages a sufficient separation of the legislature and the executive, in spite of the fact that the executive is formed from the majority in the main legislative body – that is, the Lower House. But because the Upper House, which is staffed through direct elections that take place in each separate state, has real legislative powers, which Colomer (2001) describes, the system manages to introduce a satisfactory level of separation between the two powers. It must also be stressed that according to Article 67 of the Basic Law the head of the executive is appointed with high certainty, and any vote of no confidence must at the same time propose a successor. Comparing this system with the French and the Austrian systems, we note that this separation of powers is achieved in spite of the absence of separate national elections for the executive. This is made possible by the fact that the system includes two direct elections – one, federal, for the Lower House and, effectively, the executive, and one in each state separately for the representation of the state in the Upper House, which yields significant powers in the legislative process.

In other countries, such as Sweden and Denmark, the preservation of monarchies ensures that governments are powerful enough to govern, but this comes at the cost of maintaining an unelected head of state. The most impressive example among these countries is probably Australia, which copies basic elements of the American system, but manages to reduce the effective separation of powers by introducing the requirement that the ministers gain the support of the House of Representatives, which is one of the two legislative bodies. An interesting question to ask here is whether the American system would survive without such a fusion of the legislature and the executive in the absence of the filibuster, which ensures that, at the end of the day, the legislature will also govern – even if that means that often the legislature has to overcome disagreements with the majority that elected the executive. Italy requires the government to maintain at all times the confidence of both legislative chambers. If this vote of confidence is revoked, and no new government can be formed, the president calls for new elections, which means that forming strong governments is very difficult in this system. Similarly, a law that is proposed by one of the two houses of the parliament needs to be approved sequentially by the other house as well. If the second house proposes amendments, the first house can only accept them or reject the whole initiative; it cannot override a rejection of the second house or the introduction of these amendments.

In the case of Greece, finally, we observe a parliamentary democracy with the weakest separation of the executive and the legislature among all the countries we have examined. The Greek system best fits to the description of Moe and Caldwell (1994) of a system in which "the executive gets what it wants." According to article 26 of the Greek constitution, there is a separation of powers: the executive power is exercised by the government and the president and the legislative power is exercised by the parliament and the president. Article 82 describes the details of the executive power, which, through the government, determines and directs the general policies of the country according to the constitution and the existing laws. But this theoretical separation of the two powers is effectively canceled subsequently. First, Article 37 mentions that the prime minister is the head of the political party that has the majority in the parliament. Also, according to Article 81, the government, which is formed by a law that is adopted by the majority of the parliament, has to maintain the confidence of the parliament according to Article 84. But the most important provision is the one that reaffirms the fact that the unconditional decision-maker in the government is the prime minister. In effect he chooses, and dismisses, the members of the executive branch of the government, as well as – according to Article 73 – the ministers, who he suggests for inclusion in the law that is foreseen by Article 81. These ministers can take the legislative initiative – that is, they can directly participate in the lawmaking process by putting up for vote in the parliament fully-formed draft laws in a way that will lead to the acceptance of the draft proposals with almost complete certainty – barring some wrestling and disagreement within the political party of the government that are usually quickly resolved after some horse-trading. Therefore, the fusion of the executive branch of government and the legislature is complete. The absolute, and unchecked, head of the government is the prime minister, as Manos (2006) stresses. The warning of de Montesquieu that the executive should not be involved in the process of preparing laws seems not to have been incorporated in the Greek constitution, in spite of the fact that it has become a largely unquestionable part of western political culture, as Persson et al. (1997) mention. The executive powers of the president are essentially procedural, and are exhausted with the obligation to hand the leader of the party that has the majority in the parliament the order to form a government. That president's legislative powers are also essentially non-existent: he can only repeal laws once and he has to sign them when the parliament passes the same law with the same simple majority that passed the law in the first place. Finally, he has the obligation to sign the decrees that are necessary for the implementation of the laws the parliament has passed.

Article 86 follows as a logical consequence of this merging of the executive and the legislative powers in one body. That provision states that only the parliament, whose majority belongs, by definition, to the political party that controls the executive branch of government and which therefore determines the nature of the related laws, can allow the prosecution of a member of the government. And, according to Article 51, the party that controls the majority in parliament, and also staffs the executive branch of course, can decide, with a simple majority, on the law that determines the election of the government, as well as of the members of parliament of course. Only recently a limitation was added that stipulates that each new law will take effect after the next elections that will take place once the new election law has been adopted. It had been observed that when a governing party anticipated that they would lose an election, they often adopted an election law that would make it very difficult for the opposition to gain a majority in the parliament, even if the opposition performed very well in the elections. It should be added here that Hamilton (1788) explicitly discusses the way the US deals with the obvious problems that arise when the legislative body can, with a simple majority, decide the way that it gets elected. In the case of the US constitution, the issue that arises when the legislative body decides – by a simple majority – the manner it is getting elected has been solved by a formulation that stipulates that the state legislative bodies decide the way the members of the congress are elected, but at the same time the congress as a whole body can change the process in each separate state. And it comes as no surprise that the process which offers immunity from prosecution to Greek members of the parliament, even for unlawful acts that are unrelated to their duties and activities as members of the parliament, as we have seen in Chapter 2, has been found to injure the basic human rights of Greek citizens by the European Court of Human Rights.

The abuse of the opportunity to legislate without binding checks and balances also has affected the constitution. For example the constitutional amendment that took place in 1986 removed all the checks on the omnipotence of the executive branch of the government, and especially the prime minister. The governments that have been formed by this system are usually strong, thanks to the non-proportional way seats are allocated in the parliament to the party that wins a relative majority, and to the ability of the prime minister, and his ministers, to essentially pass any law or executive decision they want without any constraint at all – except that from the Symvoulio Epikrateias, which checks the constitutionality of laws. As a result the governments that emerge from this constitution are generally not plagued by the issues of instability that troubled many governments of modern Greece, especially before the dictatorship, as these features ensure the uncomplicated adoption of elections laws that allocate a comfortable majority to the largest party that emerges from the elections, even if it falls well short of collecting a simple majority. These features also effectively rule out any possibility of forming coalitions of parties after the election results have been announced. But the governments that are formed rarely consult minorities, or respect them. They also fail to make the decisions that best serve the needs of the country, as described in Colomer (2005), with the immediate result that many minorities will seek to obtain exceptions or other favors through the process that was described in the preceding sections of this Chapter. Therefore the price of this stability is paid in the form of governments that react rationally to the incentives and disincentives that the coincidence of the legislative and executive powers create. This leads, among other things, to the selection of candidates from party lists, and the election of members of parliament to seats that are allocated to the winning party and not according to the votes received by the various candidates in each district. But above all these governments are expected to be, rationally, autocratic and insensitive, in their everyday operation, to the justified concerns and preferences of unorganized minorities and quite susceptible to corruption from well organized minorities. Such a description is not only broadly compatible with the description of Kazakos (2007) and the findings of Transparency International for the country. It is surprisingly compatible with the detailed description of the behavior of the various interest groups and Greek politicians that was provided in the second Chapter of this book. It is also compatible with the acceptance of the privileges of the well organized minority groups of Greek self-employed workers and Greek public sector employees, as opposed to the underrepresented in the political process main contributors of tax revenue – that is, higher income private sector salaried employees and larger companies that abide by the laws, that are audited more effectively than the numerous smaller companies, and that pay most of the income taxes, as will be demonstrated in Chapter 5. This behavior is also a result of the structure of any government in which one center has all the powers to legislate and execute, and as a result all the administration looks toward this center to obtain guidance, even with regard to minor decisions. In this context soon the number of decisions that have to be made exhaust the lawmaking executive ministers and the prime minister, who needs to arbitrate all legislative and executive efforts. While the concentration of all, essentially unchecked, strong powers in the hands of the prime minister and a few high-ranking ministers may seemingly guarantee the ability to make decisions, the overwhelming need to make all these decisions soon results in a humanly inevitably exhaustion. This in turn leads to a tendency to simply try to deal with pending issues in the most expedited and immediately convenient way, which usually includes the practice to simply heed to the demands of the strongest protest voices – that is, the voices with the best connection to be heard or with the most effective control over strike and demonstration mechanisms. These voices usually belong to the well organized interest groups that have been studied in Chapter 2. Clearly this process does not favor the fine-tuning of laws and or their implementation to the needs of various minorities that are shut out of the political process and that are neither well connected nor in control of a blackmail infrastructure like, for example, the strike and demonstration mechanisms.

Finally, it should be mentioned that the weakening of the separation of powers that has been observed in Greece and France took place in order to overcome problems that arouse when the executive and the legislature represented somewhat different interests. One power took, through the legislature, the initiative to reduce the ability of the other power to check on it. In both cases therefore the initial checks and balances built into the system were insufficient to maintain the separation of powers through time; the ambitions Madison describes were not countered by opposite ambitions that were sufficiently powerful to fight off the encroachment, and the dismantlement of the separation of powers followed naturally as soon as the system was tested to a sufficiently large degree. At this point one should also recall Madison's (1788g) comments regarding the danger that, in a system with insufficient checks, the legislature will pass unchecked laws that favor itself. In particular, both Greece and France have only one legislative body that has real powers, while for example Germany and America have two distinct legislative bodies with real powers. This seems to suggest that the existence of two separate, and powerful, legislative bodies is a better guarantee that any separation of powers will withstand the test of time, regardless of whether the system is a presidential or parliamentary democracy.

3.7 Proposals for constitutional reform in Greece

The preceding analysis demonstrates that an amendment that aims to introduce into the Greek constitution "checks and balances" will have improved chances to fulfill the mandate of democracy and to support the efforts of reform-minded politicians in Greece if it incorporates the following attributes:

1. The legislative body and the executive branch should be formed as a result of separate elections.
2. The executive branch should not depend on the confidence of the legislative body, and as a result it should not be affected by shifts in the majority of the legislative body away from the party that has won the mandate for the executive in a separate election. The prerequisite of the confidence of the legislative body may provide stability to the political systems of many countries, but in most cases, with the exception of federal Germany, it also means that the executive and legislative branches of government concoincide, at least to a significant degree. On the other hand, the legislative body should be able to impeach members of the executive if they commit high crimes and breach of faith and oath. Such a possibility is easily introduced by allowing the legislative body to impeach a member of the executive, or multiple members but with a separate process for each, with an increased majority of two-thirds of the votes for example. In case there is also a separate legislative body, like a senate for example, then an agreement of both these legislative bodies would

be an appropriate requirement, especially if they are staffed through different elections. The introduction of a second legislative body that is staffed, for example, from elections in single-seat districts and that needs to also approve legislative initiatives could be used to imitate the German approach and ensure a separation of powers – especially if it were paired with the requirement to appoint a successor in the case of a motion of no confidence. Such a solution should be preferred whenever the fact that the basic articles of the Greek constitution cannot be amended proves impossible to reconcile with the simpler design of a separate mandate for the executive and the single legislative body, which will no longer be required to provide a vote of confidence for the executive branch of government.

3. The mandate to form the executive should be given according to a mechanism that leads to a certain winner after the elections. Handing the mandate to the winner of a second round, for example, would guarantee a winner and the formation of a powerful and stable executive government, but not of an omnipotent government that also controls directly, or indirectly, the legislature. Such a clear mandate is particularly important for the executive, which handles the daily affairs of society. These elections could very well be used to update at the same the mandate of a fraction of the legislative body, or bodies, as it is done in the US. Again, alternatively, the details of the German system could be adjusted to the non-federal Greek system.

4. The executive branch of government should not take part in the process of preparing and shaping the legislation. But it should have the power to oppose legislation it strongly disagrees with. Such a power will have practical meaning only if an increased majority is required when the legislative body wants to overrule the opposition of the executive. This process needs to ensure that at the end a decision is made, but that this decision requires an increased majority after the first rejection. A clause that requires the physical presence of the members of parliament, and that does not set any time limits for example on the duration of this process, like the clauses foreseen in the US Senate, could provide such a mechanism. The examples of Austria and France, where the second legislative body has no real powers to stop proposed legislation, shows that, on the one hand, the introduction of a second legislative body is meaningful only if it is vested with substantial powers, and that, on the other hand, these powers should not be limited to exceptional circumstances like motions of no confidence – they should also extent to the daily production of legislation. For example, the Senate could have the

final word when the executive opposes a legislation adopted by the parliament with a simple majority. Most importantly, the second legislative body may work as a "cooling chamber," as the US Senate is described by *The Economist* (2010), especially when proposed laws and amendments, may undermine the separation and balance of powers between the separate branches of government. Finally, the German system could, as already mentioned, also offer a satisfactory solution to this issue.

5. The two separate legislative bodies, if this solution is finally selected, should be elected in different ways. For example, one chamber could emerge from the existing system and the other from elections in single-seat districts. In each case the representation of the members of parliament should be proportional, but there should be rules to enable the body to make decisions at the end of the day. Disagreement among the members of the legislative body do not threaten the ability to govern like they do in the case of the executive, which has to take care of the everyday affairs of society. Therefore the legislative body is more appropriate to accept the proportional representation of the voting body. This also means that the separation of the executive and the legislative branches is used to introduce a proportional representation in government without undermining either the strength of the executive or the representation of minority groups in a government body that has substantial powers. In the case of two separate legislative bodies, the different methods of electing and staffing the members of these bodies will enrich the mechanism that selects the minorities that are ultimately represented in the government. Ongoing research on the topic suggests at least that significant diligence should be given to the design of these smaller details, even if the broad design of the system appears initially to be sound and on the right track. Finally, the new structure of electing regional governments should be assessed by any proposed change.

6. The judiciary should be appointed through some procedure that can be overruled by a strong, increased, majority of the legislature, for example. Meanwhile the Symvoulio Epikrateias, which examines the constitutionality of laws and decrees, has to remain as it stands today as the last bastion of defense against the omnipotence of the prime minister. This rationally leads to the pressures that body sustains, as predicted by de Tocqueville and de Montesquieu.

The proposed system, where two legislative bodies are required to reconcile the desired attributes with the limitation that the basic articles of the Greek constitution cannot be amended, is formed on the basis of three separate mandates, which are granted through two separate elections. These mandates are sufficiently distinct as to the power they vest on each center of government to exercise this mandate and to react in the case some other government branch exceeds its mandate and threatens the others' powers. The strength of the executive is guaranteed by an electoral mechanism that designates a clear winner with absolute certainty, while the representation of the minorities is ensured by the proportional representation in the legislative bodies. This system introduces sufficient checks and balances, but in order to ensure an efficient government it has also to make sure that legislative decisions will be made in spite of the proportional representation, as small minorities will have increased power to pressurize the legislative body into making decisions. Introducing the appropriate mechanisms will secure the ability of the government to exercise its mandate without ruling out the proportional representation of minorities in the system, as is the case of the Greek constitution today, which follows from the coincidence of the legislative and the executive power. The proposed design does not hide its influence by the US constitution, and the considerations of the Founding Fathers. However it adapts the basic principles of their design to the context of non-federal and much smaller Greece, which has a tradition of parliamentary democracy rather than presidential democracy. Even so, the creation of a second legislative body, which in the US addresses also concerns that are relating to the federal structure of the country may be appropriate as an additional check for significant changes, like the alteration of the balance of power among branches of government and the tie breaking of conflicts between the executive and the main legislative body. Alternatively, and to the extent that there is a reluctance to implement a system that has too many similarities with the US system of governance, the German system could be used as a blueprint, as long as the important aspects of the design of the system that range from the substantial powers of the second chamber, the separate elections for the two chambers and the fine-tuning of the process that revokes the confidence of the first chamber to the executive are not omitted.

3.8 Conclusion

In this Chapter we summarized the findings of recent works that examine the relationship between the various political systems and corruption. We also revisited seminal work that deliberated on the need to introduce checks and balances into political systems in order to secure a majority rule while protecting minority rights. The simultaneous review of the deliberations on corruption and the separation of powers indicates that the same attributes of democracies that lead to decisions that reflect the preferences of a large spectrum of minorities also create an environment that is not favorable to the emergence of corruption. This result remains to be verified empirically. But even with the current analysis, the attributes observed in Greece seem surprisingly compatible with the outcomes one can expect given the broad aspects of the design of the political system of the country. As a result this broad design will need to be reexamined if reform-minded politicians want not only to pass reforms that will increase the long-term welfare and coherence of Greek society, but also ensure that these reforms withstand the test of time. That is, if they are to be complemented in the future by policy decisions that remain in the general interest of the majority of the members of the Greek society, and that support the establishment of strong institutions in a society that will be able to prosper and enhance social coherence in the decades to come.

References

Alt, James E. and David Dreyer Lassen (2008), "Inequality and Corruption: Evidence from US States." EPRU Working Paper Series 08-02, Economic Policy Research Unit (EPRU), Department of Economics, University of Copenhagen.

Blais, A. and M.-A. Bodet (2006), "Does Proportional Representation Foster Closer Congruence Between Citizens and Policy Makers?" *Comparative Political Studies*, 39: 1243–62.

Colomer, J. (2001), *Political Institutions: Democracy and Social Choice.* Oxford and New York: Oxford University Press. Reprinted 2006.

Colomer, J. (2005), "Policy Making in Divided Government: A Pivotal Actors Model with Party Discipline." *Public Choice*, 125: 247–69.

Colomer, J. (2005b), "It's Parties That Choose Electoral Systems (or, Duverger's Laws Upside Down)." *Political Studies*, Political Studies Association, 53: 1–21.

Colomer, J. (2008), "Institutional Design," in Todd Landmann and Neil Robinson (eds.), *Handbook of Comparative Politics.* Thousand Oaks, CA: Sage.

Colomer, J. (ed.) (2011), *Personal Representation. The Neglected Dimension of Electoral Systems.* Colchester: ECPR Press.

Cooter, R. (2000), *The Strategic Constitution.* Princeton, NJ: Princeton University Press.

Economist, The (2010), "A Briefing America's Democracy." Issue of February 20.

Gerring, J. and S. Thacker (2004), "Political Institutions and Corruption: The Role of Unitarism and Parliamentarism." *B.J.Pol.S*, 34: 295–330.

Hamilton, A. (1788), "Federalist Paper 59. Concerning the Power of Congress to Regulate the Election of its Members." *The New York Packet*, Friday, February 22.

Huber, J. and P. Bingham (1994), "Congruence Between Citizens and Policymakers in two Versions of Liberal Democracy." *World Politics*, 46, 403: 291–326.

Kazakos, P. (2007), *Constitutional Amendment and the Economy*. Athens: Papazisis Publishing House.

Kunicova, J. and S. Rose-Ackerman (2005), "Electoral Rules and Constitutional Structures as Constraints on Corruption." *B. J. Pol. S*, 35: 573–606.

Laffont, J.-J. and M. Meleu (2001), "Separation of Powers and Development." *Journal of Development Economics*, 64: 129–45.

Lederman, D., N. Loayza and R. Reis Soares (2005), "Accountability and Corruption: Political Institutions Matter." *Economics and Politics*, 17(3): 1–35.

Lintott, A. (1999), *The Constitution of the Roman Empire*. New York: Oxford University Press.

Lijphart, A. (1994), *Electoral Systems and Party Systems: A Study of Twenty-Seven Democracies, 1945–1990*. Oxford: Oxford University Press.

Lijphart, A. (1999), *Patterns of Democracy, Government Forms and Performance in Thirty Six Countries*. New Haven: Yale University Press.

Madison, J. (1788a), "Federalist Paper no. 41. General View of the Powers Conferred by the Constitution." *Independent Journal*, January 19.

Madison, J. (1788b), "Federalist Paper no. 44. Restrictions on the Authority of the Several States." *The New York Packet*, Friday, January 25.

Madison, J. (1788c), "Federalist Paper no. 47. The Particular Structure of the New Government and the Distribution of Power among Its Different Parts." *The Independent Journal*. Wednesday, January 30.

Madison, J. (1788d), "Federalist Paper no. 48. The Departments Should Not Be So Far Separated as To Have No Constitutional Control Over Each Other." *The New York Packet*, Friday, February 1.

Madison, J. (1788e), "Federalist Paper no. 49. Method of Guarding Against the Encroachments of Any One Department of Government by Appealing to the People Through a Convention." *The Independent Journal*. Saturday, February 2.

Madison, J. (1788f), "Federalist Paper no. 51. The Structure of the Government Must Furnish the Proper Checks and Balances Between the Different Departments." *The Independent Journal*. Wednesday, February 6.

Madison, J. (1788g), "Federalist Paper no. 57. The Alleged Tendency of the New Plan to Elevate the Few at the Expense of the Many Considered in Connection with Representation." *The New York Packet*. Tuesday, February 19.

Madison, J. (1788h), "Federalist paper no. 58. Objection That the Number of Members Will Not Be Augmented as the Progress of Population Demands Considered." *The Independent Journal*. Wednesday, February 20.

Manos, S. (2006). "Amending the Constitution 4: Checks and Balances." *Kathimerini Journal*, May 23.

Massicotte, L. and A. Blais (1999). "Mixed Electoral Systems: A Conceptual and Empirical Survey." *Electoral Studies*, 18: 341–66.

Mitsopoulos, M. and T. Pelagidis (2009), "A Model of Constitutional Design and Corruption." Paper Presented at European Public Choice Society Meetings, Athens.

Moe, T. M. and M. Caldwell (1994), "Institutional Foundations of Democratic Government." *Journal of Institutional and Theoretical Economics*, 150: 171–95.

de Montesquieu, Baron, C. L. (1748), *De l' esprit des lois*. Livre XI (Originally published anonymously).

Norris, P. (1997), "Designing Democracies: Institutional Arrangements and System Support." For the John F. Kennedy School of Government Workshop on Confidence in Democratic Institutions: America in Comparative Perspective, August 25–27.

Neisser, H., G. Loibelsbergerand H. Strobel (2006), *The Austrian Democracy*. Athens: Papazisis Publishing House.

Niskanen, W. (1994), *Bureaucracy and Public Economics*. Cheltenham, UK: Edward Elgar Publishing.

Panagopoulos, E. (1996), *The Greek Roots of the American Constitution*. Athens: Papazisis Publishing House.

Persson, T., R. Gérard and G. Tabellini (1997), "Separation of Powers and Accountability: Towards a Formal Approach to Comparative Politics." *Quarterly Journal of Economics*, 112(4): 1163–202.

Persson, T. and G. Tabellini (2003), "Munich Lectures in Economics." *The Economic Effects of Constitutions*.: Cambridge, MA: MIT Press.

Persson, T. and Tabellini, G. (2006), "Democracy and Development: The Devil in the Details." *The American Economic Review*, 96(2): 319–24.

Persson, T., G. Tabellini and F. Trebbi (2003), "Electoral Rules and Corruption." *J. Eur. Ec. Assoc.*, 1: 958–89.

Posner, R. (1993), "What Do Judges and Justices Maximize? (The Same Thing Everyone Else Does)." *Supreme Court Economic Review*, 3: 1–41.

Sakellariou, M. (2007), "Comparing the Athenian Democracy with New Democracies." *Filologos*, 127, January–March, Malliaris Paideia, Athens.

Sartori, G. (1997), *Comparative Constitutional Engineering* (second edition). New York: New York University Press.

Svensson, J. (2005), "Eight Questions about Corruption." *Journal of Economic Perspectives*, 19: 19–42.

de Tocqueville, A. (1835), *De la Démocratie en Amérique,* republished in 1961, 1966 and 1992.

Treisman, D. (2007), "What Have We Learned about the Causes of Corruption from Ten Years of Cross national Empirical Research?" *Annual Review of Political Science* 10: 211–44.

Wagner, A., F. Schneider and M. Halla (2009), "The Quality of Institutions and Satisfaction with Democracy in Western Europe – A Panel Analysis." *European Journal of Political Economy*, 25: 30–41.

Wilentz, S. (2006), *The Rise of American Democracy: Jefferson to Lincoln*. New York, NY and London, UK: W. W. Norton.

4
Efficiency and Quality of Justice in Greece

4.1 Introduction

The significance of the presence of the rule of law, which nowadays is described as a coherent, predictable, speedy and consistent judicial decision-making process from case filing until final case disposition, on economic activity has been stressed repeatedly in economic theory – beginning with the thorough and convincing study of Smith (1762–3) and (1776), and including de Montesquieu (1748), Posner (1998), Blanchard and Giavazzi (2003), Lopez-de-Silanes (2002), Acemoglou et al. (2005) and Dam (2006), among many others. There exists also an increasing number of empirical evidence, mainly as a result of the accumulation of usable data that supports such views. Dakolias and Said (1999) cite surveys of businesses in Brazil in which 66 percent of the respondents stated that judicial uncertainty directly harmed their business. According to a survey conducted in the Slovak Republic in 2000, and cited in the World Bank Doing Business in 2004 report, 80 percent of entrepreneurs indicated the slowness of the courts to be among the main three obstacles to doing business. The World Bank Doing Business reports for 2004 and 2005 cite evidence that in the absence of efficient courts, fewer investment and business transactions take place. Dakolias and Said (1999) also mention the result of a survey in which 90 percent of the businesses in Brazil cite delay as the main problem of the judiciary. Finally German employers consider, according to work cited by the Observatory of European SMEs (2002), that the unforeseeable outcomes of court decisions form a barrier that may impede the recruitment of permanent employees.

Even though it is increasingly accepted that the rule of law is a fundamental part of the institutional framework that enables worldwide markets to operate smoothly, it is only recently that more thorough research has been conducted which not only examines the details of such a relationship, but also gives an exact definition of the rule of law that can be associated with specific quantitative measures. This follows largely from the difficulty to obtain detailed and comparable data from a satisfactory cross section and time span for the workings of the mechanisms whose role is to serve justice.

Two important projects of the past decade have collected data that has been useful for research that examines in a detailed manner the workings of the judiciary. These are the World Bank project on judicial reform and the Lex Mundi project. Djankov et al. (2002), in cooperation with the Lex Mundi law firms from 109 countries, construct a qualitative index of the procedure, in these countries, to resolve two typical disputes: the eviction of a non-paying tenant and the collection of a bounced check. The construction of the index is associated with the collection of data concerning only one qualitative aspect of the arbitration mechanism – that is, the duration of the procedure from its commencement until the final settlement of the dispute and the enforcement of the decision of the arbitration mechanism. Thus, in the work of Djankov et al. (2002) the measure used by the authors is only for one quantitative aspect that affects the rule of law – namely, the time needed to serve justice.

The World Bank has also used its significant resources in the past years to gather data and to research the workings of the judiciary – mainly in Latin American and Caribbean countries. The data has been collected both through questionnaires that measure the time it takes for justice to be served and through the construction of datasets concerning the workings of the judiciary that provide indirect measures of this duration. These datasets have led to numerous research projects that now constitute an important part of the relevant literature. The World Bank uses the experience from this work in the Doing Business reports for the years 2003, 2004 and 2005.

As a result of this work, it has been possible to build on this literature and, using data from the National Greek Statistical Service and a legal database of Greek court cases for the civil tertiary court (Areios Pagos), to establish – in Mitsopoulos and Pelagidis (2007) – an indirect measure of the time needed to conclude cases in Greek courts and to obtain – in Mitsopoulos and Pelagidis (2010) – a direct estimate of the delays suffered by the cases that reached the civil tertiary court. We summarize and juxtapose here the results from our previous work and proceed to cite also recent decisions by the European Court for Human Rights that provide further evidence that the delays we documented previously indeed are excessive and lead to the violation of fundamental human rights in Greece. Apart from updating some of the figures that were included in our previous work with more recent data, we proceed to use the details collected by Doing Business for the case of collecting a claim to identify certain attributes of the Greek judicial process that could be linked with this performance.

4.2 Measures of the judiciary's efficiency

Once the importance of an efficient judiciary has been accepted, the issue of how to measure this efficiency surfaces. The problem arises not only because of the commonly encountered lack of data, but also because the quantification of an inherently qualitative measure, like justice, poses particular difficulties and risks. Along with the bulk of the recent literature, Greek researchers also point this out. Thus Bellis (2001) writes that the efficiency of the judiciary is determined by the correctness of the decisions, the speed at which the decisions are issued and the completeness of justice – that is, the amount of illegal acts that are actually pursued in courts. More recent research, like Buscaglia and Stephan (2005) – who measure the barriers of access to the court system and examine how it relates to the efficient use of formal and informal dispute resolution mechanisms among the poorest segments of the population in Colombia – increasingly succeeds in overcoming the existing obstacles. Other works, like Buscaglia (1999), overcome the inherent weaknesses of surveys to pinpoint corrupt practices in Latin American courts. But although there is clearly more than one aspect that determines the efficiency of the judiciary, all relevant research seems to accept that the duration of dispute settlement is an important qualitative consideration. Voiklis (1998) mentions that excessive delays in the completion of the judgment process and the publication of the court rulings can undermine, to the degree of complete annulation, the practical value of the ruling; Gemtos (2001) makes a similar statement. Thus, Greek researchers take a position similar to the one expressed in Dam (2006) and Dakolias (1999), among others, that the speed of disposition is only one of the criteria to determine the efficiency of the judiciary, but that it is an important one. There is some evidence, presented in Djankov et al. (2002), that when justice is served with great delay, other qualitative measures of the judiciary's efficiency also deteriorate.

Similar conclusions are drawn in a World Bank survey mentioned in the Doing Business in 2004 report that involved 10,000 companies in 82 countries. This survey finds that lower numbers of procedures are associated with more fairness and impartiality in the legal system. The report further cites evidence, which is background-tested with the data from Djankov et al. (2002), according to which higher numbers of procedures are associated with more opportunities in the judicial system to extract bribes – a position also accepted by Buscaglia (1999). The report then presents evidence to show that the higher complexity of procedures is associated with higher costs and longer delays for serving justice.

Concerning the measuring of the time that it takes for justice to be served, we have encountered two different approaches: the indirect and the direct methods of measurement. An example of the first method is Dakolias (1996). She mentions that involved parties consider the time required for typical cases to be often excessive; she refers to counties like Bolivia, Brazil, and Trinidad and Tobago in which less than half of the cases filed each year are resolved within the year. Buscaglia and Dakolias (1999) also employ an indirect method. In particular, they study the clearance rate that shows the ratio of cases terminated to cases filed. They also note that increasing efficiency, as measured by clearance rates, may come at the cost of the overall quality of justice. However the latter statement does not follow from their main analysis: rather, it is a note of caution against relying exclusively on such quantitative measures, even though they have the advantage of being relatively easily available and of allowing relatively reliable international comparisons. Buscaglia and Dakolias (1996) jurimetric analysis of clearance rates is an indirect way to measure the delays with which justice is served. The authors measure the efficiency of courts by using a ratio that compares cases filed with cases terminated, and present relevant data for Argentina and Ecuador. Dakolias (1999) also uses an indirect method and examines both the clearance rate – that is, cases disposed to cases filed – and the congestion rate – that is, total caseload to cases resolved. She also mentions how these relate to the time needed to dispose a case.

An example of the direct method is found in Buscaglia and Dakolias (1996). They provide, among other data, the expected timeframe to resolve a case. Djankov et al. (2002) measure the duration of this process in days. They obtain their estimates from detailed questionnaires handed out to participating law firms in 109 countries. Also Dakolias

(1999) refers to sample data on the average duration of each case for Chile, the US and Germany.

4.3 Analysis of an indirect measure of the time required to dispose justice in Greece

In Mitsopoulos and Pelagidis (2007) we investigate the evolution of the sum of cases that are either postponed or remain pending at the end of the year, since our interest lies in constructing a proxy for the duration of dispute resolution from the moment a case is introduced before the courts to the moment it is terminated. In particular we use as a proxy of the time taken for dispute resolution the ratio of cases that are postponed or remain unresolved at the end of the year to the total number of cases introduced[1] during the year. Thus we assume that when the number of cases remaining unresolved compared to the number of cases introduced increases, the implied time needed to conclude a dispute increases, and vice versa.

The data concerning the annual output of the courts is made available in the annual tables of the "Statistics of Justice" publication of the Greek Statistical Service (ELSE, now renamed ELSTAT). These tables provide annual data for lower and higher civil courts of first instance, civil appeals courts, administrative courts of first instance and administrative appeals courts (administrative courts deal with cases that involve differences between the government, or government bodies, and civil parties). Even though data for the works of the Symvoulio Epikrateias and the Areios Pagos, which are the higher appeals courts for administrative and civil courts respectively, are also available, we did not expand our analysis in Mitsopoulos and Pelagidis (2007) to include them – even though we cited, for the higher administrative appeals court (Symboulio Epikrateias), work by Makris (2004) who uses this data and presents a quantitative analysis.

The data of the ESYE provides us, for each of these court types, with the number of new cases entered each year, the cases that are pending from previous years and the cases that have been subject to a postponement procedure. Furthermore the cases that are terminated during the year are grouped according to the kind of termination, which can be dispute resolution agreed by the parties, cancelation, discussion of the case by the court, postponement to the next year and, finally, cases that remain pending for the next year. We stress that the discussion of the cases that are tracked by the data we have does not imply the publication of the court decisions. The publication of the decisions usually occurs after some delay of up to four months.

The data is provided not only for the whole of the country, but also separately for each appeals court district. The appeals court districts for the civil and administrative courts are not the same, and neither type of appeals court district coincides with the administrative division of the country into prefectures.

Figures 4.1, 4.2 and 4.3 present our indirect measure of the time needed to terminate cases, over a period of time ranging from 1970 until, according to the court type, up to 2006 (unfortunately data for the administrative courts has not been published since 2000). We see in Figures 4.1 and 4.2 that the ratio of remaining cases to introduced cases in the civil first instance courts, both lower and higher, has increased uninterrupted since the 1970s, and especially after the mid-1990s. For

	Civil low fi	Civil high fi	Civil appeals	Admin. fi	Admin. appeals
1970	14.53	14.10	43.87	44.80	6.32a
1980	20.37	17.59	45.12	45.95	49.77
1986	23.28	19.84	43.86	58.37	54.07
1987	25.41	20.70	41.78	51.20	49.72
1988	26.83	22.85	41.02	50.12	48.85
1989	24.43	21.19	42.68	50.84	51.76
1990	28.33	22.77	45.08	48.68	63.10
1991	27.14	23.82	47.14	48.93	61.39
1992	*	32.36	30.05	60.10	73.31
1993	31.05	26.50	24.12	59.16	67.37
1994	35.75	24.36	32.25	62.01	71.65
1995	31.12	24.14	32.53	49.73	62.11
1996	36.68	30.63	34.60	50.19	66.77
1997	33.14	31.29	41.30	48.60	61.98
1998	34.23	39.13	34.56	49.70	63.88
1999	31.47	40.50	36.83	52.53	63.95
2000	37.49	44.46	44.47	58.82	51.09
2001	39.72	49.41	43.14		
2002	39.89	54.83	50.19		
2003	38.78	60.82	50.40		
2004	42.46	64.31	50.50		
2005	45.59	66.66	49.67		
2006	44.81	68.94	54.50		

Note: * = Data not published by the ESYE.

Figure 4.1   Remaining cases and postponed cases as percentage of total cases introduced (Fi = First instance)

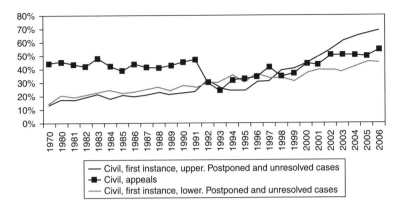

Figure 4.2 Unresolved and postponed cases to total cases introduced. Civil courts

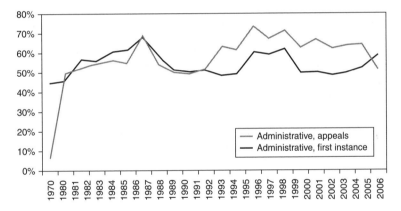

Figure 4.3 Unresolved to total cases introduced. Administrative courts

civil appeals courts the data implies persistently larger time periods to terminate cases with respect to the civil courts of first instance. A separation of the cases postponed and unresolved at the end of the year reveals the impact of a restructuring effort of civil first instance courts around 1992, as can be seen in Figure 4.4. After that year the number of remaining cases significantly increases in lower civil first instance courts and, after a brief improvement, in civil appeals courts. In higher civil first instance courts the number of cases remaining increased after a more prolonged decline. The evolution of postponed cases

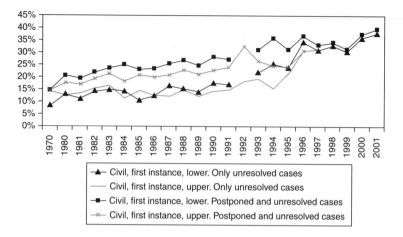

Figure 4.4   Only unresolved cases compared to unresolved and postponed cases to total cases introduced. Civil courts

shows that in the civil first instance courts, this change is to be attributed to the reshuffling of cases postponed to cases remaining, as the postponed cases were simply reclassified as cases remaining. This reshuffling, as shown by the continuous increase of the percentage of cases that have not been terminated to the cases that are introduced, was incapable of slowing down the deterioration of the time needed to dispense justice. The inability of the abolition of postponed cases to reduce the documented increase in the time needed to serve justice is compatible with the finding of Djankov et al. (2002) that efforts to cap the inefficiency of courts without tackling the underlying causes are usually not effective.

Administrative justice, on the other hand, has demonstrated over the decades a more stable performance, as can be seen in Figure 4.3 – albeit a dismal one on an absolute scale as more than half of the cases introduced during any given year corresponds to cases unresolved at the end of the year. We note that the administrative appeals courts were created in 1971 and that the low percentage of cases that remained unresolved at the end of that year is due to the novel character of the institution. Furthermore, the performance of administrative courts, both of first instance and of appeals, are compatible – with first instance courts performing as disappointing as appeals courts. Our data shows that, depending on the court type, between 70 percent and 40 percent of the cases that are introduced each year correspond to cases not terminated during that same year.

Dakolias (1996) cites as an example of ineffective judicial systems in which justice is served with excessive delays the cases of Brazil – where, in 1990, 58 percent of the cases filed were adjudicated within the year – Bolivia – where 42 percent of the cases that entered the system were terminated in the same year – and Trinidad and Tobago – where 30 percent of the cases filed were terminated in the same year. Buscaglia and Dakolias (1999) mention the result of reforms in the 1990–6 period in France, Peru, Singapore, Chile and Panama. All these countries had clearance rates, after reforms were implemented, in excess of 89 percent. This is considered by the authors to be not perfect, but much better than other countries. Finally, according to the data presented in the Statistical Abstract of the US, as well as the annual reports of the trial courts in numerous US states, clearance rates in the US courts are almost 100 percent.

4.4 Appeals court decisions – case facts as a direct proxy for the time needed to dispose justice in Greece

In Mitsopoulos and Pelagidis (2010) we use the facts of the cases judged by the Greek civil Supreme Court (Areios Pagos) that are included in the full history of these cases. These provide us with a data source with regard to the timeframe for the process that led to the appeals court decision. Unfortunately, we are not able to examine cases judged by appeals courts or lower courts, as only a selection of the cases that are judged in these courts is published in the official gazette of court decisions. The selection depends on the subjective opinion of the judge, who generally publishes only cases that are deemed to be of general interest. It can be mentioned here that this practice not only hinders our research, it also invites unlawful acts – as was demonstrated by the so-called para-legal network that proceeded with grabs of public land through a process that was based on lower court decisions that were never published and only used as references in crucial administrative acts. Transparency and information dissemination is further limited as access to these unpublished cases is restricted only to those parties that have a legal interest in obtaining a copy of the judgment. Only for the highest courts – namely, the Areios Pagos and the Symboulio Epikrateias, does Greece adopt the practice of publishing all cases. But even in these cases, the courts publish only the parts of reasonings that are relevant to their decisions. This means that all information to the previous court decisions is presented only to the extent that it is necessary to justify the present court decision. As a result, it is not possible to conduct a systematic investigation into the decisions that precede those of the highest courts. Furthermore, it is virtually impossible to get access to the preceding court decisions, as the abovementioned limitations apply. Therefore our ability to collect systematic measures of the quality of court decisions is essentially eliminated. It should be stressed that even the information we have access to, through a database that is accessible only to paying customers or to professions that are granted access by law (like lawyers and judges), was recently threatened by an effort by the then chief judge of the Areios Pagos to cancel the practice to publish all cases that are tried by this court. This initiative had to be withdrawn under the pressure of massive popular protest. Also, in the case of civil courts the decision of the highest court contains a brief summary of the history of the case, including information regarding the dates and the courts that have previously tried the case, as well as the date on which the case was first introduced before a court. In the case of administrative courts, such information is not included in the publication of the decision of the highest court. Therefore, we are able to take a random sample only from the population of cases that are tried by these courts, which means it is impossible to examine the duration of the legal process and the stages that preceded the case that is being examined.

This means that the size of our sample, which is restricted to civil cases for the abovementioned reasons, is significantly reduced as appeals courts in Greece took in the year 2005 34,726 new cases (which are added to 32,570 cases that were still pending from previous years), and heard (but did not necessarily write and published a decision on) 27,969 cases. It has to be noted that a case is first heard on the day that has been allotted, unless for some reason it is postponed to a later date. The decision is written at a subsequent date and published at an even later date. Often, after the publication of the decision, one of the defendants will make remarks that the court may take into account by writing and publishing a final decision. Of these, about 10 percent, after they are decided and published, are brought to the Areios Pagos. Civil cases that are brought to lower and higher civil courts totaled 141,441 and 140,951 respectively, with a backlog of 83,660 and 62,505 respectively. Of these 73,232 and 64,671 were heard respectively for the year we examine.

The civil supreme court, the Areios Pagos, like in all other civil law countries, does not examine the essence of the judgment of the lower courts. Instead, it examines whether the judgment of the lower level courts that is brought before it was based on a procedure that conforms with the law, and whether the reasoning of the judging court took into account all relevant laws. Therefore when the Areios Pagos asks for a retrial, it is either because the appeals court did not follow the lawful procedure, or because it ignored or misinterpreted a pertinent law. Therefore the number of cases brought before this court is dependent only on the cost of using the court and the legal flaws in the decision of the appeals court, and not on the subjective belief of the involved parties in their probability of winning that are formed on the basis of the essence of the case. Cases that do not serve justice at the level of the appeals court, and in particular cases that allocate unreasonably low damages to the injured party, but that followed procedures and laws in a way that cannot be reproached, are not taken to the Areios Pagos.

The number of cases tried in the year 2006 by the Areios Pagos was 2,251. Of these, the Areios Pagos judged that 978 should be retried by the appeals court or by the court that had ruled in place of the appeals court, which happens in some special cases. Therefore 43.5 percent of the cases had to be tried again by the appeals court. In 2005 this percentage was 42.6. In other words, given our sample of two recent years, over 40 percent of the cases brought before the Areios Pagos are found flawed, either in the procedure that was followed by the appeals court to take the decision or in that the decision was taken in spite of violating, directly or indirectly, an existing law, or even the constitution. A careful reading of a random sample of 100 cases among the 978 cases that are to be retried shows that in 66 of these cases the retrial is asked for because the proper procedures were not followed. In most cases, the retrial is asked because either evidence was taken into account that should not have been taken into account, or evidence was excluded that should have been taken into account, or evidence that was taken into account was not properly evaluated, or a verdict was issued without having sufficient evidence to do so. For the other 34 cases, the reason for retrial arises because the appeals court either ignored or misinterpreted existing laws. In most cases the appealing party puts forward multiple reasons to repeal the decision, which is also true for the cases in which no retrial is ordered and the previous court's decision is upheld.

Only 25 cases were marked for a partial retrial; the remaing 75 cases need to be retried entirely. Therefore, for the 25 cases at least, part of the verdict of the appeals court is enforceable, while only part of them is delayed awaiting retrial. On the other hand, for the other 75 percent of the cases in our sample, serving justice is delayed until the new verdict of the appeals court is issued, and under the assumption that this new verdict of the appeals court is not brought again before the Areios Pagos. Such a rate of repeals is compatible with the rate of repeals observed in other civil and common law countries, with all the caveats regarding the differences between the applicable systems of course, as pointed out by Shavell (1993). Using an appropriate measure for the quality of the appeals courts' decisions, which requires evaluating the substance of their decisions, is therefore risky, in the sense that it questions credibility. This is why we abstain from such an effort.

We note in our sample some lengthy delays in the process of serving justice, as can be seen in Figure 4.5. Specifically, 20 percent of our cases have not been settled almost ten years after they were first filed; even for these cases, the process will be delayed for at least another year before the appeals court issues a new verdict. Sixty-five percent of the cases await a new verdict from the appeals court, in spite of the fact that they were first filed between five and ten years ago. On average, at the end of the year 2006 the cases tried by the Areios Pagos and that were marked for a retrial were six-and-a-half years old. We also find a small but not insignificant number of cases (8 percent of our sample) for which we document repeated appeals to the civil Supreme Court. These originate among the 40 percent of all the cases that have been retried by order of the Areios Pagos. It seems that for a number of these cases, the new decision of the appeals court (or the court that tries in its place), is challenged anew by one of the involved parties in front of the Areios Pagos. While the total number of these cases is small (as mentioned above,

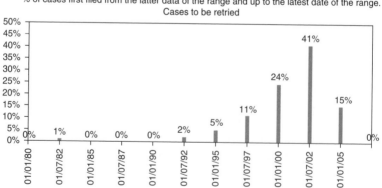

Figure 4.5   Duration of cases that have been ordered to be retried by the Areios Pagos in 2006

about 8 percent of the total), about half of the cases were initiated more than 12 years before 2006, and about one-fourth of the cases are over ten years old. This indicated that there is a small, but non-negligible, chance that a case will get entangled in a process of repeated retrials, and this process ensures that no final verdict is obtained for at least a decade. Our sample contains two cases that were judged for the third time by the Areios Pagos (and thus are due to get tried for the fourth time by the appeals court), and one case where the second verdict of the Areios Pagos was challenged and was directly brought again to the court for retrial.

Such delays also apply to cases in which the relevant supreme court reaffirms the decision of the previous court. Taking a random sample of 100 cases among those for the year 2006, we see that these cases, which form about 60 percent of the cases in the year 2006, were on average over seven-and-a-half years old at the time the decision of the Areios Pagos was published. And while 70 percent of these cases were less than seven years old, a significant 30 percent were older than seven years – with one case being first introduced almost 26 years ago and another case 33 years ago, as shown in Figure 4.6. About 25 percent of these very old cases, which were first introduced more than seven years ago, were cases that had been retried by the appeals court before, after a previous order to do so, but 75 percent of these old cases simply proceeded very slowly.

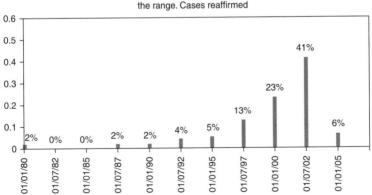

Figure 4.6 Duration of cases that have been reaffirmed by the Areios Pagos in 2006

These long delays in the process of official arbitration are not caused by the fact that one of the involved parties is not satisfied with the outcome – say, because the height of the compensation awarded did not meet its expectations. They are caused by the fact that the lower courts either do not follow procedures properly, or they ignore, or misinterpret, laws – which in itself is an objective measure of the low quality of the decisions that are taken by the lower courts. However the use of the appeals process for error correction, as opposed to first instance and appeals courts decisions that do not make mistakes, does not provide by itself information on the quality of the judicial system, as explained by Shavell (1993). Still, it remains that for a given number of cases the time needed to conclude the judicial procedures seems to be very long.

Measuring the quality is curtailed by the fact that we have a complete sample only from Supreme Court decisions that judge only the lawfulness of the preceding court decisions, as is appropriate for a civil law country. Also, since we are not always informed about the full content of all the preceding court decisions – that is, both the appeals and first instance court – or, in the case of previous retrials, the content of the initial court decisions, we cannot construct measures that compare the initial with the subsequent decisions. Furthermore the structure of civil law does not permit judges to commit errors that may be brought before the highest court and that we may use to pinpoint the low quality of court decisions that refer to issues like the height of compensation. Therefore we are left once again only with a measure of time, which allows us to assess the time needed to finally serve justice.

4.5 European Court of Human Rights decisions regarding delays in Greek courts

The European Court of Human Rights (Court) provides us with further evidence that the conclusion of judicial processes in Greece often is subject to excessive delays. It also gives us some indication of the quality of administrative justice in Greece, in particular regarding the impartiality of administrative courts. Regarding the issue of delays, a small sample of recent decision shows a recurrent pattern of excessive delays in the judicial procedures in Greece, both in civil and administrative courts. An example given is the case of *Kopsidis* versus *Greece* (Case no 2920/08, which led to the decision of the Court of March 18, 2010). According to the history of the case, in 1993 the claimant obtained two orders of payment amounting to a little over 35,000 euros against his previous associates, who filed for an annulation of these within the same year.

Until the year 2007 the case was repeatedly brought before various courts that sometimes decided that the orders of payment should be upheld, sometimes decided that they should not, sometimes overruled previous court decisions and sometimes upheld them. Often these decisions were lengthy and arcane, and dealt with lesser and complex procedural details. The claimant turned to the European Court of Human Rights and complained that his right to have access to a court had been violated. The Court concluded that the time needed to conclude this case by the Greek courts was not reasonable, and that a violation of the European Convention on Human Rights had occurred. Furthermore the Court cited its older decision (Konti-Arvaniti c. Grèce, no 53401/99, §§ 29–30, April 10, 2003) regarding the fact that the Greek state does not offer a procedure to file a complaint in the case in which a violation of the right of access to court takes place, and that this constitutes a violation of the Convention. Furthermore the Court decided that for the compensation that the Greek state has to pay it should use a commensurate interest rate, which is dependent on the marginal lending facility of the European Central Bank (ECB), thus indicating the fact that the practice of the Greek state to charge an interest that is different from the one it pays itself in such cases is not fair.

In the case of *Kamilleri* versus *Greece* (Case no 9842/08, which led to a Court decision on March 18, 2010), repeated court decisions that did not lead to a final decision within eight years were also deemed to have taken an excessive amount of time. In the case *Pechlivanidis and others* versus *Greece* (Case no 48380/07, which led to a Court decision on February 18, 2010), the claimants argue that the ability to use their plot of land has been undermined by the repeated acts of the Greek state, the first of which dates back to 1987, to expropriate their property in order for it to become a "green zone and recreation area." They furthermore complain that there is no national process to take recourse to enforce the court decision that annulled these expropriation acts in 2007, given that they had not been completed nor compensation paid, within a reasonable amount of time. The Court upheld their claim regarding the delay between the first seizure and the court decision of 2007 that overturned it, and the subsequent seizures, holding that the owners were unjustly deprived of their property, and that the process that finally annulled these seizures took too long. Notably the Court accepted that the moral distress imposed on the owners of the plot, because the court decision of 2007 was not enforced and because of the absence of a procedure to uphold their rights, should be compensated with the payment of 40,000 euros. Similarly, in the case of *Galotskin* versus *Greece*

(Case no 2945/07, which led to a court decision on January 14, 2010), the length of the criminal and administrative proceedings complained of was also found excessive and failed to satisfy the "reasonable time" requirement. Furthermore the Court considered that the applicant had undoubtedly suffered non-pecuniary damage, which cannot be compensated solely by the findings of violations. With regard to the specific circumstances of the case and ruling on an equitable basis, the Court awarded the applicant 17,000 euros, plus any tax that may be chargeable on that amount.

The length of the judicial proceedings, as well as the absence of an authority from which one can seek recourse in the case of excessive delays in these proceedings, was also relevant to the case of *Tsasnik and Kaounis* versus *Greece* (Case no 3142/08, which led to a Court decision on January 14, 2010), the case of *Gargasoulas* versus *Greece* (Case no 51500/07, which led to a Court decision on January 7, 2010), the case of *Dimopoulos* versus *Greece* (Case no 34198/07, which led to a Court decision on January 7, 2010), the case of *Pikoulas and others* versus *Greece* (Case no 1545/08, which led to a Court decision on January 7, 2010 for a case that was first filed in 1985), the case of *Mageiras* versus *Greece* (Case no 9893/08, which led to a Court decision on January 7, 2010 for a process that had started in 1999) and the case of *Karokis* versus *Greece* (Case no 17461/08, which led to a Court decision on January 7, 2010 for a process that had started in 1998). The recurrent pattern of these cases, as well as the repeated decisions by the European Court of Human Rights, verify the results of both the analysis of ESYE data for the construction of an indirect measure for the duration of the process to dispense justice in Greece and the results of the analysis of cases that have been judged by the tertiary civil court. They also demonstrate that the long timeframe often required by the Greek courts to reach a final decision actually injures fundamental human rights, while the absence of a national authority from which the injured parties may seek recourse also constitutes a violation of the European Convention on Human Rights.

Furthermore cases no 48906/06 and no 48380/07, for example, provide some tangible indications that put in question the impartiality of the administrative courts and procedures when the interests of individuals and the Greek state are opposed. Case no 48906/06 was brought before the European Court of Human Rights, leading to a judgment on May 25, 2009. The Greek court of first instance decided that a claim brought by the state against the company for damages, because allegedly the company had failed to fulfill its contractual obligations, could be claimed, under that law, by the state, within a limitation period of 20 years, while the counterclaim brought by the company against the state for damages on the grounds that the state had not fully performed the contract was subject to the one-year limitation period foreseen by the law for claims of private individuals. The Court of First Instance joined the two actions and, following this rationale, subsequently rejected the applicant company's action as time-barred and upheld the state's claim, awarding it the sums requested. The applicant company appealed, but the Court of Appeal partly upheld the decision – finding that the application of two different limitation periods for the two parties did not contravene the provision of the Greek Constitution enshrining the principle of equality, nor was it in breach of Article 6 § 1 of the Convention of Human Rights. An appeal on points of law by the applicant company was dismissed. The European Court of Human Rights, on the other hand, took the view that the application, to the detriment of the applicant company's claims against the state, of different periods of limitation to the opposing parties, which entailed a considerable discrepancy between them, contravened the principle of the equality of arms. Accordingly, the Court dismissed the Greek government's preliminary objection to the effect that the applicant company's complaint was inadmissible ratione materiae and concluded unanimously that a violation of the European Convention on Human Rights existed.

4.6 Time needed to dispose cases and resources

The examination of the relationship between the time needed to serve justice and the budget of the Ministry of Justice, as it was named until 2009, is facing the constraint that the budget includes spending beyond the operation of courts, like the budget of prisons and rehabilitation centers. Taken this constraint into account, we proceed to note in Figure 4.7 that the budget of the Ministry of Justice is a relative constant percentage of the GDP until 1991, even though between 1988 and 1991 there is a decline to the levels of 1970. This drop precedes a period of deterioration in the duration of justice dispensing in the civil courts. After 1991 a constant increase is observed, which has persisted until 2002, after which it declines again – only to grow again more recently and up to 2009.

The ESYE has published data for court activities, up until 2006 for civil courts and 2000 for administrative courts. Thus it is possible to see that, at least with the lower civil courts of first instance, the increase in spending observed since the mid-1990s had no effect, until the end of

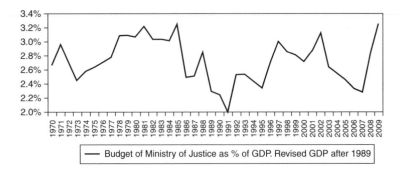

Figure 4.7 Budget of the Ministry of Justice as a percentage of the GDP

2002, on the time needed to terminate cases, as measured by the cases unresolved over cases introduced. The renewed decline in spending from 2002 until 2006 also seems not to have had any impact on the steady increase of the deterioration of our indeces. A temporary improvement in civil appeals courts, documented in Figures 4.1 and 4.2, coincides with the spending increase, but also with reforms introduced in 1992, but was short lived in any case.

This is in line with the findings of the literature. In particular, Djankov et al. (2002) find that an increase in material spending in itself does not necessarily increase the efficiency of the judicial system. A similar result is found by Buscaglia and Dakolias (1999), who concluded that while spending on capital infrastructure that increases tractability and case-tracking did, in their sample, affect positively clearance rates, increasing the general budget did not lead to any measurable effect. It should be noted here, though, that introducing case-management rolling lists in the Family Courts of the Sydney Registry did not bring the expected improvements, as documented in Matruglio (1996), because the reforms that were introduced neglected to ensure the participation of the involved parties in the process of design and implementation. This suggests that even the investment favored by the analysis of Buscaglia and Dakolias (1999) has to be well designed and properly installed. A similar cautionary note should be attached to the successful creation of specialized courts that often coincides with the significant simplification of overly complicated procedures, as is the case of landlord-tenant disputes in New Zealand cited by Cole (2001). In particular, the creation of the administrative appeals courts in Greece in 1971 came about in order to remove these cases from the civil appeals courts and accelerate their trials. The dismal performance of these Greek administrative courts after 1971 shows, though, that success cannot be attributed to the establishment of the specialized courts alone, and that the cautionary note also applies in this case.

With regard to reform through the increase of funding, Botero et al. (2003) mention that only Buscaglia and Dakolias (1996) have found that "resources allocated for court personnel" emerged as an important factor in Argentina and Ecuador, although this is a result obtained during a period in which the efficiency of courts in these countries deteriorated significantly, while the number of cases introduced also increased significantly. Botero et al. mention that Buscaglia and Ulen (1997), Church et al. (1978), Buscaglia and Dakolias (1999) and Dakolias (1996, 1999) – all also cited in Lopez-de-Silanes (2002) – found no relationship between the overall level of resources allocated and the time needed to terminate cases or the clearance rates. Botero et al. (2003) cite Neubauer et al. (1981), who find that the large injection of resources may help in the short run to alleviate backlogs, but they are unable to tackle underlying long-term inefficiencies.

Another similar result, following from the survey in Buscaglia and Dakolias (1999), stands out because it is based on the answers of judges to a questionnaire. The answers showed that judges considered insufficient staffing one of the main causes of the inefficiency of the judicial system, something that is contradicted by the statistical data the authors present in the same work. Thus the statements of the judges in Mexico given in a similar survey may also not be a reliable source. This is supported by the Doing Business in 2004 report of the World Bank, which cites the case of a pilot project in Mexico that revealed that 60 percent of the cases never progressed beyond initial filing, and thus the actual workload of the judges was much lighter that the one they claimed in the survey. But while the empirical literature suggests that staffing has no correlation with the time needed to dispose cases, one should not rule out that in cases in which staffing fails to adjust to workload, and especially in extreme cases, this may occur. Turcotte (1998) proposes a process to identify those cases in which workload exceeds the reasonable workload per judge, and thus an increase in staffing is appropriate. Dakolias (1999) mentions the existence of a saturation point after which judges are not able to work efficiently any more. Dakolias (1999) is also careful to mention that there are cases where adding judges may help reduce congestion, and cites works that examine the impact of adding a judge to different types of court. The latter observation is in line with our finding in Mitsopoulos and Pelagidis (2007) that staff numbers per incoming case are related to the speed of dispensing justice in higher courts, but not in lower courts, which – one can assume – face more standardized cases in which the actual input of judges will not be as important as in the more complicated cases that reach higher courts.

Procedural changes are supported by Djankov et al. (2002), who find from their detailed data for the two selected processes in 109 countries that the increase of material resources and the adoption of specific guidelines for the involved parties does not affect the efficiency of the judicial system as much as the formalism of the procedures that regulate the operation of courts. The same conclusion is reached in Botero et al. (2003), who suggest that chronic judicial stagnation calls for simplifying procedures rather than simply increasing material resources. Overall, the evidence at hand shows that when the increase in resources is examined, success requires the adoption of well conceived procedural changes, as also suggested by Buscaglia and Dakolias (1999), who find that organizational issues – like time spent on adjudicative activities – strongly affects clearance rates in a positive way, while time spent on administrative tasks does affect negatively clearance rates.

4.7   The increase in the appellate rate

We examine next how the number of cases that are terminated at the level of first instance courts, both civil and administrative, compares to the number of cases that are introduced for the first time in the appeals courts, again both civil and administrative. We conclude the analysis for the whole country and compare the obtained result with the evolution of our measure for the time needed to serve justice.

The appellate rate has been focused on in the literature before. Klein et al. (1981) mention the use of the number of appeals as a way to measure how changes in legal rules affect the behavior of involved parties. More recently, the World Bank's Doing Business in 2005 report mentions that in Brazil, where debtors frequently use appeals to stall enforcement, 88 percent of the judgments in commercial cases are appealed. This percentage reaches 100 percent for the cases in which the judge awards full compensation to the creditor. The same report cites appeals rates for commercial courts in Argentina at 13 percent, Peru 17 percent and Mexico 30 percent. The abovementioned World Bank survey shows that frivolous appeals may be encouraged when there are long delays in the disposition of cases in appeals courts. Particularly, appeals by the defendant are encouraged when frivolous appeals are not punished accordingly, or when they block the immediate implementation of the decision of the first instance court without appropriate compensation for time lost. As a measure for comparison, the rate of cases disposed to cases introduced in the circuit courts in Virginia, as reported by the court's webpage, is around 96 percent, while the appeals rate lies a little over 1 percent.

Blankenburg (1999) cites the case of small claims courts in the Netherlands, and asserts that even though parties may initiate ordinary proceedings after the initial case, the fact that they rarely do so suggests that both parties are generally pleased with the decision of the court. Also Cole (2001) cites the fact that only 5 percent of the decisions of Tenancy and Dispute Tribunals in New Zealand, which are proposed as an example of well working and efficient courts, are appealed. In Greece the rate of appeals has gradually increased from around 20 percent of cases terminated at the first instance level in both civil and administrative appeals courts to around 30 percent in 2000 – the last years for which data for both courts is available, while it increased for civil appeals courts until 2006, which is the last year for which data is available for these courts. Also it has to be noted that in certain years the appeals rate was as high as 50 percent in civil courts.

Klein et al. (1981), Priest and Klein (1984) and, more recently, Brown (1998), among others, describe theoretically how demand for justice is created by the propensity of involved parties to disagree and how such disagreements are forwarded to the courts. One significant factor that determines the amount of disputes that are forwarded to the formal resolution mechanisms is, according to these theories, the cost of initiating and following through the formal process. More recently, Buscaglia and Stephan (2005) show empirically that the cost of access can be important, particularly among poor populations. In any case, long delays in the process can offer the injuring party a material benefit and a sense of euphoria, and at the same time make the injured party suffer a sense of desperation and injustice.

Comparing the cases terminated at the first instance level with the appeals of a given calendar year may not be exactly right, as cases that are terminated in one year may be appealed in a subsequent year. But given the usual delay to initiate an appeal from the issuance of the first instance court decision, it is a good proxy. We see in Figure 4.8 that from 1980, that is the year from which on we examine this set, in civilian courts there is a significant increase in the number of appeals to the cases that are terminated by the first instance courts. This increase lasts until the beginning of the 1990s, at which time the situation

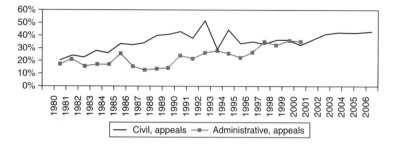

Figure 4.8 New cases introduced to appeals courts to cases concluded by first instance courts

stabilizes, but at an unfavorable level. Concerning administrative courts, the number of appeals starts rising in the beginning of the 1990s and continues to do so until the last year for which data is available – that is, 2000. In both cases, thus, the number of appeals increases.

In the data for the whole country and for administrative justice the increase in the number of appeals and the increase in the time needed to serve justice at the level of first instance in the period 1989–2000 coincides, as this is the period in which the delays increased most. Concerning civil justice, a similar relation can be seen – mainly up to the beginning of the 1990s – while the worsening of the situation as shown in Figures 4.1 and 4.2 for the 2000–6 period seems to be matched with an increase in our proxy of the appellate rate as well. In both cases the reforms of 1992 seem to have had some impact on the relationship. Finally we note that, unfortunately, the data does not provide us with more details, like in the case of administrative courts, as to whether the appeals are initiated by the private parties or by the administration.

4.8   The cost of using official arbitration

In Greece the submission fee to litigate was very low (15 euros) and in our sample the average cost that was involved, according to the award of court expenses mentioned in the tertiary court's decisions, was 1,161 euros – both for the cases that are to be retried and those that were reaffirmed. On the other hand, apart from the fact that the use of courts and legal services is obligatory and no non-court (eksodikastiki) procedure for the solution of disputes exists, the malfunctioning law services market increases the propensity of injured parties to litigate. This is because of the lack of competition in the legal services markets, which leads to asymmetries of information. The opposing parties ignore the true possibilities for winning a case as the(ir) lawyers misinform them about the chances of winning a case. This is because, in a closed legal services market, the lawyers have the incentive to increase the demand of litigations, without loosing their reputation and credibility.

Still, the height of fees may not be as important as the indirect costs that are implied by the high uncertainty regarding the time needed to dispose the case, and the possibility that the case will have to be retried many times. A study for the UK Ministry of Justice (2007) shows that the overall cost of going to court is ranked very low in the list of factors considered when going to court, especially among those who know something about court fees, and 71 percent of whose say that fees are not, or not much, a factor in their decision to go to court; among those, 52 percent of those who know about court fees consider that fees are not a factor to influence their decision. But this is influenced by the fact that often the court expenses will be paid by an insurance firm of a no-win-no-fee solicitor, or claimed back by the defendant. For 69 percent of those asked, higher court fees would not affect their decision. In Greece, the average court expense that is judged to be paid by the losing party is 1,300 euros for the cases that will be retried and 1,000 euros for the cases that are not to be retried, as shown by the analysis of individual cases in Mitsopoulos and Pelagidis (2010).

In the UK Ministry of Justice study, agents expressed a strong preference to knowing upfront the height of the court fees they will face. According to the same survey, the reason to go to court, for almost all, is to get a final decision, and to get justice. For more than the single half of the respondents, going to court was a last resort. On the other hand, respondents are not concerned by how long it will last, how much it will cost and how stressful it will be.

4.9 Rents and the judiciary: The Greek case of demand and supply for legal services

Examining first the supply side, and as far as the judiciary is concerned, it can be argued that, in economic terms, it has a natural monopoly on the supply of justice. Consequently it creates incentives to act ineffi-ciently. This would mean that, given the opportunity, the judiciary cap-tures rents, which may include simple rents like the leisurely execution of tasks, by providing less–than-optimal services. This in turn causes delays in the resolution of cases, as well as raises quality issues. Reduced effort is bound to be the most important rent for judges as, in order to shield the profession from unwanted outside pressure and to secure their impartiality, they usually have a given pay structure that is unrelated to measures of performance. This leaves effort (or time spent working productively) as the only variable that can affect their utility, in a way described by Posner (1993), and without taking into account issues of corruption and any related revenue. Thus, Posner predicts, judges will adjust their effort according to incentives that are non-pecuniary. The particular way the pay of judges is structured may therefore be the reason why the level of their pay is not found in empirical studies like Buscaglia and Dakolias (1999) to significantly affect their performance.

On the other hand, there is evidence that, as Posner (1993) predicts, judges act as rational agents when non-pecuniary variables that affect their utility are altered. Indeed, the international experience suggests that introducing measures that increase the accountability of judges and that advance caseload management render the courts – that is, the supply of judicial services – more efficient and lead to reductions in the time needed to terminate newly introduced cases. The attraction of measuring performance is that it increases accountability, and thus provides an incentive for judges to improve performance, without the need to alter the remuneration structure of judges. Hanssen (1999) finds indirect evidence that the decisions of more independent judges are more predictable. Also, Taha (2004) finds that the caseload does affect measures of time allocation, and in particular the decision of a judge to allocate time to publish his rulings. Buscaglia and Dakolias (1999) find that time allocated to administrative tasks affects the productivity of judges. Further, Morriss et al. (2005) add to existing evidence that prospects of promotion affect the behavior of judges. While it is impossible to see whether Greek judges work inefficiently because non-pecuniary incentives encourage them to do so, the documented inefficiency of Greek courts at least does not oppose such an assertion. Also, Bellis (2001) – who supports the view that the performance of judges is affected mainly by non-pecuniary factors – provides anecdotal evidence that in Greece the insufficient institutional support for the judiciary, the absence of meritocracy and the frequent legal amendments introduced to cover illegal acts by favored parties have ultimately undermined the efforts of even the most honest and motivated members of the judiciary, who – according to Posner (1993) – form an crusading minority of visionaries.

Apart from the judiciary, providers of legal services may also affect the supply – but also the demand – for justice by lobbying for measures that affect the price and quality of their services, and that make the use of courts and legal services obligatory – thus appropriating to them increased and secure revenues. Concerning the providers of the relevant services, and beyond the anecdotal evidence that there exist severe restrictions in the way legal services are supplied in Greece, the study by Paterson et al. (2003) finds that in Greece the composition of regulation index for lawyers used to be the most restrictive in the European Union, as shown in Figure 4.9.

Greece used to severely restrict entry to the market by limiting, in particular, licensing and entry routes to the profession in spite of the fact that for new lawyers there are low requirements in education, special education, practice and compulsory exams. Once these rationed and poorly educated lawyers started their professional career, the study finds, they worked in the most regulated environment of all EU countries as far as pricing of services, advertising, location, diversification, business form, intra-business cooperation and intra-professional cooperation are concerned.

	Lawyers	Notaries Public*
Austria	7.3	5
Belgium	4.6	4.3
Denmark	3	
Finland	0.3	
France	6.6	4.8
Germany	6.5	5.0
Greece	9.5	4.8
Ireland	4.5	
Italy	6.4	4.3
Luxemburg	6.6	4.6
Netherlands	3.9	3.8
Portugal	5.7	3.9
Spain	6.5	4
Sweden	2.4	
UK/E & W Barristers	4.6	
UK	3.5	

*Arethmetic mean of market entry regulation indexes.

Figure 4.9 Composition of regulation indices constructed by Paterson et al. (2003) for lawyers and notaries public

Thus, the supply of lawyer services used to be highly regulated in Greece and competition for the provision of better services at lower prices, which experience suggests would benefit the consumer through lower prices and better quality services, is curtailed to an extent that was unprecedented among the countries that were members of the European Union at the time of the study.

More recent data by the OECD on the regulation of professional services reveals, through the indicator constructed by the OECD regarding the regulatory conditions for these services, that the provision of legal services, along with the other services examined by the OECD, remained highly regulated and uncompetitive in Greece by 2008, as shown by Figure 4.10. Sub-indeces reveal that in Greece persistently stringent conduct regulation, unprecedented stringent regulation on pricing, advertising and licensing are coupled with only average requirements regarding education, which reaffirms the findings of Paterson et al. (2003), whose methodology the OECD used to construct its own indicators, as well as the persistence of these findings for Greece at least until 2008.

We also have to mention here, given the findings of Paterson et al. (2003) regarding the education and training of Greek lawyers, that Dakolias (1996) mentions that in Latin American and Caribbean countries one of the problems observed is the poor requirements on the education of the lawyers and judges, and the fact that the bar associations do not sufficiently monitor the profession and do not enforce stringent ethical standards and high quality in new, potential lawyers' treatment and final exams. So, one can easily assume that insufficient lawyers' education and

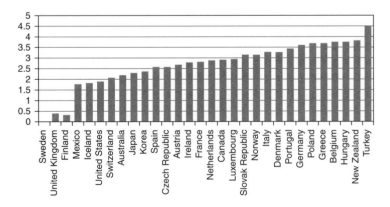

Figure 4.10 Overall indicator for legal services according to OECD indicator of regulatory conditions in professional services sectors

training have a significant negative impact on the quality of justice procedures and decisions. Data in Paterson et al. (2003) for notaries public in Greece is available only for market entry and not for market conduct. Data for market entry reveals the third most restrictive environment among ten countries, and again it is entry regulation and the licensing regulation that are relatively severe, while requirements for special education and compulsory practice are relatively undemanding. Finally, there is ample anecdotal evidence that the market conduct for notaries public is regulated in ways comparable to the market for lawyers.

A further piece of evidence that at least the professions that provide legal services in Greece indeed yield monopoly rents is the emerging reaction to any attempts to either deregulate some of the restrictions that exist on legal professions, or to reduce cases that require the participation of a legal professional by law. It therefore comes as no surprise that since the signing of the conditionality program between Greece and the EC/ECB/IMF in early 2010, the prescribed reforms regarding these issues have been among the cases where resistance to reform has been most successful. Such reaction is to be expected at the prospect of reform that may disturb existing rents, as suggested by Lopez-de-Silanes (2002) and documented for Japan by Ginsburg and Hoetker (2004), in addition to any natural bias for the status-quo, as explained in Fernandez and Rodrik (1991). So, while Bellis (2001) describes the introduction of large numbers of insufficiently trained lawyers, and the creation of rents that are sufficient to support them, Albanis (2004) promotes resistance to the introduction of automated procedures that could reduce the incidences where the involvement of notaries public is required and proposes measures to undermine the scope of the legal profession deregulation that is gradually being examined by European Union bodies. Similarly to Albanis, other legal professionals often propose resistance to the European Commission's proposals on the grounds that they only take into account the economic aspects of the workings of legal professions, and disregard the "public nature" of the profession of the notary public. It should be noted here that indeed Kornhauser (1999) comments on how Landers and Posner (1979) argue that rules are a public good, and thus the majority of disputes cannot be adjudicated by a private provider of such services. But their description of the term "public nature" implies that the rules have to be public, and may also suggest that particularities like the pay structure of judges are indeed appropriate. But they imply in no way the absence of the individual accountability of judges, nor the regulation of the fees of legal service providers, limitations on their numbers or the requirement by law to purchase their services in given circumstances.

The relevance of these issues is suggested by Botero et al. (2003), who argue that reforms that create incentives for judges, lawyers and other involved parties produce the greatest impact when they foster accountability, competition and choice. Thus they state that according to most – but not all – evidence, making judges accountable by introducing legislated time limits does not seem to work in the desired direction, while individual calendars in which judges have assigned cases that follow them from beginning to end seem to work apparently, they say, because they increase accountability and competition by allowing to measure the performance of individual judges. They also mention that according to the evidence published so far in various studies, case management – which may include pre-trial conferences, strict scheduling and shortened discovery time cut-offs – seems to work in the hands of judges who already take judicial efficiency seriously, while there is no conclusive evidence of positive results in systems that are not performing efficiently.

Botero et al. (2003) comment on the effect that the sharpening of incentives has for lawyers. The authors cite ample evidence of cases in which affected interest groups, like lawyers and attorneys, oppose reforms that may either speed up trials, fearing that this will imply less work for them or make them face competition from other professional groups like engineers and architects. While the fears of the interest groups are not totally unsubstantiated, as the evolution of fees in the cases of Japan and the Netherlands (but also the newer experience of Australia) show, the deregulation of the legal service markets improves efficiency, lowers fees and thus increases access to the judicial system and, by the last, increases also elastic demand for legal services. An increase in demand for litigation in Japan was recorded by Ginsburg and Hoetker (2004) after the increase in the number of lawyers, judges and institutional reforms that made litigation more attractive. Also, a strong increase in demand was observed in the case of the Netherlands where the deregulation of the legal services market created a flourishing mediation market in which service businesses compete directly with lawyers. And in the case of New South Wales, Australia, it has been found by Baker (1996) that the deregulation of legal services' fees led to a significant fall – from 10 percent for the fees of conveyance, which is a legal service related to real estate transactions, down to 40 percent for fees related to the issuing of mortgages related to these transactions. Deregulation in Australia included three steps. In 1991 restrictions on advertising by solicitors were eliminated. In 1992 licensed conveyances were permitted to compete with solicitors. And finally in 1994 the old scale of fees was abolished, the compulsory fee disclosure was introduced, remaining restrictions on advertising were removed and simplified procedures to handle the complaints of clients regarding fees were adopted.

Turning now to the demand for justice, this is created by the propensity of involved parties to disagree and by the amount of such disagreements that are forwarded to courts. Both of them are governed, at least in part, by the legal standards or the way these standards are applied, which determines the circumstances in which a court will grant damages for injuries to oneself or one's resources, as first described theoretically in Klein et al. (1981), Priest and Klein (1984) and, more recently, Brown (1998). One significant factor that determines the amount of disputes that are forwarded to the formal resolution mechanisms is, also according to these theories, the cost of initiating and following through the formal process. We remind that delays to terminate cases reduce the value of compensation sought by the plaintiff and, thus, are equivalent to increases in cost. In Greece we have observed the existence of such delays and, on the other hand, the lack of competition in the market of legal services – as documented above – suggests that these services are offered at a high price, at least for any given level of quality. Equally important are the beliefs of the opposed parties with respect to the applied legal standards. One aspect of these beliefs is the standard applied itself, and how it relates to the beliefs of the involved parties, as described in Klein et al. (1981), which determines the belief that each party holds regarding the probability to win the case. Gemtos (2001) makes a similar argument. But while Klein et al. (1981) presume coherent standards, Bellis (2001) and Gemtos (2001) do mention that in Greece errors and inconsistencies committed by all the parties that form the supply side of judicial services imply that these standards in Greece are not always coherent, and that as a result there is increased uncertainty regarding the rulings on comparable cases. Such inconsistencies, one may say by extending the analysis of Klein et al. (1981) in Priest and Klein (1984) and from empirical research, can indeed increase the number of cases that are litigated. Thus Hanssen (1999) relates the uncertainty of judgments with the litigation rate and finds a positive relationship. A similar relationship, again based on the same theoretical background, has also been established by Waldfogel (1995).

These theories and the associated evidence that supports them point to a paradox. Increased litigation rates may correspond to an unreliable system of legal standards and represent the qualitative failing of an unpredictable legal system to form a deterrent against injuring acts. On the other hand, increasing the cost of using the formal dispute resolution mechanism will discourage the injured parties from litigating according to Klein et al. (1981), but also according to Bellis (2001). Thus, without further research that can account for these two effects that work in opposing directions, it is not recommended to draw conclusions based on the litigation rate of countries like Greece where justice is served with excessive delays and resulting relatively high cost, and there exists in addition anecdotal evidence that the court rulings are often unpredictable – something that seems to be reaffirmed at least in certain cases that have reached the European Court of Human Rights and which have a long history of contradictory decisions as they were retried and repealed. Also, we caution that the different structure of the Greek and the US legal systems does not favor a direct comparison between the ratios of cases introduced per population member. Still we note that in the judicial system most notorious for excessive and frivolous use – the US judicial system, where the ratio of cases disposed within the year over cases introduced hover around 100 percent according to data that is found in the Statistical Yearbook of the US – Hanssen (1999) finds (using data for trial courts of general jurisdiction that go under different names in different states and for the period 1985–94) that 0.037 cases were filed per population member. In comparison in civil courts of first instance in Greece for the period 1993–7 0.26 cases were filed per population member, and if the cases of administrative courts of first instance are added, this increases to 0.031, which is comparable to the US level. Given that the public sector influences economic activity to a much larger extent in Greece than in the US, this addition may be appropriate.

Thus, if we accept that the lack of competition in the market for legal services and the documented large delays in Greece indeed reduce the propensity of injured parties to litigate, the abovementioned numbers suggest that the inconsistency of rulings may indeed be higher in Greece than in the US. This is so since apart from the cost of litigation and the uncertainty about the ruling, the only factor remaining to affect litigation is a bias for or against the plaintiff. But the theory of Priest and Klein (1984) does predict that the nature of the cases litigated will adapt to such a bias, until the documented success rate of litigants returns to around 50 percent.

4.10   Simplifying procedures and strengthening accountability

Regarding simplifying procedures, Botero et al. (2003) basically refers to the Lex Mundi project, which is presented in Djankov et al. (2002).

The mass of evidence presented suggests that the impact of simplifying procedures is particularly pronounced in countries in which they are initially very burdensome, and in particular in developing countries where this is the case. The Lex Mundi project has shown that the countries with particularly burdensome procedures are usually countries with civil law traditions. They warn though against the risk that the simplification of already simple procedures may result in frivolous litigation. Thus, it is suggested that there may exist some "optimal" level of procedural rigor, which is in any case apparently lower than the level observed in most countries with civil law traditions, and Greece in particular.

The Doing Business in 2004 report proposes several areas where procedures can be simplified. The introduction of oral procedures, the simplification of the notification process, the limitation of the number and timing of appeals, the elimination of the need of legal justification by the involved parties, the simplification of regulation on evidence are all considered. The report presents evidence that such measures are associated with a reduction in the time and the cost needed to resolve disputes. In particular oral procedures, instead of systems in which written elements are predominant, ensure that the judge has direct contact with the involved parties and witnesses. The report mentions that in some countries the defendant can be held accountable only if an appointed court officer serves the claim, while in other countries the defendant is notified directly by the plaintiff's attorney or a letter. The case of Bulgaria, in which before the 2000 revision the courts needed to notify the defendants in person, is cited to show that such formalism can, when exploited creatively, lead to delays that run into years. The report also emphasizes the importance of delaying the enforcement of a judgment until the resolution of an appeal, and shows the effect it has on reducing the value of a first instance ruling, unless the winning party is compensated appropriately for the cost of delay. The Doing Business in 2005 report also cites as one measure of the reform introduced in Colombia the fact that now a courier company, instead of a court clerk, delivers the notification to the debtor in the case of a court filing.

The Doing Business in 2005 report cites that the most common reform introduced in 2003 was the adoption of summary proceedings especially for the collection of small debt and returned checks. Also the proposal made in the Doing Business in 2004 report to take a lot of cases that are voluntary or non-disputed, like the voluntary dissolution of a company and consensual divorces, out of courts in order to reduce their workload appears more reasonable as it has similar effects to the combined simplification of procedures and reduction of case intake of existing courts but does not require the establishment of new courts. The Doing Business in 2005 report also cites the initiative taken by many countries, like Germany and Slovakia, to take the responsibility of business registration from judges and allocate them to clerks, while in the case of Serbia and Montenegro business registration was taken away from the courts. The report also mentions a number of successful cases in which the establishment of specialized, commercial and small claims courts significantly reduced the time needed to resolve disputes, and at the same time encouraged out-of-court settlements. Thus, it seems that in the end the establishment of alternative avenues of dispute resolution, if done properly, equals to, or coincides with, a well conceived simplification of procedures.

This is also the case with establishing alternative specialized courts. A good example in which the setting up of specialized courts coincided with the significant simplification of overly complicated procedures is the case of landlord-tenant disputes in New Zealand, cited by Cole (2001). One should also recall that the creation of the administrative appeals courts in Greece in 1971 came about in order to remove these cases from the civil appeals courts and accelerate their trials. The dismal performance of these Greek administrative courts after 1971 shows however that success cannot be attributed to the establishment of the specialized courts alone and usually depends on a simplification of procedures that is introduced together with the creation of these courts, like in the case of New Zealand and unlike the case of administrative courts in Greece. Even if it is the simplification of procedures that appears to ultimately accelerate dispute resolution, rather than the creation of new courts, specialized and small claims courts can help to provide both better and cheaper access to official dispute resolution mechanisms. And of course the creation of such courts presents a good opportunity to introduce simplified procedures for commonly encountered cases. When properly executed, the introduction of such courts does reduces the cost of using an official dispute resolution mechanism and therefore allows smaller cases to benefit from the advantages that an official dispute resolution mechanism offers, thus extending the scope of the protection of the law to a larger number of disputes. Botero et al. (2003) cite many specific examples of such courts, including small claims courts, courts for labor disputes, for divorces and debt collection and centers for mediation and arbitration. It should be noted that these specialized courts are appropriate for cases that are usually straightforward to resolve, and for which the simplification of procedures does not carry the risk of increasing the number of mistakes that can occur when the judgment is made through an accelerated process. Also it may be desirable to allow the optional use of regular courts in order to create competition among different court types.

Procedural changes are supported by Djankov et al. (2002), who find from their detailed data for the two selected processes in 109 countries that the increase of material resources and the adoption of specific guidelines for the involved parties does not affect the efficiency of the judicial system as much as the formalism of the procedures that regulate the operation of courts. The same conclusion is reached in Botero et al. (2003), who suggest that chronic judicial stagnation calls for simplifying procedures rather than simply increasing material resources. The evidence at hand shows that when the increase in resources is examined, success again requires the adoption of well conceived procedural changes. Buscaglia and Dakolias (1999) find that organizational issues, like time spent on adjudicative activities, strongly affects clearance rates in a positive way, while time spent on administrative tasks does affect negatively clearance rates. They suggest that the better management of the judges' workload, which also may increase the time they spent on adjudicative activities, also helps clearance rates.

Buscaglia and Dakolias (1999) show that, when seeking the best avenue of reform, it is risky to simply survey judges in order to determine the proper directions of reform, as judges tend to blame the inefficiency of courts on factors outside their responsibility and, in particular, on factors related to higher spending on courts, like better remuneration and more staff, that are now known to be largely irrelevant, for courts of first instance at least.

Buscaglia and Dakolias (1999) argue that technological infrastructure, and especially such that increases accountability and tractability of cases, and the spending on such infrastructure, was found to positively affect clearance rates. Investment in capital infrastructure, like case management systems, is often cheap and can be introduced fast, as the case of Slovakia shows. There a pilot project in a district was implemented in six months. In the case of Slovakia the time between filing and the first hearing was cut to 27 days from 73 days. The scheme was then scaled up to all districts in the next two years. In a demonstration of the importance of combining the procedural changes with the use of infrastructure, this progress was obtained with the introduction of a system of automatic case assignment, together with the reduction of procedures needed from 23 to five, as many documents that were previously managed manually could be managed electronically. They also suggest better case management to include better time management

by the judges. These proposals seem to be compatible with the proposal of Botero et al. (2003) for procedural simplification. Therefore
it is reasonable to conclude that only focused spending on infrastructure combined with organizational changes has a positive effect, in
particular since general increases in spending have not been found to
have such an effect. Furthermore, this infrastructure should be used to
address certain issues, like the fact that not all decisions are published in
Greece, which has led to the ability of certain individuals to effectively
hide illegal acts and abusive court decisions, like the ones related to
grabs of public land.

The introduction of competition in the market for the provision of
legal services, in the end amounts to a simplification of procedures as
cases where the formal presence of a legal service provider is required
and the official registration of a fee is required will become more flexible and require fewer formal procedures. This case seems relevant to
Greece given the findings of Paterson et al. 2003. It is also interesting
to note here that Bellis (2001) does not propose in the case of Greece
an increase in spending or hiring. On the contrary, he proposes, among
other measures, the drastic simplification of legal procedures and rules,
the creation of alternative mechanisms of dispute resolution, and the
provision of a judicial police force. These suggestions seem to show that
the reforms needed in Greece are indeed, as the international experience shows, of a qualitative rather than quantitative nature.

It should be noted that such reforms, when badly conceived, can
misfire, as in the cited case of Japan's pre-trial cases. Also the Doing
Business in 2005 report cites the case of Romania where reforms introduced in 2001 led to an increase in the time needed to resolve disputes.
This underlines the need to identify the reasons for the bottleneck and
take aimed measures against them, before proceeding with reform.
Finally, concerning the sharpening of incentives for litigants to avoid
procrastination in courts, Botero et al. (2003) propose that one way to
discourage long litigation is to increase the direct costs to one, or both,
parties. They cite the case of Singapore, where the first day of trial is free
and then, as the process drags on, court fees increase. While the authors
mention that such a mechanism has the drawback of allowing wealthier
litigants to win cases by outspending their opponents, the low cost to
the involved parties, and especially the injuring frivolous parties, seems
to be a factor that prolongs the conclusion of cases through appeals,
especially in the case of administrative courts in Greece.

Dakolias and Said (1999) also propose the adoption of pilot courts at
the first stages of reform. Such cases, they state, help communicate the

vision of change, permit the judiciaries to see beyond vested interests and help reformers to avoid setting unattainable goals, thus reducing the risk of failure. They finally preserve resources and fine tune reforms to the particular environment of each country. Pilot projects may also help overcome initial resistance to reform due to ignorance, as the case of the TAXIS system in Greek tax agencies shows, and that the Doing Business in 2005 report cites to have emerged in 18 countries that implemented reforms in their judiciary in 2003.

It should be noted that the Greek legal system has been influenced by both the French and the German legal systems, something that according to Balas et al. (2009) can matter significantly. As a result a comparison of the procedures needed to "enforce a contract", which are listed by the Doing Business database for Greece, Germany and France, promises to yield some interesting insights into the possible source of delays in the design of the procedures of the Greek judicial system. From this comparison, which is presented in Figure 4.11, one can observe that the Greek system adopts procedures that may exist in one of the other countries, but not in the other, with the result that on many occasions the Greek system accumulates more steps than the comparable procedures of Germany and France. This analysis seems in line with the findings of Djankov et al. (2003) that formalism is systematically greater in civil law countries than in common law jurisdictionss. In line with our previous finding regarding the Greek judiciary, they also find that this formalism is associated, among others findings regarding consistency, honesty, fairness and corruption, with higher expected duration of judicial proceedings. Related to the subject of formalism we note that, for example, in Cases 34198/07 and 2920/08, which were brought before the European Court of Human Rights, and which we examined previously, the applicants complained "of excessive formalism" in the proceedings of the Greek courts. Regarding the details of Figure 4.11, a closer inspection reveals that one of the few steps not borrowed from the German system is the meditation hearing, which is step 14 in the case of Germany in Figure 4.11. Furthermore, in Germany and France it seems that a case is assigned to a specific judge, which does not appear to be the case, according to the Doing Business database, in Greece. Furthermore, during a trial in Germany and France the judge sets a deadline for the plaintiff to answer the defendant's defense or answer, which seems not to be the case in Greece. Similarly absent are, in Greece, the court appointment of independent experts and the summoning of expert witnesses, and the setting of a date at which the judgment will be delivered and made available in written form.

Greece	France	Germany
	Filing and service	
	1 Plaintiff requests payment. Plaintiff or his lawyer asks defendant orally or in writing to comply with the contract.	1 Plaintiff requests payment. Plaintiff or his lawyer asks defendant orally or in writing to comply with the contract.
1 Plaintiff's hiring of lawyer. Plaintiff hires a lawyer to represent him before the court.	2 Plaintiff's hiring of lawyer. Plaintiff hires a lawyer to represent him before the court.	2 Plaintiff's hiring of lawyer. Plaintiff hires a lawyer to represent him before the court.
* Plaintiff's filing of summons and complaint. Plaintiff files a summons and complaint with the court, orally or in writing.	* Plaintiff's filing of summons and complaint. Plaintiff files a summons and complaint with the court, orally or in writing.	* Plaintiff's filing of summons and complaint. Plaintiff files a summons and complaint with the court, orally or in writing.
* Plaintiff's payment of court fees. Plaintiff pays court duties, stamp duties, or any other type of court fee.	* Plaintiff's payment of court fees. Plaintiff pays court duties, stamp duties, or any other type of court fee.	* Plaintiff's payment of court fees. Plaintiff pays court duties, stamp duties, or any other type of court fee.
2 Registration of court case. The court administration registers the lawsuit or court case. This includes assigning a reference number to the lawsuit or court case.	3 Registration of court case. The court administration registers the lawsuit or court case. This includes assigning a reference number to the lawsuit or court case.	3 Registration of court case. The court administration registers the lawsuit or court case. This includes assigning a reference number to the lawsuit or court case.
	* Assignment of court case to a judge. The court case is assigned to a specific judge through a random procedure, automated system, ruling of an administrative judge, court officer, etc.	* Assignment of court case to a judge. The court case is assigned to a specific judge through a random procedure, automated system, ruling of an administrative judge, court officer, etc.

* Arrangements for physical delivery of summons and complaint. Plaintiff takes whatever steps are necessary to arrange for physical service of process on defendant, such as instructing a court officer or a (private) bailiff.

3 First attempt at physical delivery. A first attempt to physically deliver summons and complaint to defendant is successful in the majority of cases.

4 Application for substituted service. Because physical delivery is typically unsuccessful, plaintiff applies for substituted service. Substituted service can include, but is not limited to, service by publication in newspapers or affixing of a notice in court or on public bulletin boards.

5 Court order regarding substituted service. The judge in a court order defines acceptable means for substituted service.

* Arrangements for physical delivery of summons and complaint. Plaintiff takes whatever steps are necessary to arrange for physical service of process on defendant, such as instructing a court officer or a (private) bailiff.

4 First attempt at physical delivery. A first attempt to physically deliver summons and complaint to defendant is successful in the majority of cases.

* Proof of service. Plaintiff submits proof of service to court.

4 Court scrutiny of summons and complaint. A judge examines plaintiff's summons and complaint for formal requirements.

* Mailing of summons and complaint. Court or process server, including (private) bailiff, mails summons and complaint to defendant.

5 First attempt at physical delivery. A first attempt to physically deliver summons and complaint to defendant is successful in the majority of cases.

(continued)

Figure 4.11 (continued)

Greece	France	Germany
6 Substituted service. Substituted service is accomplished by publication in newspapers, by affixing a notice in court or on public bulletin boards, etc.		
* Application for pre-judgment attachment. Plaintiff submits an application in writing for the attachment of defendant's property prior to judgment. (see assumption 5)	* Application for pre-judgment attachment. Plaintiff submits an application in writing for the attachment of defendant's property prior to judgment. (see assumption 5)	* Application for pre-judgment attachment. Plaintiff submits an application in writing for the attachment of defendant's property prior to judgment. (see assumption 5)
* Decision on pre-judgment attachment. The judge decides whether to grant Plaintiff's request for pre-judgment attachment of defendant's property and notifies plaintiff and defendant of the decision. This step may include requesting that plaintiff submit guarantees or bonds to secure defendant against damages. (see assumption 5)	* Decision on pre-judgment attachment. The judge decides whether to grant plaintiff's request for pre-judgment attachment of defendant's property and notifies plaintiff and defendant of the decision. This step may include requesting that plaintiff submit guarantees or bonds to secure defendant against damages. (see assumption 5)	* Decision on pre-judgment attachment. The judge decides whether to grant plaintiff's request for pre-judgment attachment of defendant's property and notifies plaintiff and defendant of the decision. This step may include requesting that plaintiff submit guarantees or bonds to secure defendant against damages. (see assumption 5)
7 Guarantees securing attached property. Plaintiff submits guarantees or bonds to secure defendant against possible damages to attached property. (see assumption 5)		
8 Pre-judgment attachment. Defendant's property is attached prior to judgment. Attachment is either physical or achieved by registering, marking, debiting or separating assets. (see assumption 5)	5 Pre-judgment attachment. Defendant's property is attached prior to judgment. Attachment is either physical or achieved by registering, marking, debiting or separating assets. (see assumption 5)	6 Pre-judgment attachment. Defendant's property is attached prior to judgment. Attachment is either physical or achieved by registering, marking, debiting or separating assets. (see assumption 5)

6 Report on pre-judgment attachment. Court enforcement officer or (private) bailiff issues and delivers a report on the attachment of defendant's property to the judge. (see assumption 5)

7 Hearing on pre-judgment attachment. A hearing takes place to resolve the question of whether defendant's assets can be attached prior to judgment. This process may include the submission of separate summons and petitions. (see assumption 5)

Trial and judgment

7 Report on pre-judgment attachment. Court enforcement officer or (private) bailiff issues and delivers a report on the attachment of defendant's property to the judge. (see assumption 5)

8 Hearing on pre-judgment attachment. A hearing takes place to resolve the question of whether defendant's assets can be attached prior to judgment. This process may include the submission of separate summons and petitions. (see assumption 5)

9 Report on pre-judgment attachment. Court enforcement officer or (private) bailiff issues and delivers a report on the attachment of defendant's property to the judge. (see assumption 5)

10 Hearing on pre-judgment attachment. A hearing takes place to resolve the question of whether defendant's assets can be attached prior to judgment. This process may include the submission of separate summons and petitions. (see assumption 5)

* Defendant's filing of preliminary exemptions. Defendant presents preliminary exemptions to the court. Preliminary exemptions differ from answers on the merits of the claim. Examples of preliminary exemptions are statute of limitations, jurisdictions, etc.

* Plaintiff's answer to preliminary exemptions. Plaintiff responds to the preliminary exemptions raised by defendant.

11 Judge's resolution on preliminary exemptions. Judge decides on preliminary exemptions separately from the merits of the case.

(continued)

Figure 4.11 (continued)

Greece	France	Germany
12 Defendant's filing of defense or answer to plaintiff's claim. Defendant files a written pleading that includes his defense or answer on the merits of the case. Defendant's written answer may or may not include witness statements, expert statements, the documents the defendant relies on as evidence and the legal authorities the defendant relies on.	8 Defendant's filing of defense or answer to plaintiff's claim. Defendant files a written pleading that includes his defense or answer on the merits of the case. Defendant's written answer may or may not include witness statements, expert statements, the documents the defendant relies on as evidence and the legal authorities the defendant relies on.	9 Defendant's filing of defense or answer to plaintiff's claim. Defendant files a written pleading that includes his defense or answer on the merits of the case. Defendant's written answer may or may not include witness statements, expert statements, the documents the defendant relies on as evidence and the legal authorities the defendant relies on.
13 Plaintiff's written response to defendant's defense or answer. Plaintiff responds to defendant's defense or answer with a written pleading. Plaintiff's answer may or may not include a witness statements or expert (witness) statements.	9 Deadline for plaintiff to answer defendant's defense or answer. Judge sets the deadline by which plaintiff will be allowed to answer defendant's defense or answer.	10 Deadline for plaintiff to answer defendant's defense or answer. Judge sets the deadline by which plaintiff will be allowed to answer defendant's defense or answer.
14 Filing of pleadings. Plaintiff and defendant file written pleadings and submissions with the court and transmit copies of the written pleadings or submissions to one another. The pleadings may or may not include witness statements or expert (witness) statements.	10 Plaintiff's written response to defendant's defense or answer. Plaintiff responds to defendant's defense or answer with a written pleading. Plaintiff's answer may or may not include a witness statements or expert (witness) statements.	11 Plaintiff's written response to defendant's defense or answer. Plaintiff responds to defendant's defense or answer with a written pleading. Plaintiff's answer may or may not include a witness statements or expert (witness) statements.
	11 Filing of pleadings. Plaintiff and defendant file written pleadings and submissions with the court and transmit copies of the written pleadings or submissions to one another. The pleadings may or may not include witness statements or expert (witness) statements.	

12 Adjournments. Court procedure is delayed because one or both parties request and obtain an adjournment to submit written pleadings.

* Court appointment of independent expert. Judge appoints, either at the parties' request or at his own initiative, an independent expert to decide whether the quality of the goods the plaintiff delivered to the defendant is adequate. See assumption 6-b of this case.

13 Notification of court-appointment of independent expert. The court notifies both parties that the court is appointing an independent expert. See assumption 6-b of this case.

* Delivery of expert report by court-appointed expert. The independent expert appointed by the court delivers his or her expert report to the court. See assumption 6-b of this case.

12 Adjournments. Court procedure is delayed because one or both parties request and obtain an adjournment to submit written pleadings.

* Court appointment of independent expert. Judge appoints, either at the parties' request or at his own initiative, an independent expert to decide whether the quality of the goods the plaintiff delivered to the defendant is adequate. See assumption 6-b of this case.

13 Notification of court-appointment of independent expert. The court notifies both parties that the court is appointing an independent expert. See assumption 6-b of this case.

* Delivery of expert report by court-appointed expert. The independent expert appointed by the court delivers his or her expert report to the court. See assumption 6-b of this case.

15 Adjournments. Court procedure is delayed because one or both parties request and obtain an adjournment to submit written pleadings.

* Court appointment of independent expert. Judge appoints, either at the parties' request or at his own initiative, an independent expert to decide whether the quality of the goods the plaintiff delivered to the defendant is adequate. See assumption 6-b of this case.

* Delivery of expert report by court-appointed expert. The independent expert appointed by the court delivers his or her expert report to the court. See assumption 6-b of this case.

(continued)

Figure 4.11 (continued)

Greece	France	Germany
		14 Mediation hearing. The judge during this informal meeting with the parties encourages them to settle the case. The judge acts as mediator. If the case cannot be settled, the judge may draft a pre-trial conference report, after which the case may be allocated to another judge for trial.
* Setting of date(s) for oral hearing or trial. The judge sets the date(s) for the oral hearing or trial.	* Setting of date(s) for oral hearing or trial. The judge sets the date(s) for the oral hearing or trial.	* Setting of date(s) for oral hearing or trial. The judge sets the date(s) for the oral hearing or trial.
		15 Summoning of (expert) witnesses. The court summons (expert) witnesses to appear in court for the oral hearing or trial.
16 Adjournments. Court proceedings are delayed because one or both parties request and obtain an adjournment to prepare for the oral hearing or trial.	14 Oral hearing (prevalent in civil law.) The parties argue the merits of the case at an oral hearing before the judge. Witnesses and a court-appointed independent expert may be heard and questioned at the oral hearing.	16 Oral hearing (prevalent in civil law.) The parties argue the merits of the case at an oral hearing before the judge. Witnesses and a court-appointed independent expert may be heard and questioned at the oral hearing.
17 Oral hearing (prevalent in civil law.) The parties argue the merits of the case at an oral hearing before the judge. Witnesses and a court-appointed independent expert may be heard and questioned at the oral hearing.		

* Final arguments. The parties present their final factual and legal arguments to the court either by oral presentation or by a written submission.

18 Notification of judgment in court. The parties are notified of the judgment at a court hearing.

19 Writing of judgment. The judge produces a written copy of the judgment.

20 Registration of judgment. The court office registers the judgment after receiving a written copy of the judgment.

21 Plaintiff's receipt of a copy of written judgment. The plaintiff receives a copy of the written judgment.

15 Judgment date. The judge sets a date for delivery of the judgment.

16 Notification of judgment in court. The parties are notified of the judgment at a court hearing.

17 Writing of judgment. The judge produces a written copy of the judgment.

18 Registration of judgment. The court office registers the judgment after receiving a written copy of the judgment.

19 Court notification of availability of the written judgment. The court notifies the parties that the written judgment is available at the courthouse.

20 Plaintiff's receipt of a copy of written judgment. The plaintiff receives a copy of the written judgment.

17 Adjournments. Court proceedings are delayed because one or both parties request and obtain an adjournment during the oral hearing or trial, resulting in an additional or later trial or hearing date.

18 Judgment date. The judge sets a date for delivery of the judgment.

19 Writing of judgment. The judge produces a written copy of the judgment.

20 Registration of judgment. The court office registers the judgment after receiving a written copy of the judgment.

21 Court notification of availability of the written judgment. The court notifies the parties that the written judgment is available at the courthouse.

22 Plaintiff's receipt of a copy of written judgment. The plaintiff receives a copy of the written judgment.

(continued)

Figure 4.11 (continued)

Greece	France	Germany
22 Notification of defendant of judgment. Plaintiff or court formally notifies the defendant of the judgment. The appeal period starts to run the day the defendant is formally notified of the judgment.	21 Notification of defendant of judgment. Plaintiff or court formally notifies the defendant of the judgment. The appeal period starts to run the day the defendant is formally notified of the judgment.	23 Notification of defendant of judgment. Plaintiff or court formally notifies the defendant of the judgment. The appeal period starts to run the day the defendant is formally notified of the judgment.
23 Appeal period. The defendant has the opportunity to appeal the judgment during a period specified in the law. Defendant decides not to appeal. Judgment becomes final the day the appeal period ends.	22 Appeal period. The defendant has the opportunity to appeal the judgment during a period specified in the law. Defendant decides not to appeal. Judgment becomes final the day the appeal period ends.	24 Appeal period. The defendant has the opportunity to appeal the judgment during a period specified in the law. Defendant decides not to appeal. Judgment becomes final the day the appeal period ends.
24 Reimbursement by defendant of plaintiff's court fees. The judgment obliges defendant to reimburse plaintiff for the court fees plaintiff has advanced, because defendant has lost the case.	23 Reimbursement by defendant of plaintiff's court fees. The judgment obliges defendant to reimburse plaintiff for the court fees plaintiff has advanced, because defendant has lost the case.	25 Reimbursement by defendant of plaintiff's court fees. The judgment obliges defendant to reimburse plaintiff for the court fees plaintiff has advanced, because defendant has lost the case.
	Enforcement of judgment	
* Plaintiff's hiring of lawyer. Plaintiff hires a lawyer to enforce the judgment or continues to be represented by a lawyer during the enforcement of judgment phase.	* Plaintiff's hiring of lawyer. Plaintiff hires a lawyer to enforce the judgment or continues to be represented by a lawyer during the enforcement of judgment phase.	* Plaintiff's hiring of lawyer. Plaintiff hires a lawyer to enforce the judgment or continues to be represented by a lawyer during the enforcement of judgment phase.

24 Plaintiff's approaching of court enforcement officer or (private) bailiff to enforce the judgment. To enforce the judgment, Plaintiff approaches a court enforcement officer such as a court bailiff or sheriff, or a private bailiff.

25 Plaintiff's approaching of court enforcement officer or (private) bailiff to enforce the judgment. To enforce the judgment, Plaintiff approaches a court enforcement officer such as a court bailiff or sheriff, or a private bailiff.

* Plaintiff's request for enforcement order. Plaintiff applies to the court to obtain the enforcement order ('seal' on judgment).

26 Plaintiff's advancement of enforcement fees. Plaintiff pays the fees related to the enforcement of the judgment.

27 Attachment of enforcement order to judgment. The judge attaches the enforcement order ('seal') to the judgment.

* Delivery of enforcement order. The court's enforcement order is delivered to a court enforcement officer or a (private) bailiff.

28 Judge's order for physical enforcement. The judge orders the police to assist with the physical enforcement of the attachment of the defendant's movable goods.

26 Plaintiff's approaching of court enforcement officer or (private) bailiff to enforce the judgment. To enforce the judgment, Plaintiff approaches a court enforcement officer such as a court bailiff or sheriff, or a private bailiff.

* Plaintiff's request for enforcement order. Plaintiff applies to the court to obtain the enforcement order ('seal' on judgment).

27 Attachment of enforcement order to judgment. The judge attaches the enforcement order ('seal') to the judgment.

* Delivery of enforcement order. The court's enforcement order is delivered to a court enforcement officer or a (private) bailiff.

(continued)

Figure 4.11 (continued)

Greece	France	Germany
29 Request to defendant to comply voluntarily with judgment. The plaintiff, a court enforcement officer or a (private) bailiff requests defendant to voluntarily comply with the judgment, giving the defendant one last chance to comply voluntarily with the judgment.	25 Request to defendant to comply voluntarily with judgment. The plaintiff, a court enforcement officer or a (private) bailiff requests defendant to voluntarily comply with the judgment, giving the defendant one last chance to comply voluntarily with the judgment.	28 Request to defendant to comply voluntarily with judgment. The plaintiff, a court enforcement officer or a (private) bailiff requests Defendant to voluntarily comply with the judgment, giving the defendant one last chance to comply voluntarily with the judgment.
30 Plaintiff's identification of defendant's assets for attachment. The plaintiff identifies the defendant's assets for attachment.	26 Identification of defendant's assets for attachment by court official or defendant. The judge, a court enforcement officer, a (private) bailiff or the defendant himself identifies the defendant's movable assets for attachment.	29 Identification of defendant's assets for attachment by court official or defendant. The judge, a court enforcement officer, a (private) bailiff or the defendant himself identifies the defendant's movable assets for attachment.
31 Attachment. Defendant's movable goods are attached (physically or by registering, marking or separating assets).	27 Attachment. Defendant's movable goods are attached (physically or by registering, marking or separating assets).	30 Attachment. Defendant's movable goods are attached (physically or by registering, marking or separating assets).
32 Report on execution of attachment. A court enforcement officer or private process server delivers a report on the attachment of the defendant's movable goods to the judge.		
33 Valuation or appraisal of attached movable goods. The court or court-appointed valuation expert issues a valuation of the attached property.		

34 Enforcement disputes before court. The enforcement of the judgment is delayed because the defendant opposes aspects of the enforcement process before the judge.

35 Call for public auction. The judge calls a public auction by, for example, advertising or publication in the newspapers.

36 Sale through public auction. The defendant's movable property is sold at public auction.

37 Distribution of proceeds. The proceeds of the public auction are distributed to various creditors (including the plaintiff), according to the rules of priority.

38 Reimbursement of plaintiff's enforcement fees. The defendant reimburses plaintiff's enforcement fees.

39 Payment. The court orders that the proceeds of the public auction or the direct sale be delivered to the plaintiff.

31 Enforcement disputes before court. The enforcement of the judgment is delayed because the defendant opposes aspects of the enforcement process before the judge.

32 Call for public auction. The judge calls a public auction by, for example, advertising or publication in the newspapers.

33 Sale through public auction. The defendant's movable property is sold at public auction.

34 Reimbursement of plaintiff's enforcement fees. The defendant reimburses the plaintiff's enforcement fees.

35 Payment. The court orders that the proceeds of the public auction or the direct sale be delivered to the plaintiff.

Notes: Steps with asterisk by Doing Business are not counted as separate steps.
Assumption 5 of "Doing Business" for "Enforce contract", which is cited in figure: Seller attaches buyer's goods prior to obtaining a judgment because seller fears that buyer may become insolvent during the lawsuit. Assumption 6-b regards details of the practice of giving the expert opinion.

Figure 4.11 Comparison of details of list of procedural steps necessary to enforce a contract by Doing Business for Greece, France and Germany

These details certainly should be examined and possibly incorporated in the qualitative improvements that the previous sections suggest would be appropriate for the case of Greece.

Recently the current president of the Areios Pagos (tertiary civil court) proposed the improvement of the infrastructure of courts and, in particular, the encouragement of out-of-court settlements, as well as the more frequent use of the article of law that permits the summary dismissal of cases, the reduction of postponements and the change in the law that requires court hearings even for small administrative and other violations. These proposals, especially the ones regarding the encouragement of settlements together with the practice to summarily dismiss clearly frivolous cases, seem to indicate that the fact that, according to the database of Doing Business, no meditation hearing takes place during the judicial process in Greece may indeed be a significant shortcoming of the design of the Greek judicial system. Furthermore, the removal from courts of simple violations and infractions is in line with the observation that organizational matters seem to be important for lower courts.

4.11   Preserving the independence of the judiciary during reform

The question of the efficiency with which the rule of law is implemented in a society has drawn the attention of recent studies, like Botero et al. (2003), who argue for the need for judicial independence. Such independence is necessary, they mention, to secure the judicial process against meddling by other branches of government. Such meddling may not only interfere with the normal process of the judiciary, affecting adversely the impartiality of its rulings and thus lowering the quality of the services provided by the judiciary, but they may also allow the introduction of pressures from organized rent-seeking interest groups that want to either block reform or promote measures that undermine the quality of the judicial system. LaPorta et al. (2003) provide empirical evidence to support the claim that an independent judiciary is a strong predictor of economic freedom. Dakolias (1996) proposes that the inefficiency in the administration of justice is a product of many obstacles, which include a lack of independence of the judiciary. But the case for the independence of the judiciary has been made in a compelling way before, not least by Madison in the Federalist Paper no 51 (1788). Madison states that in particular the judiciary has to be independent of the legislature. Thus, it seems reasonable to adopt the recommendation of Dakolias (1996) that the independence of the judiciary has structural, organizational and administrative aspects which must be considered during reform. Aspects that should be considered include substantive, personal, collective and internal independence. Personal independence for judges can be achieved through appropriate judicial terms, the level of the salaries as well as case and court assignments.

In addition, the procedures following which judges are appointed, evaluated, disciplined and promoted play an important role in guaranteeing independence, as well as maintaining qualified judges on the bench. Judicial independence also requires a transparent and merit-based appointment system. It is stressed that all these elements constitute the overall independence of the judiciary and must be considered during judicial reform – not only for practical reasons, but also in order to put to rest any issue raised against the introduction of organizational reforms in the name of the "public nature" of this particular service.

4.12 Conclusions

To sum up, the evidence at hand suggests that Greek society may face a substantial cost associated with the inefficiency of its judiciary and the lack of competition in legal services markets, which apparently lead to the low quality of judicial services – at least as far as the speed of justice is concerned. A number of other related indicators regarding the stringent regulation that limits competition in the provision of legal services, but also regarding the levels of accountability and the quality of the design of the judicial procedure, suggest that the demand and supply of judicial services is not optimal in Greece, contributing – as an aggregate – to the failings of the Greek judiciary. It seems likely that, as a result, in Greece injured parties often forego their right to have material and immaterial property protected, and that these parties are deprived of their right to have access to a reasonably speedy and fair trial. An even more significant cost may be associated with changes in the behavior of agents who, responding rationally to the high cost of litigation and the uncertainty of outcomes, reduce their caution to avoid acts that injure other parties, as shown by Cooter (1985) – which means that the legal system fails in its role as a deterrent. This cost is also suggested by the finding of the Doing Business in 2004 report that the inefficiency of the judiciary encourages parties to seek ways to form contracts that do not lead to disputes, although these new contracts may present other serious drawbacks. Even more importantly, the failings of the official dispute arbitration mechanism are set in Greece in an environment of generally weak institutions, low-quality laws and weak enforcement. As a result the failings of the judiciary emerge as among the most crucial elements of the institutional setting that undermine the "rule of law" in Greece and contribute to the replication of the disadvantageous equilibrium that was described in Chapter 2. It comes therefore as no surprise that once the lenders involved in the conditionality program documented the extent of these failings, they proceeded to incorporate an increasingly detailed and wide ranging reform agenda for the judiciary in the conditionality program.

References

Acemoglou, D., S. Johnson and J. A. Robinson (2005), "Institutions as the Fundamental Cause of Long-Run Growth," in P. Aghion and S. Durlauf (eds.), *Handbook of Economic Growth*. North-Holland: Amsterdam.

Albanis, A. (2004), "Increasing of the Workload of Notaries Public." *Notary Journal*, January–March.

Baker, J. (1996), "Conveyance Fees in a Competitive Market." Justice Research Centre. Law Foundation of New South Wales.

Balas, A., R. La Porta, F. Lopez-de-Silanes and A. Shleifer (2009). "The Divergence of Legal Procedures." *American Economic Journal: Economic Policy*, American Economic Association, 1(2): 138–62.

Bellis, G. (2001). "Efficiency of Justice." *Dike International*, 1277–81.

Blanchard, O. and F. Giavazzi (2003), "Macroeconomic Effects of Regulation and Deregulation in Goods and Labor Markets." *The Quarterly Journal of Economics*, 118(3): 879–907.

Blankenburg, E. (1999). "Civil Justice, Access Costs and Expedition – The Netherlands," in A. S. A. Zuckerman (ed.), *Civil Justice in Crisis: Comparative Perspectives of Civil Procedure*. Oxford: Oxford University Press.

Botero, J. C., R. La Porta, F. Lopez-de-Silanes, A. Shleifer and A. Volokh (2003), "Judicial Reform." *The World Bank Research Observer*, 18(1): 61–88.

Brown, J. (1998), "Economic Theory of Liability Rules," in P. Newman (ed.), *The New Palgrave Dictionary of Economics and the Law*. London: Palgrave Macmillan.

Buscaglia, E. (1999), "Judicial Corruption in Developing Countries: Its Causes and Economic Consequences." Berkeley Program in Law and Economics Working Paper Series Working Paper 28.

Buscaglia, E. and M. Dakolias (1996), "Judicial Reform in Latin American Courts: The Experience in Argentina and Equador." World Bank Technical Paper 350.

Buscaglia, E. and M. Dakolias (1999), *Comparative International Study of Court Performance Indicators: A Descriptive and Analytical Account*. The International Bank for Reconstruction and Development and the World Bank.

Buscaglia, E. and T. Ulen (1997), "A Quantitative Assessment of the Efficiency of the Judicial Sector in Latin America." *International Review of Law and Economics*, 17: 275–91.

Buscaglia, E. and P. Stephan (2005), "An Empirical Assessment of the Impact of Formal versus Informal Dispute Resolution on Poverty: A Governance-Based Approach." *International Review of Law and Economics*, 25: 89–106.

Church, T., A. Carlson, J. Lee and T. Tan (1978), *Justice Delayed: The Pace of Litigation in Urban Trial Courts*. Williamsburg, VA: National Center for State Courts.

Cole, M. (2001), "The New Zealand Perspective." Paper presented at the World Bank Conference on Legal Structure and Judicial Efficiency. Washington, DC, October 25.

Cooter, R. (1985), "Unity in Tort, Contract and Property: The Model of Precaution." *California Law Review*, 73: 1–45.

Dakolias, M. (1996), *The Judicial Sector in Latin America and the Caribbean Elements of Reform*. World Bank Technical Paper 319.

Dakolias, M. (1999), "Court Performance around the World: A Comparative Perspective." World Bank Technical Paper 430.

Dakolias, M. and S. Said (1999), "Judicial Reform, a Process of Change through Pilot Courts." Legal and Judicial Reform Unit, Legal Department, World Bank.

Dam, K. (2006), "The Judiciary and Economic Development." John M. Olin Law & Economics Working Paper 287.

Djankov, S., R. La Porta, F. Lopez-de-Silanes and A. Shleifer (2002), "The Practice of Justice." World Bank World Development Report.

Djankov, S., R. La Porta, F. Lopez-de-Silanes and A. Shleifer (2003), "Courts." *The Quarterly Journal of Economics*, 118(2): 453–517.

Doing Business Reports of the World Bank (2003, 2004, 2005). World Bank.

Fernandez, R. and D. Rodrik (1991). "Resistance to Reform: Status Quo Bias in the Presence of Individual-Specific Uncertainty." *American Economic Review*, 81(5): 1146–55.

Gemtos, P. (2001), "Economic Analysis of the Civil Trial." *Dike International*, 1251–76.

Ginsburg, T. and G. Hoetker (2004), "The Unreluctant Litigant? An Empirical Analysis of Japan's Turn to Litigation." University of Illinois College of Law. Law and Economics Working Paper No 14.

Hanssen, A. (1999), "The Effect of Judicial Institutions on Uncertainty and the Rate of Litigation: The Election Versus Appointment of Judges." *Journal of Legal Studies*, XXVVIII (1).

Kornhauser, L. (1999), "Judicial Organization and Administration." Author's manuscript. No 7100.

Klein, B., K. Murphy and G. L. Priest (1981), "Litigation v. settlement: A Theory of the Selection of Tried Disputes." University of California Los Angeles Department of Economics Working Paper 197.

Landers, W. M. and R. A. Posner (1979), "Adjudication as a Private Good." *Journal of Legal Studies*, 8: 235–84.

LaPorta, R., F. Lopez-de-Silane, C. Pop-Eleches and A. Shleifer (2003), "Judicial Checks and Balances." NBER Working Papers 9775, National Bureau of Economic Research.

Lopez-de-Silanes, F. (2002), "The Politics of Legal Reform." G-24 Discussion Paper UNCTAD 17.

Makris, D. (2004), *Organization and Acceleration of Legal Protection at the Administrative Higher Appeals Court during the Years 1990–2002*. Athens: Sakkoulas Publications.

Matruglio, T. (1996), *Case Management Rolling Lists in the Family Court, Sydney Registry*. Justice Research Center, Law Foundation of New South Wales.

Mitsopoulos, M. and T. Pelagidis (2007), "Does Staffing Affect the Time to Dispose Cases in Greek Courts?" *International Review of Law and Economics*, 27: 219–44.

Mitsopoulos M. and T. Pelagidis (2010), "Greek Appeals Courts' Quality Analysis and Performance." *European Journal of Law and Economics*, 30(1): 17–39. Published online.

de Montesquieu, Baron, C. L. (1748), *De l' esprit des lois*. Livre XI. (original published anonymously.)

Morriss, A., M. Heise and G. Sisk (2005), "Signaling and Precedent in Federal District Court Opinions." *Supreme Court Economic Review*, 13.

Neubauer, D. W., M. J. Lipetz, M. L. Luskin and J. P. Ryan (1981), *Managing the Pace of Justice: An Evaluation of LESS's Court Delay Reduction Programs*. US Department of Justice, Washington, DC.

Observatory of European SMEs (2002), "Recruitment of Employees Administrative Burdens on SMEs in Europe." European Commission Observatory of European SMEs 7.

Paterson, I., M. Fink and A. Bogus (2003), *Economic Impact of Regulation in the Field of Liberal Professions in Different Member States, Regulation of Professional Services, Final Report – Part 3*. Study by the Institute für Höher Studien, Wien, for the European Commission, DG Competition.

Posner, R. (1993), "What Do Judges and Justices Maximize? (The Same Thing Everyone Else Does)." *Supreme Court Economic Review*, 3: 1–41.

Posner, R. A. (1998), "Creating a Legal Framework for Economic Development." *World Bank Research Observer*, 13(1): 1–11.

Priest, G. L. and B. Klein (1984), "The Selection of Disputes for Litigation." *Journal of Legal Studies*, 13: 1–55.

Shavell, S. (1993), "The Appeals Process as a Means of Error Correction." *The Journal of Legal Studies*, XXIV(2): 379–426.

Smith, A. (1762–3), 'Lectures on Jurisprudence', unpublished original notes taken through his lectures of 1762–3.

Smith, A. (1776), *The Wealth of Nations*, Volume IV–V republished in 1999 and volume I–III in 2003, London.

Taha, A. (2004), "Publish or Paris? Evidence of How Judges Allocate Their Time." *American Law and Economics Review* 6(1): 1–27.

Turcotte, J. W. (1998), "Review of the Two Tiered Trial Court System and the Process of Certifying Judges." Office of Program Policy Analysis and Government Accountability, Florida Legislature.

UK Ministry of Justice (2007), "What's Cost Got to Do with It? The Impact of Changing Court Fees on Users." Ministry of Justice Research Series. No 04/07.

Voiklis, E. (1998), "The Work of Tactical Administrative Courts-Institutional, Operational and Other Shortcomings that Affect Them." *Nomiko Vima*, 46(13).

Waldfogel, J. (1995), "The Selection Hypothesis and the Relationship between Trial and Plaintiff Victory." *Journal of Political Economy*, 103 (2): 229–60.

Part II

5
Strong Growth and Weak Institutions: The Greek Paradox Reconsidered

5.1 Introduction

In Greece, certain positive developments led to the strong growth rates performance observed between the mid-1990s and the onset of the current crisis. These include, primarily, Greece's accession to the eurozone, the creation of competitive credit and capital markets, the satisfactory deregulation of the telecommunications industry and the improvement resulting from productivity-enhancing infrastructure especially in the Athens, "Olympic Games," greater area. These were financed largely by the EU structural funds, but also through the adoption of concessions for the private sector to operate certain infrastructure projects for some period of time in return for their construction. What makes the case of Greece unique is that the creation of an efficient credit market coincided with the establishment of the macroeconomic stability that followed the accession to the European Monetary Union (EMU): in all other countries that have experienced significant credit growth in the wake of either financial sector deregulation or macroeconomic stabilization, these two events had never, until then, coincided in the same way as they did in Greece.

During the same period of time a wide range of factors persisted, and still persist, contributing to the poor performance of certain other aspects of the Greek economy. Lack of competitiveness, to name just the most important of these aspects, is not only documented by numerous databases and surveys by international organizations and researchers, but also by the persistent deficit of the current account in double-digit numbers as a percentage of the GDP, the persisting positive inflation differential with the eurozone and the unattractiveness of Greece to foreign direct investments (FDIs) (inflows minus outflows) – these are practically nil. Recent research by institutions like the OECD and the World Bank, as well as a detailed presentation of numerous pieces of evidence indicate that the wide range of institutional weaknesses that prevail in Greece account, as a whole, for this dismal performance – a performance that seems to be compatible with the inability of the labor market to create a sufficient number of high-skilled jobs and, as a result, to contribute to the enhancement of social coherence and the employment of the young and talented. This performance, when closer investigated, seems to fit well with initially contradicting patterns that range from the coexistence of low wages and high labor costs to the coexistence of a high inflation differential when compared to the eurozone and an indifferent, at best, profitability for the non-financial corporate sector.

In the second section of this Chapter, we present all the available pieces of evidence that are needed to show how, when one takes account of the positive developments in the Greek economy, as well as its documented weaknesses, one actually can reconcile the case of Greece with the conclusions of existing research and the facts that are observed in other countries. These pieces of evidence will also help to explain subsequently, in sections 5.3–5.5, numerous paradoxes of the Greek economy, as for example the rapid growth of labor productivity in the face of dismal competitiveness, certain aspects of the labor market that merit further investigation and aspects related to the reality of Greek non-financial, as well as financial, corporations. Finally we present certain basic attributes of the Greek pension system and give examples of how reforms that might benefit the competitiveness of the economy and the consumers of the country are not promoted.

The related presentation of numerous institutional rigidities, namely labor and product market rigidities, that remained in Greece at least till the initiation of the conditionality program allows us to justify a general observation regarding the prevalence of "weak institutions" and "weak governance," with a description of a wide range of separate facts. Such a process is compatible with recent work, as well as with the facts documented by international institutions on this subject. This process also allows us to identify Greece as a textbook case, as described by Kaufman and Kraay (2002), in which "growth does not lead by itself to the establishment of good institutions." It allows us to ultimately describe modern Greece as a relatively "closed/rigid markets" country in which prosperity has risen to a level compatible with that of the average of OECD member countries as a result of certain factors and reforms, while the quality of the institutions and governance remains largely compatible with that of developing countries. Thus, according to the approach suggested by Rodrik (2007), the country can be described most accurately as a country that has covered some of the distance toward becoming a developed nation, and that has secured in that way rapid growth for a given period of time. At the same time it has not yet implemented the significant reforms that are needed in order to secure the establishment of the advanced and well working institutions that would be capable of putting the country onto a path of sustainable, and high, long-term growth.

5.2   Greece: Rapid growth over the past years

The OECD (2007) draws accurately the picture of modern Greece (Figure 5.1), which boasted a good performance during the past decade resulting from an upward revision in the GDP and the strong per-capita growth of the GDP. As a matter of fact, between 1993 and 2000 Greece was able, for the first time since the beginning of the 1980s, to keep up with the growth performance of the benchmark economies, which today make up the eurozone. And then, at the beginning of the 2000s, when Europe – and the eurozone – saw their performance burdened by a weak conjecture, Greece clearly outperformed the benchmark eurozone economy.

The driving force behind this very strong performance during the past decade, as correctly mentioned by the OECD (2007) and further

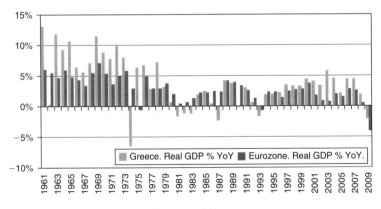

Figure 5.1   Real GDP growth in Greece and Europe

elaborated in Mitsopoulos and Pelagidis (2009), includes a number of factors, among which some stand out:

1. The proper liberalization of the financial markets, which started at the beginning of the 1990s and whose completion was accompanied by accession to the EMU, and which has led to a steady increase of private credit between 2000 and 2008.

2. Some improvement in the regulation of product markets, which has been reduced from a very high level, even though it still remains very high compared to other OECD countries according to Conway and Nicoletti (2006). And as reflected in Figure 5.2, the OECD structural indicators database for energy, communications and transport, if investigated in its details, accurately shows that the improvement observed is to be attributed to the deregulation of the telecommunications market at the beginning of the 1990s, while the energy and transport markets remained essentially regulated and uncompetitive – the first in spite of a deregulation that has happened only on paper and the second since the existing legislation still explicitly prohibited a competitive transport market, till the deregulation that was implemented in the end of 2010 according to the conditionality program.

3. The fiscal stimulus created by the 2004 Olympic Games and, one should add, the associated improvement in certain infrastructure

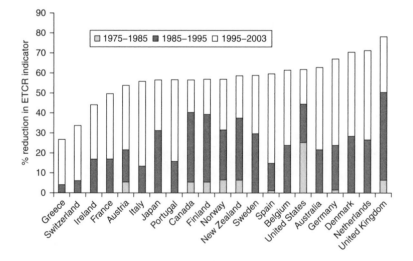

Figure 5.2 Timing of reforms in energy, transport and communications (increase in reform effort)

facilities. These were added to the improvement of the telecommunications services as a result of the satisfactory deregulation of the sector; they benefited cumulatively the productivity of the economy of the greater Athens area.

4. The influx of funds from the European Union, which also contributed largely to the improvement of infrastructure facilities.

As Figure 5.3 shows, the expansion of private sector credit in the wake of the financial services market deregulation and EMU accession complemented the inflow from the EU structural funds and the Common Agricultural Policy during the past years. One should also stress that the expansion of private credit replaced after the beginning of the 1990s the government deficit spending as the main way to finance the expansion of consumption in Greece. As Figure 5.3 shows, the impact of these developments on the GDP rate was important for every year of a prolonged period that spans the entire duration of Greece's strong performance. Therefore, in the case of Greece, the inclusion of this data is appropriate and necessary in order to reach the most useful conclusions from an analysis of the macroeconomic developments of the country. Figure 5.3 measures the change in stocks, as a percentage of the GDP, for private sector credit and public debt, as well as the net inflows from the EU budget into Greece as a percentage of the GDP of the relevant year. Figure 5.3 aims to give an approximation of the size of the importance certain developments that helped to finance domestic consumption

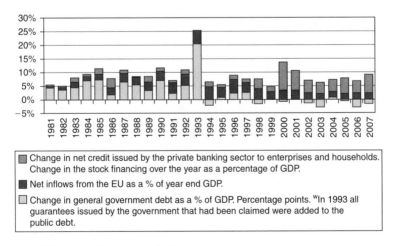

Change in net credit issued by the private banking sector to enterprises and households. Change in the stock financing over the year as a percentage of GDP.

Net inflows from the EU as a % of year end GDP.

Change in general government debt as a % of GDP. Percentage points. ᵂIn 1993 all guarantees issued by the government that had been claimed were added to the public debt.

Figure 5.3   Demand injections in Greece

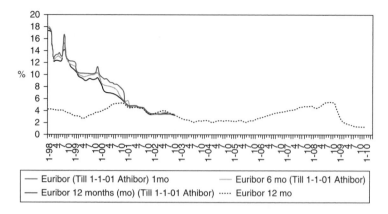

Figure 5.4 Interbank rates

in Greece had in the past decades, and thus captures the relative magnitude of these measures given the GDP of each year. For example an increase in the general government debt-to-GDP ratio from 60 percent to 70 percent in year x+1 with respect to year x is depicted as a demand injection of 10 percent for year x+1, while an inflow of EU funds of 2.5 percent of the GDP in year y is depicted as a demand injection of 2.5 percent of the GDP during that year.

The contribution of the stabilization of the macroeconomic outlook of Greece in the wake of the EMU accession to the expansion of private credit was significant. This is not only shown by the rapid fall of interbank rates after 1998 (Figure 5.4), which reflect also the decline in the rates offered by commercial banks to households and businesses, but also by the respective fall in the inflation differential between Greece and the eurozone average during the same period of time (Figure 5.5). However, the size of the growth contribution of this macroeconomic stabilization has to be controlled by the fact that until 1994 and 1999, when the last phase of the implementation into the Greek national law of the EU banking directives, which was initiated in 1992, was completed, the Greek economy was essentially unbanked. That is, the total amount of loans issued by the Main Financial Institutions (MFIs) did not exceed 24 percent of the GDP. The expansion of private credit in the wake of all these events was explosive, raising the level of financing issued by the main MFIs to households and businesses to over 80 percent of the GDP by the end of 2008; only recently has the rate of this credit expansion started to slow down, as shown in Figure 5.6. This trend has been further affected by the current crisis, but a gradual

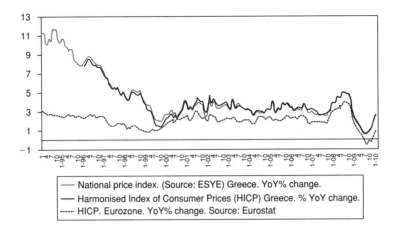

Figure 5.5   Price index changes as a percentage, year-on-year

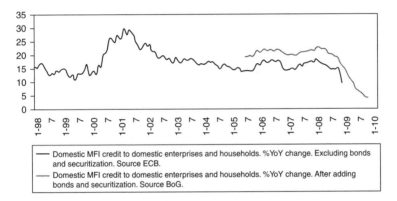

Figure 5.6   Yearly percentage change in financing of households and businesses from domestic MFIs

convergence of the credit growth rates with the eurozone growth rates was anyhow to be expected in the next years, in spite of the fact that the level of credit issued to households and businesses still remains below eurozone averages. This is so since the high level of government debt more or less compensates for this difference. In other words, at the onset of the current recession, the level of indebtness of both the private and public sectors were already at levels comparable with those of the eurozone countries (Figures 5.7, 5.8 and 5.9). This implied a limited ability of private sector credit to continue to grow at rates that

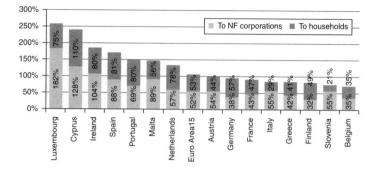

Figure 5.7   Loans by MFIs as a percentage of the GDP. November 2008 data. NF: Non-financial

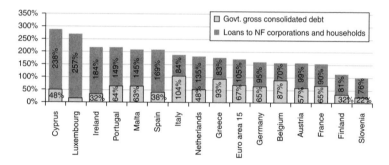

Figure 5.8   Government gross consolidated debt and loans by MFIs as a percentage of the GDP. November 2008 data. NF: Non-financial Eurozone member countries

significantly exceed the growth rate of the nominal GDP even if policy mistakes had not led Greece on a path of a deep and prolonged recession, unless of course the general government debt as a percentage of the GDP starts falling rapidly.

The important growth contribution of the creation and subsequent expansion of private credit within a stable macro-environment should not lead to the underestimation of the contribution of other reforms, such as the deregulation of the telecommunications market, first through the proper establishment of a competitive market for mobile telecommunications in 1992 and then, under pressure from EU legislation this time, through the less willing and more hesitant deregulation of the market for fixed line telecommunications. The fact that during a period of time (when Greece had persistently higher inflation than the other eurozone countries) the sub-index for telecommunication services, as

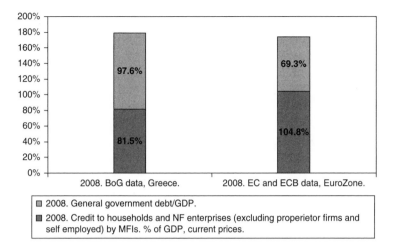

Figure 5.9 Total indebtness as a percentage of the GDP. Greece and eurozone average

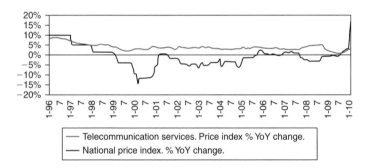

Figure 5.10 Year-on-year percentage price index changes. General price index and index for telecommunication services

shown in Figure 5.10, was steadily declining reflects only one aspect of the positive contribution this deregulation had to economic development. It should be noted here that the increase in the price of telephone services after 2009 follows from the increase in the taxes on mobile phones and mobile internet. These taxes have been repeatedly raised in the past decade, to a level that is now the highest in the EU. Thus these increases are a result of government initiatives and not market developments. Unfortunately these increases are not the only regulatory retraction in a market that so far has provided the sole positive contribution for Greece to the structural indicators database of the OECD. For example,

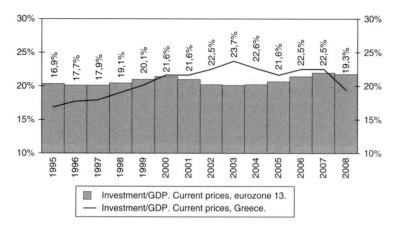

Figure 5.11 Investment-to-GDP ratio. Greece and eurozone

the new law that requires all mobile telecommunications antennae to be relicensed under a cumbersome procedure that is, often unlawfully, not followed by the responsible administration offices means that the majority of the mobile telecommunications, and therefore mobile internet, infrastructure is at this time unlicensed, which means in effect that it is illegal. As a result substantial existing investment is put at risk, and new investment is in effect discouraged at a time when the tax burden on the services provided by this infrastructure increases and mobile internet, supposedly, is actively promoted and even subsidized by government initiatives. In addition the significant efficiency gains that have been made in the economy over the past years as a result of the sector's deregulation are currently put at a completely unnecessary risk.

With regard to the gains accruing from the sector's deregulation, besides the fall in prices and, of course, as long as the repeated and very high tax increases on mobile telecommunications services did not wipe these gains out entirely for consumers, it has been documented by Terrovitis (2005) that in the ten years that followed this deregulation, sustainable private sector jobs were created even while employment in the fixed line state monopoly declined. At the same time the improvement in the quality of the services provided contributed crucially to the ability of other sectors of the economy to modernize, with the financial sector – which was rapidly developing at the time – being just one such example.

The rapid increase in new investment (Figure 5.11) also reflects the impact of the infrastructure investment that was largely financed, or indirectly encouraged, by the EU structural funds. The fact that a large

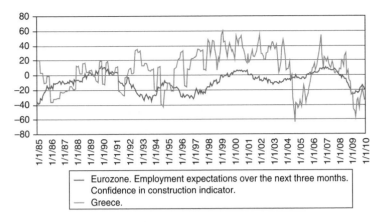

Figure 5.12 Employment expectations in construction. Greece and eurozone

part of the total investment was related to infrastructure projects, and the projects directly or indirectly related to the 2004 Olympic Games, is not incompatible with the fact that the information and communication technology (ICT) share of the total investment in Greece is one of the lowest in the OECD, as documented by Arnold et al. (2008), and that a significant portion of private investment has been so far in buildings. This is also reflected by the fact that since the onset of the current crisis investment has fallen rapidly from its previous high levels – in line with the stagnation of the construction and housing market.

The sharp drop in the employment expectations documented by the European Commission's monthly survey for the construction sector at the time of the completion of the infrastructure projects that were set to finish before the Olympic Games of 2004 gives an indication of the positive effect these projects had on job creation, at least in this sector (Figure 5.12). Positive effects seem to peter out, though, as the large infrastructure projects are gradually completed, the housing market weakens as a result of the conjecture and repeated policy mistakes and businesses face a weakening conjecture along with a declining competitiveness of the economy together with an increasing tax burden.

Still the rush into EU-financed infrastructure investment did not only contribute to the direct creation of new jobs, as in the end many of these projects, when finished, actively boosted the productivity of the Greek economy – especially in the area surrounding Athens, which hosts about half the population and economic activity of the country. Therefore the impact on the productivity of the whole economy that followed from the Athens area infrastructure projects probably has been significant for the whole economy, even though there does not seem to exist so far a study that has attempted to quantify these effects more precisely. It should be added here that, in addition to these developments, over the past years private investment also has increased significantly, especially in the growth sectors of banking and telecommunications. In certain cases this development was also accompanied by the development of a production infrastructure and know-how that supported the ability of the economy to produce and export goods and services.

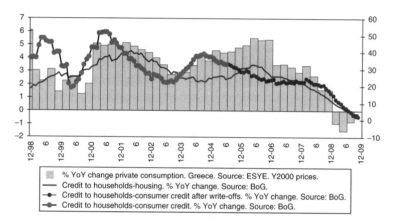

Figure 5.13   Credit expansion and private consumption yearly change. Greece

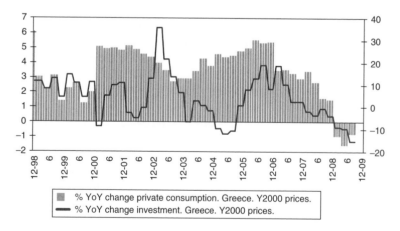

Figure 5.14   Year-on-year percentage change in private consumption and investment

In Figure 5.13 it can be seen clearly how the expansion of credit to households fueled the growth of private consumption over the past years, and how during the period preceding the completion of the infrastructure projects that were prepared to be ready for the 2004 Olympic games private consumption kept accelerating in spite of a gradual slowdown of the explosive growth of private sector credit, thus making up for the fall in the contribution of investment toward the GDP growth at that time. Figure 5.14 shows clearly this pattern.

5.3 Low competitiveness combined with a weak labor market

5.3.1 Low competitiveness

In spite of the impressive 4 percent average growth performance of the last 15 years, four pieces of information illustrate how the Greek economy retained certain severe weaknesses that undermined its competitiveness. First, the inflation differential with the eurozone, second the continuous and persisting excessive trade balance deficit, and third the consistent ranking of Greece by all competitiveness surveys – including the World Bank Doing Business and governance indicators, the World Economic Forum Competitiveness Index and the Corruption Perception Index of Transparency International – at a level that is disproportionally low compared to the country's per-capita GDP, as shown in Figure 5.20. Finally, we also add the low level of FDI that flows into Greece, proportionally to the size of the economy.

The interesting part about the inflation differential of Greece with the eurozone (Figure 5.15) is not that it is there – something that many

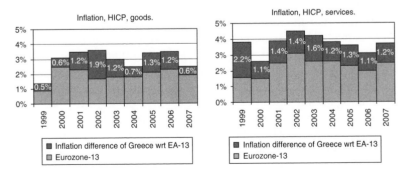

Figure 5.15 Inflation differential. Goods and services. Greece versus eurozone (EA-13)

have tried to explain with the Balassa-Samuelson effect because of the rapid growth rate of the country. Rather, it is that it seems to emerge more or less equally both in the goods and services subindices, something that initially seems to refute the Balassa-Samuelson argument.

An expository comparison with Ireland, where the inflation in goods prices was much lower than the inflation in prices for services during the period that preceded the current crisis, which thus emerges as a textbook Balassa-Samuelson case, is most revealing (Figure 5.16).

The high inflation in Greece therefore seems to emerge as a result of the increase in demand, which is largely driven by the expansion of credit and the inflows from the EU structural funds, as well as inflows from the tourism and merchant shipping industry. This rise in demand is not matched by a similar increase in the domestic supply of goods and services. This differs from the case of Ireland, for example, in which the surplus of the goods balance seems to finance a deficit in the services balance following, again, a pattern that fits well the standard predictions of the Balassa-Samuelson model.

The second piece of evidence that supports this argument is the excessive deficit of the Greek goods trade balance, as a percentage of the GDP (Figure 5.17).

As a matter of fact the Greek current account deficit has so far been of a magnitude that has never been seen in any country without the subsequent emergence of serious consequences. In the case of Greece, the participation in the eurozone seems to have initially averted developments such as the onset of a spiral of high inflation and currency devaluations, in spite of the size of this deficit. As a result, the trade and services deficit in Greece can clearly demonstrate the existence of a serious discrepancy between the growth in domestic demand and the increase in the domestic supply of both goods and services. It should be stressed that in the case of non-tradable services (tourism-related services that could be interpreted to be tradable are a small proportion of the harmonized consumer price index), the inflation differential is sufficient to document the discrepancy between supply and demand, but the emergence of such a differential for goods also suggests the peculiarity of the case of Greece. Therefore, the evidence at hand would make it more appropriate to label Greece a unique case of "quasi Balassa-Samuelson," where the inflow of the exporting sector is replaced by EU transfers and domestic credit expansion, and the price level is pushed upwards both in the goods and in the services sector – which would actually be in line with the conclusions of recent research on the topic by Gibson and Malley (2007), and also Pelagidis and Toay (2007).

123

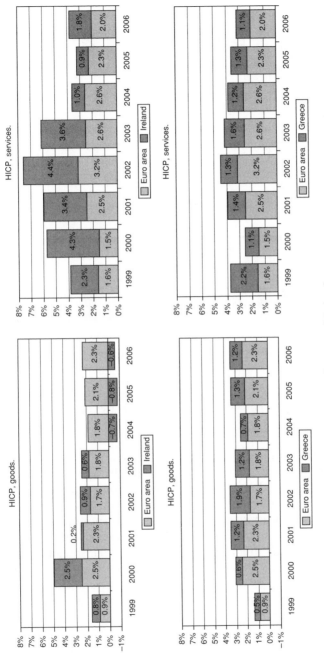

Figure 5.16 Inflation differential. Goods and services. Greece and Ireland versus eurozone

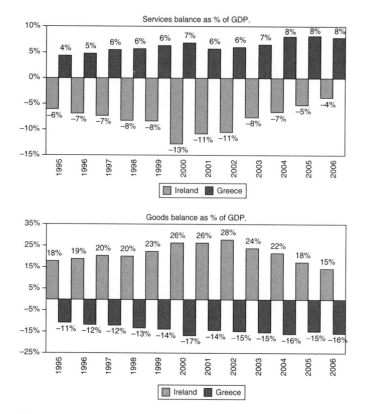

Figure 5.17   Goods and services balance as a percentage of the GDP. Greece and Ireland

The increase in the goods deficit follows as a natural consequence in this case, as increases in demand are satisfied by competitive and available imported goods as there is no sufficient competitive domestic supply of goods to compete with these imports.

This persistent deterioration of the goods balance has been financed by – besides the surplus of the services account (Figure 5.18), which mainly originates from inflows related to tourism and merchant shipping – foreign inflows in both Greek government bonds, as well as into the stocks of Greece companies, at least until the start of the present financial turmoil and the implementation of the conditionality program. The latter replaced these inflows, at least for the part that is financed by the general government deficit. However it should be noted that these inflows were rarely FDIs. FDIs during the recent past

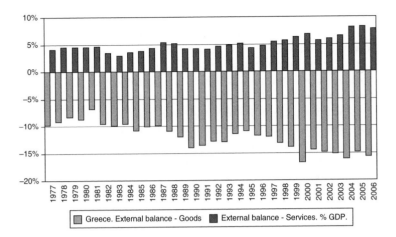

Figure 5.18 Goods and services balance as a percentage of the GDP. Greece

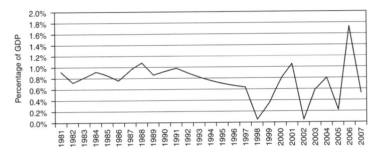

Figure 5.19 Direct investment in reporting economy. FDI inward (net flow change in billion euros)

were rather negligible, with the exception of 2006, when controlling stakes in some major Greek companies were sold to foreign shareholders (Figure 5.19), and thus registered as FDIs.

The performance of the goods balance, together with the inflation differential with respect to the eurozone for tradable goods, suggests also that the cost of importing and distributing these competitive imported goods is higher than in the eurozone. This seems to follow from the highly regulated transport services market, which we will examine in Appendix 1, and the high administrative burden faced by the economy, as shown in Figure 5.21. Furthermore, it suggests that the imports remain competitive in the domestic market in spite of this high cost of importing and distributing, which seems to be really damning for the competitiveness of the domestic supply of goods.

Notwithstanding the mitigating effect of the surplus of the services balance, the current account balance has remained for many years at a level, compared to the GDP, that – as already mentioned – in any other country would have been unsustainable for an equally long period of time. As to the two sectors that contribute to the services account surplus, it should be noted that they are less affected by the regulatory environment of the Greek economy, either because they operate almost completely outside the Greek jurisdiction and administrative reality, in the case of merchant shipping, or because they draw their competitive strength largely from the geographical attractiveness and cultural heritage of Greece, in the case of tourism. The story of the Greek merchant shipping relocation to London, in the wake of a number of attempts to tax the property and revenue accruing from the business, as documented by Harlaftis (1995), and the related common saying of merchant ship-owners that "one should not own even a kiosk (periptero) in Greece," are most revealing of the way the merchant shipping industry benefits from its ability to operate outside the Greek jurisdiction. The "prejudice" appears to be verified each time some ship-owner decides to contribute to the development of the country through some substantial new investment on the mainland, with the story of a large investment in tourism infrastructure in the Peloponnese that has been dragging on for decades being just one example.

These pieces of evidence are matched by the low competitiveness of the Greek economy that is documented by a number of surveys (Figure 5.20). The important part to note here is that a wide selection of different surveys, including those that measure governance and corruption, rank Greece in a roughly similar way, even though the methodologies they employ often differ significantly. This is consistent with the findings presented by Kaufmann and Kraay (2006) that an evaluation should be based on both objective and subjective measures, despite the fact that they also argue that the margins of error that arise from the use of different methods (either based on the evaluation of hard evidence or subjective responses to questionnaires) are rather similar.

Therefore is not surprising that the OECD regulation database, the World Economic Forum competitiveness survey, the World Bank Doing Business reports and estimates of the European Commission (2006), to name a few, all find that in Greece the administrative burden is exceptionally high (as shown in Figure 5.21), that regulation of product markets is excessive, that government intervention limits competition as well as resource allocation and pricing decisions in crucial

Doing Business in 2010		World Economic Forum (WEF), Globel Competitiveness Index 2009–2010		Transparency Internationall (TI), Corruption Perceptions Index 2008		UN, per capita GDP $, 2007	
Rank		Rank		Rank		Rank	
1	Singapore	1	Switzerland	1	Denmark	1	Liechtenstein
2	New Zealand	2	United States	1	New Zealand	2	Luxembourg
3	Hong Kong, China	3	Singapore	1	Sweden	3	Bermuda
4	United States	4	Sweden	4	Singapore	4	Norway
5	United Kingdom	5	Denmark	5	Finland	5	Qatar
6	Denmark	6	Finland	5	Switzerland	6	Iceland
7	Ireland	7	Germany	7	Iceland	7	Ireland
8	Canada	8	Japan	7	Netherlands	8	Denmark
9	Australia	9	Canada	9	Australia	9	Cayman Islands
10	Norway	10	Netherlands	9	Canada	10	Switzerland
	...		...		...		...
16	Finland	13	United Kingdom	11	Luxembourg		
18	Sweden	14	Norway	12	Austria	13	Sweden
22	Belgium	16	France	14	Germany	14	Netherlands
25	Germany	17	Austria	14	Norway	15	Finland
28	Austria	18	Belgium	16	Ireland	16	Australia
30	Netherlands	21	Luxembourg	16	United Kingdom	17	United Kingdom
31	France	25	Ireland	18	Belgium	18	United States
44	Bulgaria	31	Czech Republic	18	Japan	19	Austria
48	Portugal	33	Spain	18	USA	22	Belgium

(*continued*)

Figure 5.20 Continued

(Continued)

Doing Business in 2010		World Economic Forum (WEF), Globel Competitiveness Index 2009–2010		Transparency International (TI), Corruption Perceptions Index 2008		UN, per capita GDP $, 2007	
Rank		Rank		Rank		Rank	
62	Spain	43	Portugal	26	Slovenia	24	Germany
64	Luxembourg	46	Poland	28	Spain	26	France
73	Turkey	48	Italy	31	Cyprus	30	Singapore
74	Czech Republic	58	Hungary	32	Portugal	31	Italy
78	Italy	61	Turkey	45	Czech Republic	32	Japan
82	Albania	64	Romania	47	Hungary	34	Spain
...		...		...		...	
107	Ethiopia	69	Colombia	55	Italy	37	Turks and Caicos
108	Lebanon	70	Egypt	55	Seychelles	38	Hong Kong
109	Greece	71	Greece	57	Greece	39	Greece
110	Guatemala	72	Croatia	58	Lithuania	40	Cyprus
111	Seychelles	73	Morocco	58	Poland	41	Bahrain
...		...		...		...	
181	Guinea-Bissau	131	Chad	178	Iraq	211	Zimbabwe
182	Congo, Dem. Rep.	132	Zimbabwe	178	Myanmar	212	Congo
183	Central African Republic	133	Burundi	180	Somalia	213	Burundi

Figure 5.20 Competitiveness ranking, corruption ranking and income ranking. All countries

	AT	BL[2]	CZ	DE	DK	ES	FI	FR	UK	GR	HU	IE	IT	NL	PL	PT	RE[2]	SK	SI	SE	EU-25
Administrative cost share in GDP (in %)[1]	4.6	2.8	3.3	3.7	1.9	4.6	1.5	3.7	1.5	6.8	6.8	2.4	4.6	3.7	5.0	4.6	6.8	4.6	4.1	1.5	3.5

[1] Based on Kox (2005): Intra-EU differences in regulation-caused administrative burden for companies. CPB Memorandum 136. CPB, The Hague.
[2] BL combines Belgium and Luxembourg; RE combines the Baltic Member States, Malta and Cyprus; EU-25 figures are GDP-weighted averages.

Figure 5.21 Administrative cost as a percentage of the GDP by EU member state

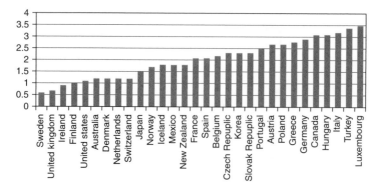

Figure 5.22 OECD regulation index for professional services

network industries and that the regulation of professional services is high as far as entry and price setting is concerned. These reports also find that qualitative standards for professional services are excessively lax, as documented by Paterson et al. (2003) and as reflected in the updated OECD indicator for regulation in professional services (Figure 5.22), and that the business environment – as an aggregate – is, plain and simple, unattractive. These findings are complemented by more general statements that indicate weak institutions besides the business environment, as well as poor governance – as documented by Kaufman et al. (2005) and Kaufman and Kraay (2006) – and high levels of corruption, as documented by Transparency International. The latter in turn seems to follow from the high administrative burden, poor governance and overregulated product markets according to evidence presented in the existing literature, as summarized by Lambsdorff (2006). As demonstrated in Chapter 2, the inability to promote reforms, or the frequent withdrawal of reforms – as was the case for telecommunications, but also for shop opening hours (which is analyzed in Appendix 2) – even when they clearly would benefit consumer welfare, is deeply rooted in the setting of inadequate governance and weak institutions that this unattractive business environment complements. It is furthermore highlighted by the unsatisfactory progress in the implementation of the part of the conditionality program that prescribers exactly these reforms.

The very low level of FDI Greece attracts (Figure 5.19) is in line with these findings, especially since it seems that the unattractive business environment documented in Greece is directly related to the low level of FDI that Greece attracts according to Hajkova et al. (2007), who argue that the business environment is actually more important for the attraction of FDI than the tax rates.

All the recent research previously mentioned and the detailed presentation of numerous pieces of evidence indicate that the wide range of institutional weaknesses that prevail in Greece account, as a whole, for this dismal performance. As a matter of fact, the magnitude of the weaknesses documented by these pieces of evidence is the only observation available that has a magnitude that could match the size of the competitiveness deficit shown for Greece by the inflation differential with respect to the eurozone, the current account deficit as a percentage of the GDP and the low level of FDIs. It has to be added that, not surprisingly, Greece is found to be the OECD country which has the most to gain from rectifying these proven deficiencies, including product market regulation, in terms of increased productivity, as suggested by Conway et al. (2006) – but as also pointed out by Mylonas and Papaconstantinou (2001). The performance of Greece on these aspects can be labeled "dismal," not because of its absolute level, but because of the large discrepancy between the performance of the country on all these aspects and the per-capita GDP that it has achieved in the past years. In particular, following the strong performance until the 1970s and over the past years, the per-capita GDP is relatively close to that of the other OECD and EU-member countries. And while Greece remains among the poorer members of these groups, it still can distance itself clearly from most other countries that do not participate in these two groups of privileged countries. On the other hand all the other performance indicators are clearly much weaker than the performance of all other OECD and EU-member countries. Here Greece clearly is placed, repeatedly, in the middle of the ranking of all the countries in the world, and not in the top 20 percent of the countries, as is the case with its per-capita GDP. Greece, ultimately, emerges as a country with almost first-class per-capita GDP, but clearly second-class governance, institutions, business environment and corruption (Figure 5.23).

The factors that were analyzed previously and that show why Greece grew so fast in spite of these shortcomings can also reconcile the recent performance of Greece with the now extended literature, mainly of OECD Economic Department Working Papers,[1] that directly link the performance of an economy with the quality of the regulatory framework and the prevalence of competitive markets. In a similar way one can reconcile also almost all of the other weak performances of the country, which range from research and innovation, as documented by Bassanini et al. (2000), to the protection of the environment, the

Corruption and Regulation

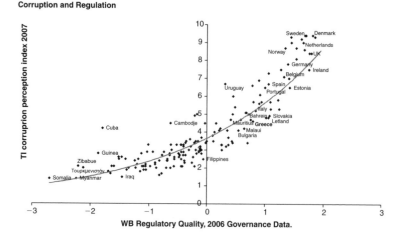

Figure 5.23   Corruption and regulation, all countries

quality of public health services and schools and the performance of the higher education system, as documented by Bassanini and Scarpetta (2001) and, more recently, Sutherland and Price (2007). Even the weak and deteriorating performance of the judiciary – as documented by work like Djankov et al. (2002), and Mitsopoulos and Pelagidis (2007, 2010) – can be ultimately linked to this pattern.

In the end though, product and labor market rigidities still complement, and – according to work like Nicoletti and Scarpetta (2005) – may reinforce, in certain circumstances, each other in Greece today, reducing competition in a wide array of economic activities and creating sufficient rents to keep satisfying the various interest groups that earn these rents, as discussed in Chapter 2 of this book. A depiction of regulatory and institutional rigidities in Greece's economy that is based on the OECD Structural Indicators Database reveals the pattern of state intervention and high administrative costs that secure these rents in greater detail.

The indicators included in the graphs below tie down the definition of business and product market regulation, as measured by the OECD summary indicator of regulatory impediments to product market competition, which itself quote "structural/institutional changes" as changes in these indicators, as explained in Conway and Nicoletti (2006) and presented with their update by the OECD product market regulation homepage.

Figure 5.24 concerns the state involvement in business operations via price controls and Figure 5.25 shows this involvement via the use

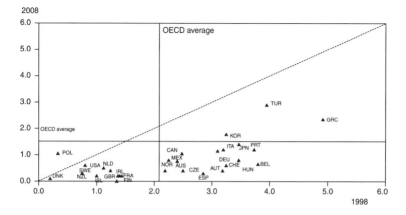

Figure 5.24 State control – price controls

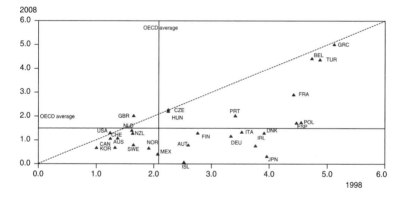

Figure 5.25 State control. Use of command and control regulation

of command and control regulation. "Command and control" includes a lot of administrative mechanisms of hindrance to entrepreneurial activity/organization, in sectors such as road and railway transports, and retail trade. The index also includes mixed government/administrative bodies that check the quality of regulations that are passed by the legislature. These bodies include the British Better Regulation Task Force and Regulatory Impact Assessment-RIA and the Dutch Advisory Board on Administrative Burden. In both Figures 5.24 and 5.25, we observe different scores across EU member states, Greece being clearly the most heavily regulated OECD member country.

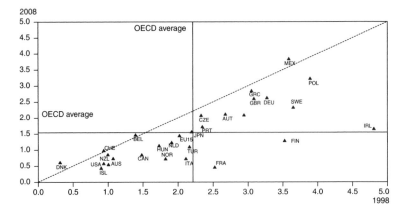

Figure 5.26 Administrative burdens on start-ups

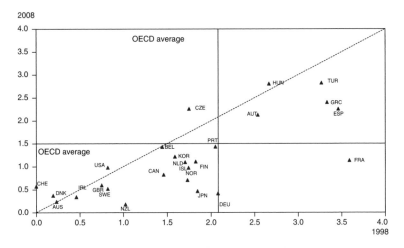

Figure 5.27 Barriers to entrepreneurship – Sector-specific administrative burden

With regard to administrative burden on start-ups and sector-specific administrative burdens (Figures 5.26 and 5.27), the picture continues to be unfortunate for Greece, which scores badly in both indexes and demonstrates a limited improvement during the past decade.

In the same context, barriers to entry in services (Figure 5.28) and barriers to FDIs (Figure 5.29), concerning the complexity of governmental communication of rules and procedures, the license and permit

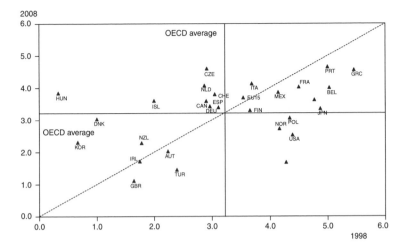

Figure 5.28 Barriers to entrepreneurship – Barriers to entry in services

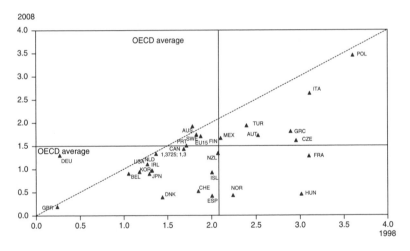

Figure 5.29 Barriers to FDI

system and barriers to FDI as described by Koyama and Golub (2006), presents the extensive diversity of EU member-states administrative procedures needed for domestic and foreign business to act in case of an asymmetric shock. They also highlight the Greek economy as one with the most complex administrative procedures and ownership

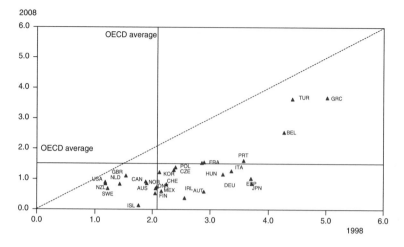

Figure 5.30 State control. Involvement in business operation

barriers among OECD countries. It also reaffirms the difficulty faced
by the successive Greek governments to effectively address these obstacles to entrepreneurship during the past decade.

Figure 5.30 summarizes the product market regulation regarding state
control through the involvement in business operation. Once again
Greece appears to both have the most stringent state involvement in
the operation of businesses and to have maintained these practices
throughout the past decade.

Among the structural indicators of the OECD, Greece scores poorly
also in the summary indicators for regulation in road and rail transport,
professional services and certain aspects of retail services – especially
with regard to the licensing process, large stores and opening hours.
On the other hand, the indexes for communications, in the wake of
the deregulation of the 1990s, is much more favorable, as are also
a number of other indicators, like antitrust exceptions. Yet the sub-
domains Greece scores so badly in collectively form a tight web of
constraints on the ability to start a new business that is able to compete
with incumbents, and to freely design the production process, the supply and distribution chain and the pricing of inputs and outputs. In
effect, the existing regulation actively constraints efforts to improve
these processes in a quest for increasing efficiency, and as a result the
competitiveness of the economy. It has to be added that regarding these
issues, documented progress at the end of the second year of the implementation of the conditionality program is scarce.

5.3.2 A weak labor market

It is unlikely that the wide range of competitive disadvantages that is documented for Greece by such an impressive array of sources leaves unaffected the labor market, and in turn that it is by itself unaffected by the significant weaknesses of the labor market.

The Greek labor marker also mirrors the abovementioned contradictions that emerge from the combination of fast growth, which has led to a high per-capita GDP, and, on the other hand, weak institutions and stringent market regulation. First of all, the Greek labor market has to be labeled "weak" in spite of the documented increase in employment during the years before the onset of the current crisis. It should be stressed here, before proceeding with the analysis, that this performance of the recent past must be contrasted with the period of the 1980s when fiscal expansion by the government led to a significant increase in public debt. That period, unlike the period of expansion of private credit, was linked to a further increase in the structural weaknesses of the economy, as summarized by Bryant et al. (2001), and a general regulatory deterioration, poor growth performance and an increase in unemployment and high inflation.

It also has to be stressed that the fiscal stabilization of the beginning of the 1990s marks the end of the period during which the growth performance of Greece clearly lagged behind the growth performance of the benchmark European countries. And that, after the accession of Greece to the eurozone, the per-capita GDP and average family earnings converged rapidly to the European averages (as shown in Figure 5.31), in coincidence with the increase of the private sector-driven financing of domestic demand, in the given context of reforms and strategic choices that has been described. This period of strong growth performance is also paired with data on employment that shows how after 2000 the employment rate starts for the first time in decades to increase, albeit at a rate that seems very slow when compared to the rapid growth of the GDP, as revealed by Figure 5.32.

Comparing now the performance of the labor market with the growth performance of the economy, we can see how from 2001 until 2007 the performance of the labor market has improved markedly as far as the employment to the population aged 15–65 years is concerned (Figure 5.32). But in spite of this significant improvement, the situation differs from the time Greece last had such employment-to-population ratios for this age bracket, as shown in Figure 5.33. That is because a significant proportion of the population is now aged over 65 and, as a result, monitoring the performance of the labor market for the age bracket of 15–65 years does not cover the full extent of the problems

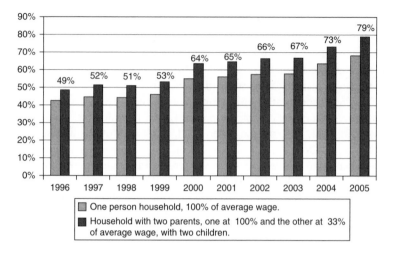

Figure 5.31   Wage earnings in Greece as an average of EU-15 for comparable household

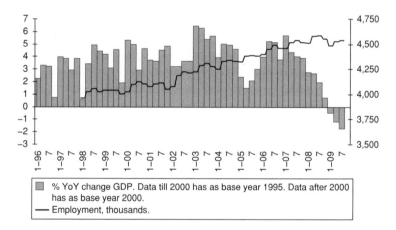

Figure 5.32   GDP and employment growth. Greece

associated with an ageing society, which aggravate the deficiencies of the pension system we present in section 5.7.

Furthermore, the low capacity to employ the young, and especially young women, indicates that the rise in employment for the age bracket 15–65 years and the fall of the unemployment rate mainly signal the improvement of the trend in the labor market, and not the achievement of a well functioning labor market (Figure 5.34). The low

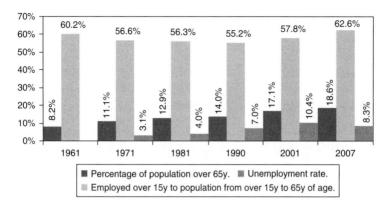

Figure 5.33 Employment, old age population and unemployment rate in Greece

Harmonized unemployment rates, Eurostat, 2008			
	Greece	EA-16	US
Males, under 25 years	17	15.3	14.4
Females, under 25 years	28.9	15.5	11.2
Total population, all age groups 15–65	7.7	7.5	5.8

Figure 5.34 Unemployment in Greece, Eurozone 16 (EA-16) and the US

employment-to-population ratio, relatively to not only the eurozone average but also the US, is disproportionally linked with the low employment of the young (and especially young women), which therefore seems to indicate the persistence of some serious qualitative failures in the workings of the labor market in spite of the gradual decline of the unemployment rate. It is this array of attributes that warrants the labeling of the Greek labor market as "weak", something that is also supported by the rapid increase of unemployment during 2010 and 2011.

We can see (Figure 5.35) how the improvement of the labor market during the years till the onset of the current crisis had not been able to bridge the significant gap, as far as the employment rate of the population aged over 15 years is concerned, with the other major EU countries. The weak performance of Greece becomes especially obvious when compared with the sizeable progress of, say, Spain until the year 2006 – that is, before the onset of the current crisis. Looking at the employment rate for all the population over 15 years old, and not only the 15–64 age bracket,

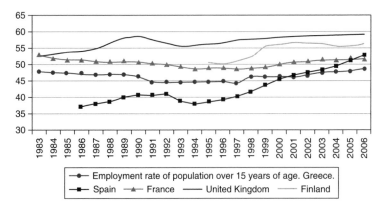

Figure 5.35 Employment ratio for the population over 15 years of age for various European countries

we can also see the burden imposed on the Greek economy by both the ageing population and the practice to allow employees of, mainly state-controlled, companies and public sector branches to retire early and generously – a burden that is not revealed sufficiently by the evolution of the unemployment rate in the 15–64 age bracket. But keeping in mind how the weak labor market performance mainly reflects the employment terms faced by the young, and especially young women, we can see the failure of the labor market to create new jobs that will employ those who enter the labor market for the first time, a fact that seems to be in accordance with the lack of dynamism of the supply side of the economy, which the excessive regulation and administrative burden seems to cause. As a result this attribute seems to fit well with the observation that the competitiveness of the economy is low. An economy that is not competitive will, according to related labor economics theory and evidence, first shun the least productive workers, which include certainly also the young who have not acquired any work experience. Further, an economy that does not expand its production base will not be able to offer new jobs to the cohorts that enter the job market – that is, again, the young – as is now documented by an extensive literature. And in the case of Greece, as the population ages and the portion of the population that is over 65 years old increases, and as a large number of the older workers are offered attractive packages by state-controlled companies and entities to retire early, the unemployment rate declines as an overall index in spite of these fundamental weaknesses. Therefore, in order to correctly monitor the ability of the economy to create jobs, one needs to closely watch the employment rate among the young, where any determined effort to deal with the deep

Figure 5.36 Adjusted wage share. Greece and EU-15

and widespread structural problems of the economy should be reflected most prominently.

The low ability to employ the young is not the only clear indication of the weak performance of the Greek labor market. The rise of the per-capita GDP during the years of rapid growth, while at the same time employment remained relatively low, has been accompanied by a failure to reverse the long-term trend of a declining wage share in the Greek economy (Figure 5.36), which is well below the (already low compared to the US) levels of the EU-15 average. The rise in investment as a proportion to the GDP, which has already been documented in Figure 5.11, matches well the picture of an economy that increasingly uses capital and self-employment as an input, as Figure 5.38 will show, and that tries to limit the use of the input of "salaried labor," which is measured by the "wage share," as much as possible.

This picture of low employment and a shrinking income share of wages is paired with impressively long working hours, which seem to result primarily from the long working days of a large population of self-employed (Figure 5.37), since the working hours of dependent labor are simply a little above average, as opposed to the working hours of all the workforce, which includes numerous self-employed, and which is much higher than the average of the other developed countries. These long workdays of the self-employed reinforce the picture of an economy that tries to limit the number of employed people, while at the same

	Hours of employment, annual, dependent labor. Data for year 2008	Hours of employment, annual, dependent and independent labor
Austria	1,483	1,631
Belgium	1,469	1,568
Czech Republic	1,923	1,992
Denmark	1,576	1,610
Finland	1,610	1,728
France	1,461	1,542
Germany	1,352	1,432
Greece	1,803	2,120
Ireland	1,522	1,601
Netherlands	1,301	1,389
New Zealand	1,731	1,753
Poland	1,940	1,969
Portugal	1,686	1,745
Spain	1,619	1,627
UK	1,638	1,653
US	1,797	1,792

Figure 5.37 Hours of employment. Various countries

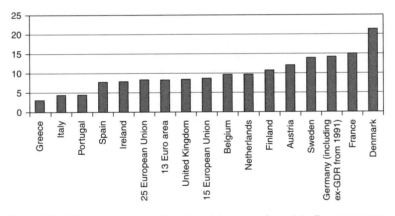

Figure 5.38 Wage earners to self-employed (non-employers) in European countries. Q1 2007 data

time stretching to the limit the use of each individual who is actually employed. Such an extreme choice, so many hours for the numerous self-employed with so few salaried employees, strongly suggests the existence of some very strong incentives for the labor market to behave in this peculiar way, which we now attempt to identify.

As already mentioned, the long working hours, which according to the OECD and International Labour Organisation (ILO) data follow

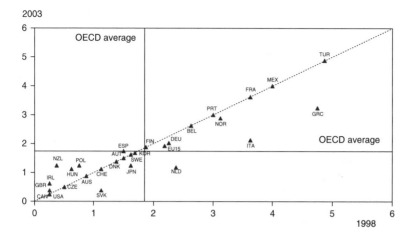

Figure 5.39 EPL. Restrictiveness and diversion of protection legislation on temporary employment

mainly from the long hours worked by the self-employed, seem to affect to such a large extent the number of total hours worked because of the unusually large number, for a eurozone country, of self-employed in the Greek economy (Figure 5.38).

We also have to take into account the indicators that record the regulation of job markets that are compiled by the OECD. Figure 5.39 shows Greece to be among the OECD countries with the most restrictive employment protection legislation (EPL). It should be noted here that the market for non-permanent, temporary employment in Greece is the main reason for the exceptional rigidity of the Greek labor market overall, and that the rigidity of the market for permanent contracts was also relatively rigid – a little over average when compared with other OECD countries, until the implementation of a number of measures prescribed by the conditionality program in late summer 2010.

Given the extensive research undertaken by the OECD Economics Department, as for example Nicoletti and Scarpetta (2005), regarding the relationship between product and labor market regulation, we will not investigate further the interdependence of labor and product market regulation. However, we still would like to emphasize that the biggest deficit observed in Greece is documented with regard to temporary contracts, which are of rather limited prevalence according to Eurostat data. In addition, the emergence of a two-tier labor market in countries that have introduced flexible temporary contracts while maintaining relatively strict regulation for permanent contracts is now being evaluated as a not very positive occurrence. There is also further evidence to suggest that labor market problems in Greece seem to be very particular when one examines this market in more detail. For example, when comparing with other OECD countries, one observes certain aspects that are particular to Greece, like the difference between the costs of firing blue collar workers and white collar employees, which is mentioned by the OECD (2007) and included in the measures taken according to the conditionality program in summer 2010. Also, the OECD reports that often existing legislation is not implemented, or is ineffective, like the reduced social insurance costs for low wage employees, in which case now the threshold has been overtaken by the minimum wage, thus making it irrelevant. However, the labor market in Greece seems to have even more remaining peculiarities than those suggested by the documented broad indexes of stringent regulation. Some, like the obligation for employers to distribute to employees who work in machine rooms a monthly ration of milk and woolen shoe covers, are more arcane and less well known.

Summarizing these findings, we draw the picture of an ageing society that fails to employ the young, limits as much as possible the use of salaried employment but, at the same time, has an impressively large number of self-employed who work very long hours. The latter, it should be noted, do not face a tax wedge of the size imposed on better paid salaried labor, as we will see subsequently, nor the restrictions imposed on temporary and part-time employment, that prevail in Greece, on the duration and allocation of the hours worked. The high investment rate and the low income share of salaried labor complete the picture of an economy that seems to go to great pains to avoid the use of the input "salaried labor." It is in that context that the relatively firm progress regarding labor market regulation that has been documented during the implementation of the conditionality program, in spite of the fact that it definitely has been an important step in the right direction, has not removed a major binding constraint to the improvement of competitiveness and growth, as would have been a similar progress in the improvement of product market regulation and professional services regulation.

5.4 Taxation and labor market paradoxes

5.4.1 Facts of personal income taxation

One of the most salient differences between Greece and the other OECD countries regarding taxation at the onset of the current crisis seems to be the impressive progressivity (Figure 5.40) of personal income taxation as measured by the OECD.

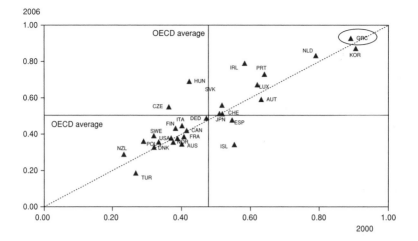

Figure 5.40 Progressivity of income taxes (without social security contributions)

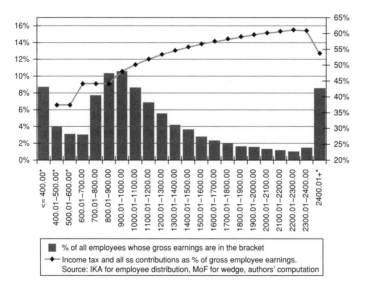

Figure 5.41 Distribution of monthly wages and corresponding tax wedge

Keeping in mind the OECD observation regarding the progressivity of the tax wedge, we proceed to look at data for June 2008 provided by the Greek Institution for Social Security (IKA), where all salaried private sector employees are insured. This data shows, in Figure 5.41, how the distribution of wage earners in the different income brackets corresponds to the wedge introduced by income tax and social security contributions. Here average income tax is computed as a percentage of the earnings gross of tax and net of social security contributions for each income brackets, where these brackets stand for monthly wages. To this tax, as a percentage of these earnings, we then add the social security contributions for the employer and the employee, as a percentage of the wage gross of taxes. In any case, regardless of how the wedge is computed, it is clear that a significant mass of wage earners belongs to a small band of monthly remunerations, for which the burden of the tax and social security contribution wedge is minimized, as a result of the low income tax burden, as social security payments are a constant percentage of salaries up to a certain high threshold. Furthermore, this concentration abruptly falls off at the level of the minimum wage, which strongly suggests the existence of a binding constraint as the one suggested by Neumark and Wascher (2008). The existence of a significant population of dependent employment with remuneration below the minimum wage is explained by, on the one hand, the proliferation of special programs, which are exempt from social security payments and for which a lower minimum wage applies, to hire young graduates as trainees, mostly in the central and general government, and on the other hand, by the fact that some individuals work less than the full month, as for example construction workers.

We can also see that after a gross salary of about 2500 euro per month for workers who were first insured before 1993, and about double for those insured after that date, pension rights and the related contributions are no longer increasing, and as a result the wedge as a percentage of earnings starts declining. In Greece the annual earnings in the private sector are the monthly earnings time 14, while the height of the additional two cash handouts have been recently reduced for the public sector. Given that the salary forms a smaller part of the total remuneration in the public sector, where cash payments on top of the salary are numerous and widespread, this reduction has a rather limited, when compared as a proportion of these extra two monthly earnings in the private sector, to the impact on total public sector "take home" remuneration. Not surprisingly, there seems to be a large number of earners of such high salaries, which however form a gradually falling tail of the distribution if one extends fully the income brackets of the salaried income over 2400 euros per month. As a result the finding of the OECD regarding the impressively high progressivity of income taxation seems to be complemented by the finding, first, that a large concentration of private sector employees is in the income bracket with the smallest wedge (that wedge covers the minimum wage right up to the upper limit of a wage bracket that remains close to the minimum wage) and, second, that a very large proportion of earners is concentrated at high wages, where the wedge declines again as a percentage of the total earnings. This is in line with the finding that the OECD documents, as shown in Figure 5.40, that is, the rapid increase of the wedge between the low income earners and the earners that are at about 160 percent of the average wage, and this finding is very relevant to the reality faced by a very large number of wage earners. It should be added that in the fall of 2008 the legislation regarding the tax treatment of stock options and bonuses for high income earners was made more stringent, and therefore it will be interesting to observe whether there are any changes in the distribution of the declared incomes of these high income earners in the future, especially since the tax rate for the bonuses of bank executives has now been set at 90 percent. It remains though that until 2009 Greece had one of the most progressive personal income taxation laws among the main European countries, as can be seen in Figure 5.42. Not only did Greece until recently set probably the highest level for tax-free income (with the exception of much wealthier France and some wealthy Scandinavian countries, which have significant local taxes though), but it also applied the top income bracket to relatively high incomes, even though this also has changed in a new tax law that will apply from 2011. It has to be stressed though that the new tax law provisions not only retain, but on the contrary aim to further enhance, the overall progressivity of the income taxation legislation, even though that progressivity is already unusually pronounced. Regarding the relatively high level set for tax-free income, that was reduced only at the end of 2011 to more reasonable levels as part of measures to reign in the deviations from set budgetary targets, it should be noted that many other countries prefer the introduction of tax credits or deductions if certain prequisites are met, which differs from the unconditional Greek approach of setting a tax-free income up to a certain level.

It seems therefore that the minimum wage emerges as very important in Greece, not so much because of its absolute level, which is about average when one takes into account the minimum wages of other countries in which there is a minimum wage (Figure 5.43), but because of its proximity to the main mass of the distribution of wage earners. It has to be stressed of course that since the countries that have higher minimum wages than Greece are also generally wealthier countries and with a higher competitiveness ranking, Greece does not appear to

Income bracket from level up to next bracket	GR	AT	FR* Tax-free up to 11.265	IRL* Tax deductions	PT * Tax credits	ES	IT* Tax credits	DE + solidarity tax of 5.5%	UK	FL + local taxes	S + local taxes
0	0.0%	0.0%	0.0%	20.0%	10.5%	24.0%	23.0%	0.0%	0.0%	0.0%	0.0%
4,639					13.0%						
5,614			5.5%								
6,500					23.5%				20.0%		
7,017											
8,004		38.3%						14.1%			
10,000											
11,198			14.0%								
12,000	25.0%										
12,600							27.0%			8.5%	
15,000											
17,000						28.0%					
17,401					34.0%						
20,800										19.0%	
25,000		43.5%	30.0%								
28,000							38.0%				
30,000	35.0%										
33,000						37.0%					

Income											
34,000										23.5%	
35,400	41.0%						40.0%				20.0%
40,200		36.0%	50.0%								
51,000						42.0%					
52,152				43.0%							25.0%
53,000					41.0%						
55,000		40.0%									
58,000									31.5%		
62,000			40.0%								
66,674	40.0%				43.0%						
75,000						45.0%					
250,000											

Figure 5.42 Personal income tax brackets. European countries, 2009

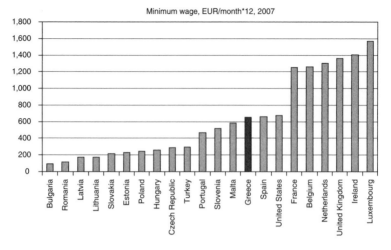

Figure 5.43   Minimum wages. European countries

have a low minimum wage once one adjusts for the competitiveness of the economy or per-capita income. Also, a significant number of EU member countries, which are not included in Figure 5.43, do not have a national minimum wage at all, but use other approaches to secure a minimum level of satisfactory pay for low wage employees.

This observation, together with the aversion to employ the young, could also be used to explain the proportion of workers earning the minimum wage. That way we can take into account both the aversion to employ young and inexperienced workers at a wage that is close to the wage of more experienced workers and, making the adjustments needed, to reflect the fact that the proximity of the minimum wage to the main mass of the distribution of employees is expected to increase the number of those who receive it (Figure 5.44). The popularity of the "stage" programs – that is, training programs for the young – even though the pay offered is significantly lower than the minimum national wage, seems to support this argument. Of course the aspiration harbored by the numerous participants of these programs who are employed in public service – where they often simply perform chores for the permanent public employees – that they may ultimately bypass the law and themselves be hired by the public sector, further contributes to the attractiveness of these programs, in spite of their low pay.

It should be further added that this particular structure of the tax wedge emerged in Greece during the early 1980s, a time that is associated with a fast rise in unemployment and very poor macroeconomic performance (Figure 5.45), as is described by Burtless (2001).

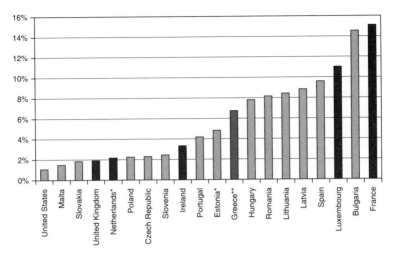

Figure 5.44 Proportion of full-time workers earning minimum wage

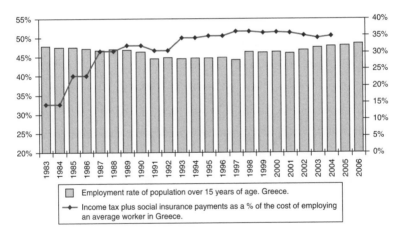

Figure 5.45 Employment rate and tax wedge in Greece

This peculiarity of the distribution can also explain the proximity of the low minimum wage to the median wage (Figure 5.46) and the high income inequality documented in Greece (Figure 5.47). It also seems to be very relevant to the attractiveness self-employment has especially for skilled middle-class professionals, who seem to actively avoid salaried employment and the high wedge that is associated with salaried employment in higher income brackets – something that was also pointed out by Burtless (2001), whose observations regarding the Greek labor market seem to be verified by all the data and evidence we were able to collect.

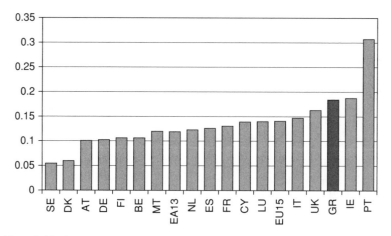

Figure 5.46   Average income to median income. Percentage difference. European countries

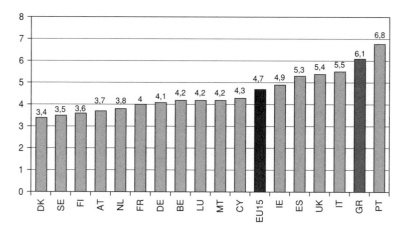

Figure 5.47   S80/S20 income quintile share ratio. European countries

The analysis of these pieces of information seems to strengthen the case for reducing the progressivity of the wedge on salaried labor for middle incomes, especially since other reform proposals may be politically more difficult to support. To support this case, we also point out that data of the Ministry of Finance and Economy regarding the tax revenue shows how tax revenue in the different income brackets seems to respond to the changes in the tax rates of each bracket (Figures 5.48 and 5.49). Please note that in Figure 5.49 each tax return includes the

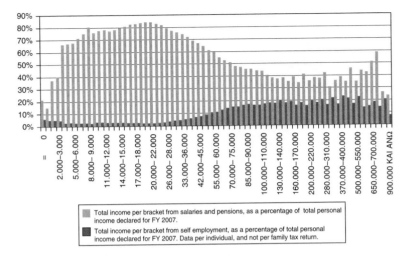

Figure 5.48 Income from salaries and wages, and self-employment to total income per bracket. Greece for financial year 2007

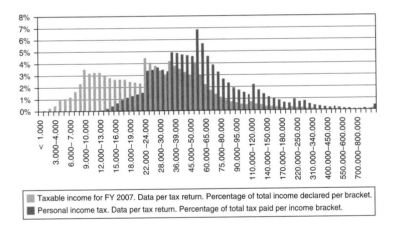

Figure 5.49 Taxable income and personal income tax per income bracket. Greece for financial year 2007

income and tax of both household members when they both earn an income.

One can clearly see how, for the fiscal year 2007, income derived from salaries and pensions mainly contributes to the income of the lower income brackets, and how higher income brackets bear the main tax

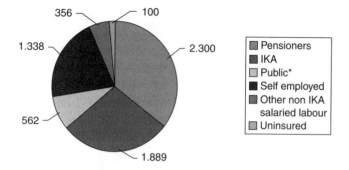

Figure 5.50   Greek workforce by insurance type
* In 2011 a census of government employees counted over 1 million civil servants. Yet a large portion of these is not directly insured by the Central Greek Government, as also shown in Alpha Bank (2010).

burden, in spite of the rapid decline of the population of high wage earners documented in Figure 5.51. Matching this information with the high occurrence of self-employment, as shown by Figure 5.38 and Figure 5.50 in Greece, suggests that the tax revenue should be fairly elastic with respect to the total wedge on wage income, as a reduction in the progressivity of the tax burden for middle and upper middle incomes probably will remove a strong and binding disincentive for salaried employment for these income brackets. It should be noted that the distributions of Figure 5.49 document family income, and therefore the form of the distribution is affected by the coincidence of data for households with one and two earners, which explains the double peak in the distribution of declared income that is observed around the tax-free annual income for one-earner and two-earner families.

The annual data issued by the General Secretariat for Information Systems of the Ministry of Finance presented in Figure 5.51 gives indeed very detailed information on the distribution of the tax burden across income brackets for individuals and corporations. This data shows in many ways how a disproportionately large share of the population declares an income that effectively makes it exempt from income taxation. Out of 5.5 million personal income tax declarations issued by heads of households for the fiscal year 2007, 3 million declared an annual income below 12,000 euros (for salaried employees this should be divided by 14 to obtain the monthly salary measured by IKA, while for self-employed the monthly income would be this number divided by 12). As a group they represent 54 percent of the tax returns filed, declared 21 percent of the income declared by personal income tax returns; they

Income bracket for family income	Number of returns	%	Income	%	Total tax paid	%	Average income	Average tax
Up to 12,000	3,008,908	54.41%	18,434,000,882	21.34%	33,188,539	0.40%	6,126	11
12,000–30,000	1,830,203	33.09%	34,202,227,796	39.59%	2,087,015,250	25.09%	18,688	1,140
30,000–75,000	632,352	11.43%	27,004,877,237	31.26%	4,202,657,012	50.52%	42,705	6,646
75,000 +	58,964	1.07%	6,755,109,652	7.82%	1,995,470,906	23.99%	114,563	33,842
Total	5,530,427	100.00%	86,396,215,567	100.00%	8,318,331,707	100.00%	15,622	1,504

Figure 5.51 Personal income declared and tax paid per income bracket. Greece for financial year 2007

paid 0.4 percent of the total personal income tax paid, which amounts to 0.18 percent of the total income declared for this group.

The 1.8 million returns that declared an annual income between 12,000 and 30,000 euros amount to 33.1 percent of all personal income tax returns filed, declared as a group 39.59 percent of all personal income and paid 25.1 percent of all personal income taxes for that year. The average tax burden of this group was 6.10 percent.

The 632,352 tax returns with a declared income of between 30,000 and 75,000 euros, which amount to the 11.43 percent of all returns filed, declared 31.26 percent of all the personal income and paid 50.52 percent of the total personal income tax collected by the state. The tax paid by this group amounted to 15.56 percent of their declared income. Those declaring above 75,000 euros in income paid 29.5 percent of their income as taxes. And even though they amount to 1.07 percent of all income tax returns filed they declared 7.82 percent of all personal income tax and paid 23.99 percent of all income tax collected by the state in this year.

According to the Bundesfinanzministerium (Ministry of Finance) of Germany in 2006 25 percent of the population that belonged to the top income bracket paid 76.3 percent of all personal income taxes, the 25 percent belonging to the income bracket immediately below paid 17.4 percent of this tax and the bottom 50 percent, which form the lowest income bracket, paid 6.3 percent of the total income tax. In France according to data from the Direction Générale des Impôts for the financial year 2005, 20 percent of the wealthiest households paid 75 percent of the personal income tax while 48 percent of the poorest households paid 4.5 percent of the personal income tax, with the rest being paid by the middle group of households, which amounted to 32 percent of all households and which paid the 20.5 percent of the personal income tax. Respectively in Greece 25 percent of the population with the highest income paid 92 percent of the personal income tax. The next 25 percent paid 7.9 percent of the total personal income tax collected by the government and the 50 percent that declared the lowest income paid only 0.028 percent of all personal income tax. Therefore, it seems that the bottom and middle part of the income distribution in Greece contributes, proportionally, quite little personal income tax, at least in comparison to France and Germany.

It is also impressive to note how in Figure 5.49 the distribution of income declared, and tax paid, seems to drop from the left of the level that coincides with the end, of the level that coincides with the tax-free income, for a one-earner family and respectively for a two-earner family. Similarly, in Figure 5.52 one sees how the number of individuals, not

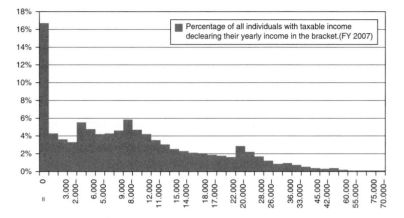

Figure 5.52 Percentage of individuals according to declared income per income bracket in financial year 2007

families this time, declaring income that is higher than the allowed tax-free annual income starts falling quite rapidly. Please note that Figure 5.49, which documents the declared income from all sources in brackets of annual income, does not contradict Figure 5.41, which documents the number of salaried employees per bracket of monthly wages registered by IKA, and which may not form all the income of an individual who receives in addition to his salary, for example, some rent, dividend or other income.

To further comment on the distribution of declared income one would need to have access to additional information to the already exhaustive, we must admit, data published by the General Secretariat for Information Systems, Ministry of Finance and Economy. In particular, we would need to know not only the income of each member of the two-earner households, but also the tax that corresponds to salaried labor, and not only the tax that corresponds to the whole family income. With access to such data we could better examine the relationship between the structure of income taxes and the income declared per earner of salaried income by identifying exactly the amount of income tax that is generated by salaried labor. Also, a separation of income from salaries and pensions would help us improve the comparison between income declared by salaried labor to the income declared by non-salaried labor. Still Figure 5.48 shows quite clearly how the aggregate income from salaried labor and pensions drops after an yearly income of about 20,000 euros (about 1,500 euro per month), while at the same time the proportion of declared income from self-employment for each successive income bracket starts to increase. Therefore the question posed should not be why the self-employed declare low incomes, as clearly a significant number of self-employed declare high incomes. The question should rather be whether the income declared by self-employed is high enough. It seems puzzling that while the self-employed tend to have an income that is closer to that declared by salaried employees in higher income brackets, the small number of salaried employees in these higher brackets, along with the large number of the self-employed, their relatively lower social security contributions and their long working hours, do not correspond to higher revenues than the ones declared by the salaried employees. In addition, one can expect that in a society where half the households pay no personal income tax at all, any self-employed probably does not feel as an outlier when he pays either no taxes or nothing higher than some token personal income tax, according to a mechanism similar to the one that encourages petty crime in areas where many windows broken, as claimed by Keizer et al. (2008) and Kelling and Coles (1997). We can reasonably assume that a high-income self-employed individual would probably ask himself some questions if he declared enough income to place himself among the small group of individuals who contribute most of the personal income taxes. A further interesting fact is that for the fiscal year 2007, according to the data of the General Secretariat for Information Systems, the average individual (among 8.2 million individuals) declared an income of 10,057 euros, and the average income declared by 5.5 million households per household tax return was 15,551 euros. At the same time the Household Income and Living Conditions Survey of the Greek National Statistical Service estimated for the year 2007 an average personal income of 12,130 euros and an average household income of 21,150 euros. This suggests that indeed tax evasion may be a problem among the 8.2 million individuals who have a tax number and the 5.5 million households that file tax returns. This data also suggests that the extent of the undeclared income probably is in excess of 20 percent, but it is also reasonable to say that, contrary to aggregate income, most of this undeclared income would imply the obligation to pay at least some tax – that is, every euro of the undeclared income would be taxable if declared properly, as it makes little sense not to declare an income as long as one remains below the threshold for tax-free income.

European Commission data shows that while, following the recent reduction of the corporate tax rates, the total direct taxes paid by corporations have declined in 2006 toward the eurozone average from the high levels of the previous years, the direct taxes paid by individuals remain, as a percentage of the GDP, much lower than in the other eurozone countries. As a matter of fact, this low contribution of personal income taxes is largely responsible for the low level of tax revenue, as a percentage of the GDP, in Greece relative to the other European countries (Figure 5.53). This observation appears to link the abovementioned attributes of the Greek personal income tax legislation and reality with the weak performance of the Greek government's finances, both over the past years and during the current conjecture, especially when one takes also into account the fact that the (relatively numerous) self-employed seem to contribute the same social security payments as the self-employed of the eurozone as a whole, even though the latter represent a much lower proportion of the total workforce, as also shown in Figure 5.53.

These attributes may not only lead to a reallocation of salaried labor toward self-employment, and a substitution of self-employment for temporary employment. To the extent that administrative barriers of entry to self-employment make it unattractive to choose it unless one has a sufficiently high income to cover this cost and to take advantage of the potential benefit of tax evasion, as well as the savings from the social security payments that effectively increase for higher incomes, this setup could also work as a barrier to increase aggregate employment, and not only as a motive to substitute self-employment for salaried employment, or part-time employment. This is probably true especially for the less skilled or for the younger entrants to the labor market, who are less able to face the process of starting the special tax books that are required for the self-employed – a process that usually triggers sooner or later the need to deal with corrupt tax officials. Also they may be less willing to accept the relatively flat rate social security contributions of the self-employed, which are very advantageous for high incomes but may be, proportionally, onerous for self-employed with small incomes. Similarly, the under-development of a market for temporary or part-time employment may further discourage the groups that usually voluntarily choose such work arrangements, like working parents – and especially mothers – as suggested by Neumark and Wascher (2008), and that are not highly skilled or not able to reach the income needed to cover the expense of self-employment. These groups may under the given circumstances also choose to leave the job market rather than to become self-employed.

	2000	2001	2002	2003	2004	2005	2006	2007
TOTAL TAXES. % GDP. EXCLUDING SOCIAL SECURITY CONTRIBUTIONS								
GREECE	24.1	22.6	22.1	20.5	20.1	20.4	20.3	20.4
EUROZONE*	26.7	25.9	25.5	25.3	25.1	25.4	26.1	26.4
INDIRECT TAXES. % GDP.								
GREECE	14.2	13.7	13.3	12.5	12	11.8	12.3	12.9
EUROZONE*	13.9	13.5	13.5	13.5	13.5	13.7	13.9	13.8
VAT. % GDP.								
GREECE	7.2	7.5	7.6	7	6.8	6.8	7.1	7.2
EUROZONE*	6.9	6.8	6.7	6.6	6.6	6.7	6.8	7
DIRECT TAXES. % GDP.								
GREECE	10	8.8	8.7	8	8.1	8.6	8	8.1
EUROZONE*	12.9	12.5	12.1	11.9	11.7	11.8	12.3	12.7
DIRECT TAXES – PERSONAL INCOME TAX. % GDP.								
GREECE	5	4.5	4.5	4.4	4.4	4.6	4.6	4.7
EUROZONE*	9.2	9.1	8.9	8.8	8.4	8.5	8.7	8.9
DIRECT TAXES – CORPORATE TAXES. % GDP.								
GREECE	4.1	3.4	3.4	2.9	3	3.2	2.7	2.6
EUROZONE*	2.6	2.4	2.2	2	2.2	2.4	2.7	2.9
SOCIAL SECURITY CONTRIBUTIONS OF SELF-EMPLOYED. % GDP.								
GREECE	1.5	1.5	1.6	1.7	1.6	1.7	1.6	1.8
EUROZONE*	1.8	1.7	1.8	1.8	1.8	1.8	1.8	1.8

Note: *15 COUNTRIES – weighted average.

Figure 5.53   Taxation trends in the EU. Tax contributions by source as a percentage of the GDP

5.4.2 A summary of the facts on personal income taxation

The above-mentioned evidence helps us draw the following picture:

First, in Greece a disproportionally large percentage of personal income tax returns declared such low income as to ensure that about half the households that file tax returns essentially did not pay any income tax. At the same time Greece has a very large number of self-employed, which both face per capita lower social security payments and have more opportunities to evade taxes, in particular when their actual income is higher than the average income. As a result it seems very probable that both the popularity of self-employment and the large number of tax returns that declare such low income are related to the ability of the self-employed to effectively avoid taxes, especially for middle and higher middle incomes. While trying to support earners of low salaries, it seems that the progressive wedge on salaried labor encourages self-employment in particular with (undeclared) higher incomes. In addition it provides a possible place for other undeclared income to hide – say, through the purchase of services from these self-employed. If this is true, then salaried labor faces stiff and unfair competition from self-employment, which could explain both the unwillingness of the economy to expand the use of salaried labor as an input, and its disproportionate reliance on the long working hours of the self-employed, together with a relatively small contingent of salaried labor positioned predominantly in those income brackets in which salaried labor faces the least wedge relatively to the alternative of self-employment. This analysis shows this is not so much a case of reducing the absolute wedge on average wage income, which is a little higher than the OECD average, as it is a case of equalizing the effective wedge on salaried employment and self-employment. A marginal reduction in the wedge on salaried labor will have little effect as long as an alternative with a much lower wedge persists, especially for higher income brackets.

Second, the tax wedge used to be too progressive, especially for middle incomes. This progressivity of the tax wedge on salaried labor makes things worse for the Greek labor market because of the fact that this wedge starts to increase at a level that is too close to the minimum wage. The result is that a disproportionally large number of salaried employees are squeezed between a narrow income range that ranges from the minimum wage to the point where the wedge starts to increase. Below this narrow range the minimum wage rules out legal salaried employment and above this narrow range self-employment is encouraged over salaried employment. Changes in the tax wedge and in the minimum wage therefore affect the core of the distribution of employees, and as a result have the potential to cause much more damage than in other countries where the minimum wage is further distanced from the main mass of this distribution. Reducing the minimum wage, especially for young and inexperienced individuals, as suggested by the OECD (2007) and authors like Neumark and Washer (2008), is one part of the solution. It should be added that labor market reforms introduced by the conditionality program regarding collective bargaining will also remove bottlenecks, especially in certain industries and sub-sectors. But the documented increase in the progressivity of the tax wedge for incomes up to 30,000 euros should also be drastically reduced in order to encourage a migration of the mass of the distribution of salaried workers to higher income brackets that are more distanced from the minimum wage. Such a measure could lead to an increase in the average declared wage to the extent that indeed a significant proportion of salaried employees migrates to these higher income brackets; it is probable that the net tax receipts from income tax would also increase, even if tax rates are reduced, as long as they will apply to the increased salary of an increased population of middle income earners who declare most of their income. At the same time, the documented income inequality would decrease and both salaries and employment would rise, as the distance between the median and the minimum wages widens, which encourages the hiring of those who enter the job market close to the minimum wage, which in turn adds also to the increase of the share of wage income. It should be noted that while reducing the wedge for middle incomes would be one way to proceed, the same effect could also be achieved by raising the wedge on lower incomes, as with the reduction of the tax free income that has now been legislated. This alternative approach to reducing the progressivity of the income tax legislation can better align the Greek tax legislation with that of other European countries. Also it is in conformity with the fact that even though the OECD finds that the progressivity of the tax wedge is extremely high in Greece, the average level of this wedge is simply a little above average for upper middle incomes. Such an alternative approach was previously suggested by a proposed law that intended to abolish the zero tax rate on the 12,000 euros of annual income declared by many self-employed. This law was never adopted because of pressure from the unions for the self-employed on the government that proposed the measure. Also, tax laws initially put forward by the current government aimed to make tax payers collect receipts from the services of self-employed and professions who either seem to evade taxes or used to be exempt from declaring their true income by law, like taxi drivers and gas station owners for example. Even though these measures could help to reduce the inequalities of a tax system that so far put the personal income tax burden disproportionally on a small number of average to high-income salaried employees who predominantly declare all their income, these measures could not reduce the excessive progressivity of the income tax system and therefore they could not remove the incentive to employ salaried labor only in the narrow income bracket between the minimum wage and the level of the tax-free income.

Third, we have to stress, once again, that these issues, which relate essentially to the efficiency and the marginal incentives for the reallocation of the workforce in the economy, operate besides the reality of the low competitiveness of the economy. This means that any visible and substantial improvement of the labor market performance will follow only after a sizeable improvement in the competitiveness of the economy has been achieved, in line with the findings of Nicoletti and Scarpetta (2005) that stringent product market regulation indeed seems to severely reduce the ability of an economy to increase employment. Changes in the progressivity of the tax laws, together with the abolition of morally unjustified tax exemptions for special interest groups, including taxi drivers and public sector employees who receive cash handouts that were so far taxed favorably, a relaxation of binding constraints of the minimum wage – especially for the young – and a relaxation of the restrictions on temporary and part-time employment for working parents, for example, can help, and probably will after their implementation according to the conditionality program. However they cannot compensate for the lack of measures to increase the competitiveness of the economy through the deregulation of product markets and a reduction of the administrative burden, and the corruption these invite. This comment seems to be supported by the gradual deepening of the Greek recession in 2010 and 2011, in spite of the numerous reforms in the tax laws and the labor market regulations.

Finally, the issues relating to personal income taxation seem to be directly related to the state of the public finances of the country, as the revenue shortfall of personal income tax as a percentage of the GDP is approximately of a size that is comparable with the structural deficit of the general government budget deficit during the period that preceded the current crisis. As such the equalization of the contribution in income taxes and social security contributions of salaried labor and self-employment, the reduction of tax evasion and marginal improvements in the personal income tax legislation, along with the rise in employment (and therefore in taxable personal income) as a result of an improved regulatory setting that increases the competitiveness of the economy, are all directly, and crucially, related to the unraveling of the current grave situation for Greek public finances.

5.4.3 Paradoxes of the Greek labor market explained

The strong demand growth, which is not driven by an increase in supply following from an increase in employment, directly affects the reliability of productivity indexes that measure the GDP to labor input in various forms. This occurs as the increase in the numerator, the GDP, matches a limited increase in the denominator, thus measuring a large rise in the productivity per worker or, even, per hour worked, in spite of the low documented competitiveness of the Greek economy (Figure 5.54). It follows from this description that the use of such indicators is not correctly capturing the variety of the parameters that shaped the performance of the Greek economy during the past decade, often depicting Greece in a position that does not favor the drawing of reliable conclusions.

Another example is the evolution of the real labor cost relatively to the EU-15 countries (Figure 5.55). An economy that limits the number of society members who are employed may offer, in an environment of high growth – in particular if that growth does not have as a prerequisite the increase of employment – its few employees increased compensation. To the extent that the economy remains uncompetitive, as in the case of Greece, and the higher compensation of dependent labor encourages

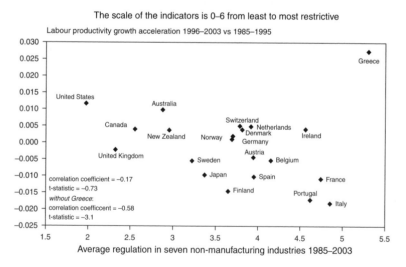

Figure 5.54 Product market regulation and total economy labor productivity acceleration in OECD countries

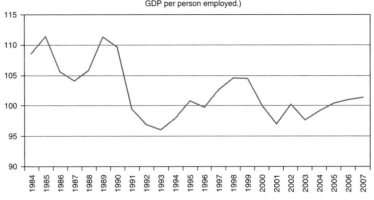

Figure 5.55 Real unit labor cost in Greece relatively to rest of EU-15

the further proliferation of self-employment, the increase in the unit labor cost for the economy, which is measured by dividing the compensation per employee with the nominal GDP per person employed, will not provide an accurate picture of the realities and mechanics of the labor market. For example, we note the paradox of having in Greece, after the 1990s, both an increase in the real unit labor cost presented in Figure 5.55 and a reduction in the income share of dependent labor income, which was presented in Figure 5.36. An increase in the compensation per capita, but an even larger fall in the number of employees per nominal GDP, as is the case in Greece, quickly resolves this paradox.

These observations, together with the earlier comments, highlight the fact that wage increases that are following the rise in productivity per labor unit (per capita or per hour GDP, that is) may favor those, mainly middle aged, who already are employed as their real compensation grows along with the increase of the GDP (Figure 5.56 and 5.57). However their true cost to society in an environment of a non-competitive economy, like the Greek economy, is the exclusion of many others from the labor market, and especially the young, less skilled or particular groups such as working parents, that seek salaried labor. Again, one must stress that a reduction in the compensation for labor, and especially low income labor, will not contribute to the resolution of the causes of these paradoxes. Only an increase in the competitiveness of the economy, assisted by the other measures also mentioned with regard to the equal treatment of income from dependent and independent labor, and the reduction in the progressiveness of personal income taxation can unwind these paradoxes

166

Labour productivity (real GDP per occupied person) (percentage change on preceding year, 1992–2011)

	5-year averages			2005	2006	2007	2008	2009		2010		2011	
	1992–96	1997–01	2002–06					IV-2009	X-2009	IV-2009	X-2009	IV-2009	X-2009
Belgium	1.4	1.3	1.3	0.4	1.6	1.3	−0.8	−2.3	−2.1	1.2	2.0	:	1.4
Germany	2.8	2.0	1.7	1.3	2.9	0.9	−0.1	−3.9	−4.6	2.5	3.1	:	2.0
Ireland	3.3	3.3	2.2	1.4	1.0	2.4	−2.2	−0.1	0.3	1.5	2.6	:	2.0
Greece	0.2	3.1	2.4	1.3	2.4	3.1	1.9	0.3	−0.2	0.2	0.5	:	0.9
Spain	1.8	0.2	0.5	0.4	0.7	0.7	1.5	2.3	3.1	1.8	1.5	:	1.4
France	1.6	1.2	1.2	1.3	1.2	0.8	−0.1	−0.8	−0.4	1.1	2.1	:	1.1
Italy	2.2	0.9	0.1	0.5	0.5	0.6	−0.9	−1.1	−2.1	0.7	1.1	:	1.0
Cyprus	:	2.6	0.3	0.3	2.3	1.2	1.0	0.7	−0.3	0.6	0.2	:	0.7
Luxembourg	0.1	1.5	1.4	2.5	1.9	2.0	−4.5	−3.5	−4.7	0.9	2.4	:	1.8
Malta	3.5	2.6	1.3	2.5	2.4	0.5	−0.3	−0.4	−1.6	0.0	0.4	:	1.0
Netherlands	1.4	1.4	1.8	2.1	1.7	1.3	0.8	−2.5	−4.4	2.5	2.4	:	2.5
Austria	1.8	1.8	1.6	1.2	2.4	2.0	0.2	−1.3	−2.3	0.8	1.8	:	1.2
Portugal	2.7	1.6	0.7	1.2	0.9	1.9	−0.5	−2.3	−0.6	−0.2	0.8	:	0.9
Slovenia	:	4.0	3.7	4.6	4.2	3.7	0.6	1.3	−4.9	1.4	3.4	:	2.3
Slovakia	:	3.8	5.0	5.1	6.1	8.1	3.4	−0.9	−3.9	0.2	1.9	:	2.0
Finland	3.7	2.3	2.0	1.4	3.1	2.0	−0.6	−1.8	−4.1	1.0	3.4	:	1.5
Euro area	2.1	1.5	1.2	1.1	1.7	1.1	0.1	−1.4	−1.8	1.5	2.1	:	1.5
Bulgaria	−1.2	2.4	3.5	3.5	2.9	3.3	2.7	0.6	−3.9	0.9	0.3	:	2.2
Czech Republic	:	2.0	4.1	5.2	4.9	3.3	0.9	−1.1	−2.8	1.6	2.2	:	2.0
Denmark	2.5	1.4	1.5	1.4	1.3	−1.0	−2.0	−1.0	−1.9	2.3	3.7	:	1.9

Estonia	:	8.5	6.3	7.5	4.1	6.4	-3.7	*-3.2*	-5.1	*2.6*	2.4	:	2.6
Latvia	-1.5	6.0	6.7	8.7	7.2	6.2	-5.2	*-4.6*	-6.9	*0.1*	1.7	:	2.2
Lithuania	-5.8	6.9	5.9	5.2	5.9	6.9	3.3	*-3.6*	-10.8	*-2.4*	-1.5	:	2.7
Hungry	:	3.2	3.9	3.1	3.0	1.1	1.9	*-3.5*	-3.6	*1.8*	0.3	:	2.1
Poland	:	5.5	3.6	1.4	2.9	2.3	1.2	*1.0*	1.9	*2.3*	2.9	:	3.1
R omania	4.3	0.9	7.3	5.8	7.1	5.9	5.9	*-1.9*	-4.9	*-0.6*	-0.3	:	1.7
Sweden	3.1	1.8	3.0	3.0	2.5	0.4	-1.1	*-1.6*	-2.4	*3.1*	3.2	:	2.1
United Kingdom	2.5	2.1	1.6	1.1	2.0	1.9	-0.2	*-1.4*	-2.6	*1.1*	1.8	:	0.5
EU	:	2.0	2.0	1.6	2.2	1.6	0.4	*-1.3*	-2.0	*1.4*	2.0	:	1.5
USA	1.5	2.0	2.1	1.7	0.6	1.0	0.9	*0.6*	1.1	*1.8*	2.8	:	1.6
Japan	0.9	1.1	1.9	1.5	1.6	2.0	-0.3	*-2.4*	-3.0	*1.3*	2.3	:	0.6

Source: See note 6 of reference on concepts and sources where countries using full time equivalents are listed.

Figure 5.56 Labor productivity. European countries

Real compensation of employees per head[1] (percentage change on preceding year, 1992–2008)

	5-year averages			2002	2003	2004	2005	2006		2007		2008	
	1992–96	1997–01	2002–06					X-2006	IV-2007	X-2006	IV-2007	X-2006	IV-2007
Belgium	1.6	1.0	0.4	2.5	0.0	-0.5	-0.5	0.1	0.5	0.3	0.7	0.5	0.7
Germany	2.8	1.3	0.1	0.7	1.0	-0.1	-0.8	-1.1	-0.2	-1.4	0.0	0.6	1.2
Ireland	1.6	1.0	2.5	0.5	1.3	5.1	3.8	2.4	2.2	2.2	1.9	2.5	2.1
Greece	-0.7	2.9	3.4	7.3	1.7	3.2	2.7	2.3	2.4	1.9	2.2	1.9	1.9
Spain	1.0	-0.3	-0.1	0.5	0.5	-0.4	-0.8	-0.5	-0.2	0.1	0.6	0.1	0.3
France	1.1	1.2	1.4	2.1	1.0	1.4	0.8	1.6	2.0	1.3	1.8	1.2	1.2
Italy	-0.3	-0.3	0.4	-0.1	0.9	0.7	0.7	0.4	-0.2	0.6	0.5	0.5	1.2
Luxembourg	1.0	0.9	0.7	3.3	-0.5	1.6	0.0	0.9	-0.9	1.5	0.7	1.7	0.3
Netherlands	0.6	1.2	1.2	2.1	1.8	3.0	-0.1	-0.5	-0.9	1.9	1.9	0.9	1.8
Austria	1.1	0.5	0.4	0.9	0.4	-0.2	-0.1	1.1	0.9	0.6	0.9	0.5	1.0
Portugal	2.3	2.7	0.0	1.0	-0.2	0.0	0.4	-0.1	-0.9	0.5	0.4	0.7	0.5
Slovenia		2.9	2.2	0.6	1.2	4.2	3.1	3.0	2.3	3.3	2.6	3.1	2.9
Finland	0.6	0.8	2.1	-0.4	3.2	2.6	3.6	1.8	1.4	1.0	0.9	1.6	1.9
Euro area		0.6	0.4	0.9	0.7	0.4	-0.1	0.0	0.1	0.1	0.6	0.7	1.0
Bulgaria		2.2	2.0	1.7	4.8	0.5	0.7	3.5	2.5	6.6	5.6	6.5	5.8
Czech Republic		2.4	4.5	6.4	9.0	2.7	2.6	3.1	1.8	3.5	1.5	2.9	1.1
Denmark	1.4	1.7	1.7	2.0	2.7	1.2	1.1	1.7	1.7	2.2	2.5	1.0	2.1

Estonia	:	7.1	9.1	6.0	12.5	10.6	8.4	8.0	8.4	7.0	9.5	6.4	7.4
Cyprus	:	2.2	1.1	2.4	3.3	0.1	-1.1	0.3	0.9	1.0	1.6	1.0	1.1
Latvia	:	3.1	8.8	1.8	8.0	6.8	15.5	10.7	12.4	8.7	9.3	6.2	8.0
Lithuania	:	6.0	8.3	5.1	9.9	11.2	4.6	10.5	10.8	9.0	10.9	9.5	7.2
Hungary	:	2.1	5.3	8.5	5.7	6.6	2.5	2.5	3.5	-0.1	-0.4	-0.1	1.0
Malta	:	2.9	0.4	0.7	3.3	0.1	-1.4	-1.2	-0.8	-0.8	0.2	-0.3	-0.2
Poland	4.7	4.4	0.0	1.0	1.3	-1.1	-0.1	2.6	1.1	2.6	3.1	2.1	1.4
Romania	0.0	5.7	7.3	3.7	6.5	3.4	11.4	10.1	12.1	8.5	11.9	7.7	9.8
Slovakia	:	3.5	2.7	5.8	1.3	1.7	2.5	3.2	2.4	3.7	4.5	3.7	3.5
Sweden	1.3	2.7	1.5	1.1	1.2	2.9	1.9	2.2	0.3	1.8	3.1	2.3	2.6
United Kingdom	0.2	3.0	2.2	1.7	2.9	2.6	2.1	2.4	1.8	2.2	2.0	2.5	2.3
EU27	:	1.4	0.7	1.3	1.2	0.7	0.3	0.6	0.1	0.8	0.8	1.2	1.3
USA	0.7	2.4	1.6	2.1	2.3	1.5	0.8	2.7	1.5	2.6	2.1	3.3	3.3
Japan	0.9	0.3	0.2	-0.1	-0.5	-0.6	1.0	0.9	1.0	1.1	1.4	1.0	1.4

[1]Deflated by the price deflator of private consumption. European Commisson spring 2006 forecasts.

Figure 5.57 Real compensation per employee. European countries

in a way that will at the same time increase employment and the wage share, and thus foster social coherence instead of further jeopardizing it.

5.5 Private sector salaried employment attributes, corporate taxation and corporate profitability

5.5.1 Private sector salaried employment, employer size and the relative attractiveness of public sector employment

The general preference of Greek society and the political establishment for small and medium enterprises, self-employment and public sector employment, which is paired with a general aversion for "big business," is usually reflected by an outright hostile attitude toward larger business units. This attitude needs to be compared with the fact that is documented by Figure 5.58, which shows that those larger business units offer better remuneration to their employees than the smaller business units, which are nevertheless looked upon more favorably by the Greek society and political establishment. The fact that their higher productivity allows them to offer these better salaries has been documented in the literature by research like the recent work of Leung et al. (2008). This has not only significant implications for the welfare of the employees of these larger companies, who receive these higher salaries. It has also an important effect on the revenue of the general government, since the average salary paid by the larger employers translate into an annual income for their

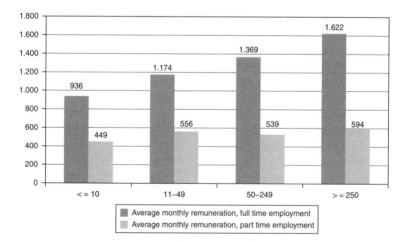

Figure 5.58 Average monthly remuneration, full-time and part-time employment. By employer size. Greece. In euros

employees who have to pay a substantial personal income tax, beside the constant proportion of social security contributions, which are naturally higher as they are computed on a larger salary. This comment becomes now increasingly pertinent, as the failure to implement product market reforms and reforms in professional services, has put the country on an adjustment path through the so called "internal devaluation". The latter encompasses reductions in particular in those salaries, and as a result in the tax and social security revenue that form a significant part of the governments tax revenue. On the other side, small and medium-sized employers pay salaries of such low height that the annual income of their average employees remained below the threshold for tax-free annual income. As a result no personal income tax was paid to the central government, on average, by the employees of small and very small employers, even though the reduction of the tax free income level from 2012 will change that. At the same time the social security contributions paid are computed on this lower salary, which means that the income of the general government is also lower, even though as a percentage these contributions are similar to those computed for the salaried employees of larger employers. Finally, the same data shows in Figure 5.61 that the smaller employers use partial employment more intensively than larger employers, which means that the yearly income, and the related taxes and social security contributions are also, respectively, smaller.

The implications on the social security payments paid are depicted in Figure 5.59 and Figure 5.60. They show that the employment of

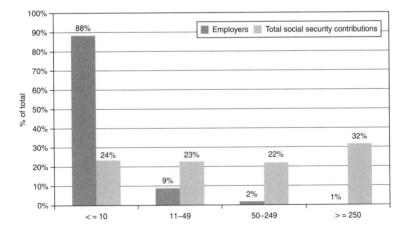

Figure 5.59 Employers and total social security contributions by employer size. Greece

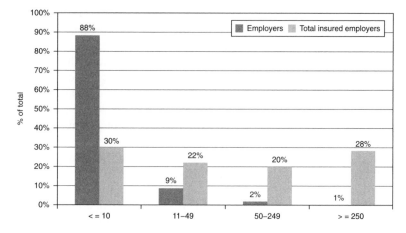

Figure 5.60   Employers and insured employees. By employer size. Greece

48 percent of the employees and workers insured with IKA by employers with over 50 employees lead to the payment of 54 percent of all contributions received by IKA.

We can use the abovementioned data also to suggest why public sector employment in Greece may be so popular, along with self-employment. Given that beside those higher skilled individuals who can take advantage of the realities pertaining to self-employment, about half the core of the private sector salaried employees face on average employment terms in the private sector that are disadvantageous when compared to the employment terms that can be offered by a larger organization, government employment may appear rather attractive. The average annual remuneration of the 506,000 public sector employees of 2008 mentioned in the government budget for 2009 (a census of public sector employees conducted in 2011 showed that their number exceeds 1 million, even though many of them are not insured directly as central government employees, as shown by Alpha Bank (2010)), and when taking the total expenditure for salaries, salaries of public hospital staff and related salary expenses of the government budget in the year 2008, reached a total of 16.5 billion euros. Dividing it with the number of registered public employees, appears to be rather attractive when compared with the remuneration offered by all but the largest private sector employers – 32,614 euros for 2008 (or 2330 euros per month times 14 at the time). That is a net payment, as neither the civil servants nor the public sector pay social security contributions for their main pension at a level that can be compared

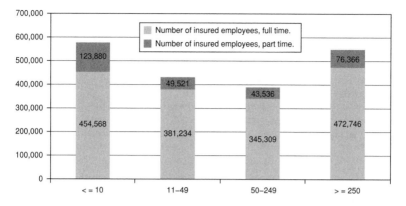

Figure 5.61 Full-time and part time employment according to employer size. Greece

to the private sector contributions for salaried employment, even though their contribution will increase significantly from 2012 on. They only pay for the additional optional pension scheme, since the government guarantees their basic pensions and therefore there is no need for such commensurate payments. Therefore the gross income for public employees includes fewer social security contributions than the gross salary of private sector employees, which includes the employees' social security contributions, as documented by IKA for the typical private sector employee. The latter is about half the gross salary of a public sector employee and equals 1277 euros per month for a full-time permanent employee insured with IKA, which should again be multiplied by 14 to get the gross annual wage income. Actually, only the employees of large employers with above average wages seemed to be able to compete with the average income of public sector employees, according to the data that is drawn from the government budget and that is in line with the data for the average gross salary estimated by Eurostat for the private and public control in Greece. The data by Eurostat, shown in Figure 5.62, further reveals that in Greece the average monthly salary and related payments per public employee was about 45 percent higher than the average private sector salary, the fourth largest such difference among the 27 member countries of the EU and much above the difference that exists on the eurozone average, which is about 12 percent. Even though recent government expenditure cuts and a new remuneration system have reduced the public sector salaries, the rapid fall of private sector salaries, especially among above average earners, during 2010 and 2011 probably implies that this wedge has remained

Data for 2006	Public control	Private control	Δ%
Estonia	573.00	653.79	−12.36%
Slovakia	487.28	543.12	−10.28%
Finland	2406.19	2657.15	−9.44%
Sweden	2702.51	2964.60	−8.84%
Netherlands	2422.84	2633.04	−7.98%
Denmark	3154.57	3334.87	−5.41%
Lithuania	460.71	478.12	−3.64%
Czech Republic	705.99	731.30	−3.46%
Iceland	3324.90	3345.45	−0.61%
EU 27	2261.88	2210.42	2.33%
Hungary	641.34	623.64	2.84%
Latvia	476.52	459.07	3.80%
United Kingdom	3378.36	3254.23	3.81%
Norway	4097.03	3888.27	5.37%
Poland	712.12	648.18	9.86%
Malta	1355.36	1231.36	10.07%
EA 16	2545.92	2266.22	12.34%
Italy	2304.88	2031.88	13.44%
Belgium	3192.51	2769.73	15.26%
Germany	3125.81	2708.94	15.39%
Bulgaria	218.98	187.52	16.78%
France	2855.00	2434.61	17.27%
Austria	2744.27	2280.57	20.33%
Spain	2165.52	1641.92	31.89%
Slovenia	1438.79	1090.71	31.91%
Ireland	4144.45	3096.82	33.83%
Luxembourg	4360.95	3191.97	36.62%
Romania	427.94	297.61	43.79%
Greece	**2136.41**	**1473.15**	**45.02%**
Cyprus	2601.16	1625.07	60.06%
Turkey	1028.72	596.54	72.45%
Portugal	1848.63	1015.50	82.04%

Figure 5.62 Monthly gross salary for private and public control. European countries

so far intact. In addition the generous public sector pension terms, which are documented by Tinios (2003), early retirement and job security, have all to be added to the general scarcity of private sector jobs that follows from the low competitiveness of the economy and, in the end, lead to the rational relative attractiveness of public sector employment over private sector salaried employment for a significant portion of the labor force. Finally, when moving away from salaried labor, the unattractive business environment severely limits the employment options for entrepreneurial activity, leaving basically, after public sector salaried employment, self-employment as the second most attractive employment option, which is true in particular for higher skill professionals.

5.5.2 Corporate income tax contribution in Greece

The low usage of labor, which we have already documented, is paired – as we have already seen in Figure 5.11 – by a constant increase in the investment-to-GDP ratio, to a level that exceeded the eurozone average in the years leading to the current crisis. According to Eurostat most of these investments originated from the private sector, and in particular construction, in spite of the large budget for public investments that is financed through the EU structural funds. This inflow of course also affects and encourages private investment, which often is subsidized and so far has taken place within the setting of a fast growing economy with macroeconomic stability and rapidly expanding private credit. In this context the picture of the 1990s in which investment lagged behind the eurozone average was gradually reversed until 2007.

But this analysis, in particular in the case of Greece, requires us to make a distinction between capital that is invested and not operating and capital that is not just invested, but also operating and generating revenue. The distinction has to be made because in Greece the cost of making it possible to operate the invested capital is often very high, and fraught with significant uncertainties regarding the total monetary cost incurred, as well as the time required to achieve the operational status of the installed and invested capital. Administrative uncertainly, delays, inability to predict shifting and vague legislation or even the ability to enforce existing legislation mean that from the time the investment is disbursed until the time one can operate the investment to generate revenue not only the investment often turns out to be much more expensive than initially anticipated, but sometimes it is even put entirely at risk. The cost of these delays, even if they entail no other cost than the interest on the tied-up capital, is rarely added to the cost of investment, and definitely not accepted by the Ministry of Economy, Competitiveness and Shipping (to which the former Ministry of Development belongs) in its assessment of the mandatory requests that companies submit when they want to increase the prices of the products and services they offer. Yet these delays are most likely significant as one can expect them to be positively correlated with the height of the administrative burden faced by the private sector. The latter is among the highest in the EU-27 according to estimates made by the European Commission, as was shown in Figure 5.21. We remind

	2000	2001	2002	2003	2004	2005	2006	2007
DIRECT TAXES – CORPORATE TAXES. % GDP.								
GREECE	4.1	3.4	3.4	2.9	3	3.2	2.7	2.6
EURO ZONE*	2.6	2.4	2.2	2	2.2	2.4	2.7	2.9

Figure 5.63   Taxation trends in the EU. Direct taxes, corporate taxes as a percentage of the GDP

that these estimates put the administrative cost faced by the economy at almost 7 percent of the GDP, twice the European average that is.

The latter cost is of course only the static cost. The total cost to the economy, besides the static cost, includes also the dynamic implication that this increased uncertainty and actual cost has on business initiatives that are never undertaken. The total cost to the economy includes also the cost of waiting for the permit to turn the key on the installed machinery, which often may exceed the interest on the tied-up capital, especially if the tied-up investment ages, depreciates or looses its competitive edge or, for example, a favorable seasonal or cyclical conjecture. Of course, often binding agreements that are taken up during the phase when the investment is made may have clauses that lead to further losses in the case of such delays. The effect of these implications on the economic activity can be estimated, but this requires advanced econometric techniques that are applied on comprehensive and innovative databases, like the work undertaken by Conway et al. (2006) for example. Other works, like d'Auria et al. (2009), estimate separately the impact of uncompetitive markets and administrative burden. Unsurprisingly, Greece is found to be the country which has the most to gain, with regard to productivity increases in the private sector of the economy, from removing such regulation and burdens that limit competition and at the same time increase the administrative burden on the economy. Preliminary results from the Institute for Economic and Industrial relations (IOBE), a Greek think-tank, which has developed such an econometric model to estimate the potential impact of such reforms, also seem to verify these results.

It remains though that in spite of the fact that the profits generated by businesses in Greece are contributing, as a percentage of the GDP and according to Figure 5.63, a corporate income tax revenue to the government that was up until 2005 above the eurozone average, the business activity has to incur in addition the cost of increased administrative uncertainly and the cost of delays that are often not counted among the tangible costs of businesses in Greece, and that definitely are not accepted as expenses by the Greek tax authorities and the authorities that impose indirect or direct restrictions on the prices or requested price increases of goods and services.

At this point we have to mention once again the prevalence of self-employment in Greece. This attribute affects not only many computations for the income share of salaried labor, as the income share of self-employment is often added to the corporate sector at this point. This inaccuracy is often also extended to computations regarding the tax burden of corporate profits. This happens to the extent that (significant) income and (scant) taxes not associated with dependent labor are allocated to the corporate sector, along of course with all measurement and other statistical errors and residuals. For example, Carey and Rabesona (2004) apply a method that does not automatically add the numbers that are associated with self-employment to the corporate sector. As a result the low estimate for the tax burden of the corporate sector, as labeled in this work, in Greece immediately increases by 45 percent, which is the fourth largest increase in a sample of 23 countries. These methodological challenges faced by researchers who use data for Greece mean that simple indicators, like taxes as a percentage of the GDP, have improved reliability. On the other hand, numbers that either bundle self-employment with the corporate sector or that do not provide a convincing methodology to identify the contribution of each separate sector need to be scrutinized more carefully before their results are used to draw conclusions.

As a result of these cautionary notes we put our emphasis on the European Commission's data that shows that until 2006, at which time the corporate income tax started to fall to levels that were more compatible with the respective levels in many other European countries, the corporate sector used to contribute, as a percentage of the GDP, more taxes in Greece than it did on average in other – much more competitive – European countries. This changed in 2007, when this contribution fell slightly below the European average. Data for 2008 when it becomes available will probably demonstrate a further decline, if one takes into account, first, the data for the main and supplementary tax paid in that year, as shown in Figure 5.66, which stayed constant at 4.7 billion euros, and, second, the fact that the GDP still increased briskly in 2008. It has to be stressed though that in many other European countries there exists already a double taxation on corporate income, as after the corporate income tax there is in addition a tax on dividends, according to the data presented in Figure 5.64. Such a tax was introduced in Greece in 2008, and as a result it will be reflected in the data for the 2008 fiscal year. This tax was initially set at 10 percent

Dividend taxation, upon distribution to individuals (*with option to tax in income bracket)

	GR	AT	FR*	IRL	PT*	ES	IT	DE	UK	FL	S	BE
	10.0%	25.0%	29.0%	20.0%	20.0%	18.0%		26.4%	10–32.5%	28.0%		

Taxation of corporate income, 2008.

	GR	AT	FR	IRL	PT	ES	IT	DE	UK	FL	S	BE
Small companies	**		15.0%		20.0%	25.0%			22.0%		25.0%	25.0%
Baseline	25.0%	25.0%	25.0%	12.5%	25.0%	30.0%	27.5%	29.8%	28.0%	26.0%	28.0%	34.0%
Large companies			28.3%									

Note: ** For proprietor companies half the income is taxed at the corporate level with 20 percent and half the income is taxed as personal income of the proprietor, or the proprietors, according to the income bracket of each of them. According to the new tax law, dividends in Greece will be taxed from 2011 as personal income.

Figure 5.64 Dividend taxation, upon distribution to individuals, and taxation of corporate income. European countries

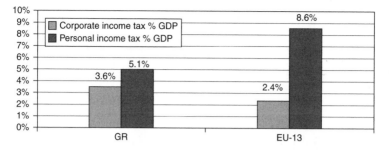

Figure 5.65 Corporate and personal income tax as a percentage of the GDP. Greece and EU-13, FY 2005

on distributed dividends, and is expected to yield according to the 2010 budget a revenue of 640 million euros, almost double the revenue of 2009, which was 360 million euros. In 2009 this tax amounted to an approximately 7 percent increase in the corporate income tax collected in 2008. Alternatively, one can interpret it, in terms of Figure 5.67, as an increase of the effective tax rate on corporate income for the year 2008 from 24 percent to 26 percent, given that the dividends of 2009 are based on the corporate income of 2008. This tax has been further raised in the latest tax law, especially for dividend income accruing to high-income individuals as now it is taxed according to the personal income tax bracket of the individual shareholder. At the same time the exemption of smaller shareholders with low declared income from this tax, as is foreseen by the latest tax law, may actually mean that the revenue collected by the government will fall at the same time.

At the same time of course, the introduction of a flat tax of 10 percent on dividends has replaced in part the reduction of the corporate income tax that was introduced in 2006 and 2007. The further increase of this dividend tax is set to effectively take the taxation of corporate profits again to the levels of the previous years, simply now part of this tax will accrue to personal incomes as it does in other countries that already tax dividends. Taxation of corporate income and dividends will be aligned, as a result, with the taxation that prevails in a number of developed European countries, but which at the same time offer a much more attractive business environment according to comparative international surveys, such as the Doing Business Reports for example, and that have generally much more liberalized economies and open markets and in which the administrative burden is estimated, as a percentage of the GDP, to be much lower. At the same time in a number of other

Public limited company

	Taxable corporate income	Verified tax	Main and supplementary tax	Verified tax as % of taxable income
2008	44,135	15,328,919,690	3,313,230,490	3,815,601,946	21,6%
2007	42,549	13,457,733,355	3,662,140,631	3,878,022,625	27,2%
2006	39,914	11,207,709,486	3,462,573,212	3,582,245,347	30,9%
2005	39,233	11,437,394,300	3,765,858,599	3,952,900,226	32,9%
2004	39,340	11,338,184,135	3,634,255,409	3,905,650,893	32,1%
2003	39,329	10,302,624,017	3,250,230,566	3,558,009,671	31,5%
2002	36,457	9,472,453,498	3,212,171,301	3,483,441,295	33,9%

Private limited company

	Taxable corporate income	Verified tax	Main and supplementary tax	Verified tax as % of taxable income
2008	24,668	1,173,638,715	279,718,548	296,113,207	23,8%
2007	23,719	1,010,525,397	287,083,656	293,836,865	28,4%
2006	22,129	875,044,826	277,041,214	280,380,922	31,7%
2005	21,492	871,872,848	299,577,036	305,592,435	34,4%
2004	21,273	819,248,032	314,027,224	286,726,957	38,3%
2003	20,074	549,071,831	192,437,244	197,598,286	35,0%
2002	19,386	494,188,868	171,992,979	173,503,571	34,8%

General partnership

	Taxable corporate income	Verified tax	Main and supplementary tax	Verified tax as % of taxable income
2008	144,665	2,900,199,570	511,748,990	601,983,218	17,6%
2007	137,631	2,521,021,805	496,084,573	575,039,643	19,7%
2006	129,765	2,343,911,437	508,235,745	584,301,253	21,7%
2005	124,231	2,448,660,598	573,382,477	650,963,414	23,4%

181

	All companies	Taxable corporate income	Verified tax	Main and supplementary tax	Verified tax as % of taxable income
2004	121,129	2,190,789,877	499,991,483	582,645,577	22,8%
2003	113,964	2,129,135,916	465,893,310	537,339,355	21,9%
2002	110,227	1,761,742,487	391,377,117	465,198,326	22,2%
2008	213,468	19,402,757,975	4,104,698,028	4,713,698,371	21,2%
2007	203,899	16,989,280,557	4,445,308,860	4,746,899,133	26,2%
2006	191,808	14,426,665,749	4,247,850,171	4,446,927,522	29,4%
2005	184,956	14,757,927,746	4,638,818,112	4,909,456,075	31,4%
2004	181,742	14,348,222,044	4,448,274,116	4,775,023,427	31,0%
2003	173,367	12,980,831,764	3,908,561,120	4,292,947,312	30,1%
2002	166,070	11,728,384,852	3,775,541,397	4,122,143,192	32,2%

Figure 5.66 Profits and tax according to legal form of enterprises. Greece

European countries, which do not belong to the small core of developed European countries, tax on corporate profits and the distributed dividends are much lighter than those Greece is about to introduce.

Finally it has to be recalled that the main deficit in the income tax revenue, as a percentage of the GDP, of the Greek general government is mainly identified among individuals and direct personal income taxes, as shown by Figure 5.65, rather than among corporate income tax. As such, and given that the corporate sector generally creates the job opportunities that are associated with the highest value added, the equalization of the taxation of the corporate sector with the taxation that prevails in some of the core European countries ahead of the equalization of the business environment and the quality of the regulation of the economy with these core European countries may not yield the anticipated results, especially as long as the quality of the regulatory environment does not even yield a prospect of rapid and substantial improvement. The latter, we must remind, seems to be more important for foreign investors than the prevailing tax rate, according to works such as Hajkova et al. (2007). In other words, the unwinding of the fiscal imbalances of the country, as far as the revenue side of the problem is concerned, does not seem to depend as much on the taxation of corporate profits as it seems to depend, according to our preceding analysis, on the increase in the competitiveness of the economy, the rise in employment and taxable income and, of course, the resolution of certain attributes of personal income taxation that really stand out when compared to the reality of the more advanced European economies. As was with the case of labor market reforms, the extensive increases in taxes that have been implemented, contrary to product market reforms, and the continuing acceleration and deepening of the Greek recession seem to support this observation.

The data of the General Secretariat for Information Systems also shows us that the largest part of the corporate income tax is paid by a small number of public limited companies, according to the definition of the European Commission (2006), that also declare the largest share of the aggregate corporate profits, as shown by Figure 5.66. This data documents the fall of the corporate income tax after the fall of the related tax rate between 2006 and 2008, but also the increase in 2007 of the total taxes received as a result of the rebound of corporate profits in that year. It has to be stressed that the profits of proprietary firms (general partnerships) are taxed for 50 percent of the profits with a tax rate of 20 percent, less than the corporate income tax rate, and for the remaining 50 percent at the rate corresponding to the income bracket of the proprietor. As a result, if there is more than one proprietor, as is often the case, then each of them can easily declare a personal income that is below the level over which personal income tax is paid. This explains also why the tax rate of these smaller proprietor companies is significantly lower than the tax rate of capital-based corporations, as shown in Figure 5.66. Also, one should note that the verified tax follows from the income declared and that the main and supplementary tax also includes additional taxes that are charged once past fiscal years are controlled by the authorities, as well as the increase, or return, of receipts of tax advances and other adjustments. As such the tax rate that is best compared with the official tax rate is the ratio of verified-tax-to-corporate income, but in the end companies pay the main and supplementary tax, which generally is higher, as shown in Figure 5.67. Tax advances, it should be noted, generally are not paid back, say, if the corporate profits fall, as for example this year the law changed postponing, canceling or replacing with new taxes the return of tax advances to banks whose profits fell during the past fiscal years. So one should expect that in 2009 and 2010 the discrepancy between tax verified, and main and supplementary tax will further diverge, following the trend of 2008.

We can see therefore not only that a small number of larger companies offer better salaries, as we have already seen, and that they generate thus taxable personal incomes, but they also contribute the majority of the corporate income taxes, which in the end are close to the European average in spite of the lower competitiveness of the Greek economy. The latter has become even more pertinent since 2009, as it is the larger companies that pay the extraordinary taxes imposed on corporate profits, and that in an environment of vanishing profits form an ever increasing part of corporate income taxation.

5.5.3 Profitability of Greek companies

The abovementioned data concerning the contribution of larger companies to both the total profits declared and the total corporate income tax paid demonstrates the seriousness of the tendency to underestimate entrepreneurship, regardless of size, as a mechanism for creating value-added and quality jobs. As a result of the reservations that Greek society has about the market economy, it is often overlooked that the larger companies make a very significant contribution to the job market, employee incomes and the public tax revenue. Among a healthy population of enterprises, there is usually a complicated relationship of cross-dependencies or subcontracting that links the success of each

Fiscal year, GSIS data.	Official tax rate	Corporate income, million euros	Verified corporate income tax, million euros	Effective tax rate on verified tax	Tax paid, million euros	Effective tax rate on tax paid
2008	.25	19.403	4.105	.21	4.414	.24
2007	.29	16.989	4.445	.26	4.747	.28
2006	.32	14.426	4.247	.29	4.447	.31
2005	.35	14.757	4.638	.31	4.910	.33

Figure 5.67 Official and effective tax rates per fiscal year. Greece

enterprise with the success of other enterprises. This healthy population can only prosper if both the subsets of larger and of smaller companies are healthy and profitable. Finally we need to take into account that many times larger companies have started out as small companies that grew exactly because they introduced an innovation, either as part of a process or as a product or service, that was very popular and in great demand. These success stories are an integral part, but not the only part, of the process that finances and incorporates innovation in the production base of the economy through many different processes – some of which are described in Lamoreaux and Sokoloff (2007) – that lead to the increase in productivity, the increase in competitiveness, the creation of value-added, according to the process documented in Nicoletti and Scarpetta (2006) – which includes profits – and of course the creation of good and well paid jobs that use the skills of the workforce in order to create these innovations. Larger companies also contribute in many different, and often unpredictable, ways toward the process of innovation, as described by the various examples presented in the work edited by Lamoreaux and Sokoloff (2007). The acceptance of entrepreneurship therefore should not come with conditions on the size of companies, as long as they abide by the laws and act responsibly toward society.

It should finally be noted that in spite of the rapid growth of the economy during the past years, the total profitability of the Greek corporations in manufacturing, as documented by the published accounts of manufacturing corporations, seems not to be high, with the exception of a spike around 1999 and 2000 (Figure 5.68). Still many studies for profitability, as for example from the European Commission (using data provided by the Greek National Statistical Service), may overestimate, unintentionally, Greek corporate profits. For example, the income of the self-employed may be misinterpreted as the primary data is less reliable for this type of labor than, say, the published accounts of corporations and the data for salaried labor. Or the computation of corporate profitability may be affected by base effects that follow when the expense for the services provided by self-employed is deducted from the value added of the corporate sector and not added to the wage bill. As a result high, or at least average (according to substantially revised data recently provided by the Greek National Statistical Service), levels of profitability may be estimated for the corporate sector when comparing Greece to other European countries. Therefore the use of direct sources of data, like corporate balance sheets, seems once again to be the most reliable way to overcome the challenges that the case of Greece poses. For example,

Figure 5.68 Profitability of Greek manufacturing

use of the Bureu van Djik database to explore deeper these assertions would indeed be a fruitful avenue for future research. Alternatively, one can use the Bank of Accounts, Harmonised (BACH) database of the European Commission and match it with comparable data from the Greek ICAP database. The use of such data in Figure 5.69 reveals that the profitability, as measured by profit before tax to sales, of non-financial corporations in Greece is consistently below the one achieved in many of the main European countries, and this is in spite of the relatively higher growth rate of the economy during the past years.

The available and reliable evidence shows that of course the absolute magnitude of profits has risen with the fast growth of the nominal GDP, but that at the same time the profitability ratio has not risen to high levels. This may of course also follow from the intensive use of capital, which drives down the marginal yield of investments, but it seems reasonable that the very high administrative cost measured by the European Commission and other institutions also contributes significantly to the reduction of the Greek profitability ratios, in spite of the high inflation differential with the eurozone that is often blamed by the media and politicians on the supposedly "excessive and immoral profitability" of large (mainly) corporations. It seems more plausible that the administrative burden – which is documented by hard and difficult to-deny facts to be indeed excessive and higher, on average, by about 3 percent of the GDP when compared to the European average – contributes equally

Profits before tax and extraordinaries to sales, non-financial companies.

Sectors NACE A-K and M-O. Germany C-I only. Italy except M-N. All companies of sample for each year (BACH definition of Variable Sample). Data for all countries except Greece BACH. Data for Greece from ICAP, yearly edition of Guide to the Greek Company. Full yearly sample, comparable to BACH Variable Sample and same NACE sectors and definition for profit before tax and extraordinaries.

	Greece	Weighted average all countries except Greece	Belgium	Germany	Spain	France	Italy	Netherlands	Austria	Portugal
2003	5.43%	4.45%	5.54%	3.43%	7.67%	4.00%	3.28%	6.72%	5.08%	6.47%
2004	4.97%	5.38%	5.84%	3.42%	7.66%	5.41%	5.05%	8.39%	5.62%	6.85%
2005	3.86%	6.01%	8.25%	3.73%	9.10%	5.58%	4.28%	12.93%	6.37%	7.79%
2006	5.04%	6.53%	7.58%	4.07%	10.11%	6.97%	4.66%	12.43%	5.29%	7.01%
2007	5.68%	7.17%	9.57%	5.98%	10.28%	7.51%	4.74%		7.84%	9.49%
2008	3.06%									

Figure 5.69 Profitability of non-financial companies. European countries

to the reduction of profitability ratios and the increase in the inflation differential. This seems plausible especially if one adds the inefficiency cost imposed by regulation that restricts competition in network industries like transportation and energy, and that reduces significantly the productivity of the private sector according to the work of Conway et al. (2006), for example. The high administrative burden and the predominance of regulation that harms competition, in particular in network industries, is in Greece of a size that should suffice to account for both a reduction of the profitability ratio among the 35,000 largest corporations by 2–3 percentage points, relatively to their European peers, and, at the same time, account for the persistent inflation difference with the other European countries. That is, these inefficiencies of the economy, which mainly stem from government regulations, succeed in securing both low profitability for corporations and high prices for consumers and companies that purchase inputs at the same time, which seems to be, at best, a very unfortunate achievement that does not appear to serve well the broader interests of Greek society. The accelerating collapse of corporate profitability during 2010 and 2011, along with the widespread implementation of measures to increase taxes, labor market reforms and failure to implement product market reforms once again seem to support this observation.

The database of the General Secretariat for Information Systems (GSIS) and the database of IKA are probably the best government databases available in Greece today; they are compiled using the best infrastructure of information technology of the Greek administration, and as such can be considered to be the most reliable databases available from the public sector. Furthermore, the data of published accounts, especially of the largest companies that are usually under the closer scrutiny of authorities, is the most reliable source of data regarding the activities of corporations. This means that it should be almost impossible to source data that can be judged objectively to be more reliable than the data presented so far, and as a result the conclusions drawn from the presentation of this data should be able to withstand most attempts to formulate counterarguments against their validity and soundness.

5.6 The current crisis and the Greek financial system

During the current conjecture the documented weaknesses of the Greek economy are held in the spotlight of international markets – as is justified by the analysis of Haugh et al. (2009), who investigate the factors that affect sovereign debt premiums. This happens in spite of

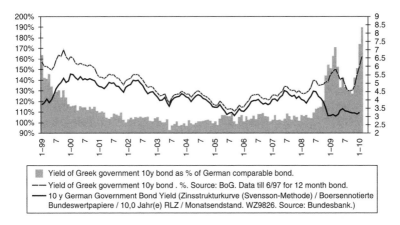

Figure 5.70   Greek and German ten-year government bond yields

the achievements of the past decades that attracted the interest of the international markets since the accession of the country to the EMU and until the start of the current crisis. This follows as the strong growth of the previous years, which highlighted the successes rather than the failings of the country, seems to peter out at the same time that the creditworthiness of the Greek government is put under scrutiny (and even doubt). Furthermore, this happens at a time when globally solvency risk has been transferred massively from the private sector to the public sector and, at the same time, sovereign risk is being reassessed by markets along with private sector risk. All these factors are reflected for example, as Figure 5.70 shows, by a significant increase in the spread of the Greek ten-year government bond compared to the German ten-year government bond.

These concerns are basically fueled neither by the high debt of the Greek government nor by the low competitiveness of the economy, but rather by the extent of the size that both these problems appear to have at the same time in Greece. Indeed, as Figure 5.71 shows, Greece is not alone regarding either the level of government debt or the balance of payments deficit, which can be used as an approximation of the competitiveness deficit of the economy. But Greece stands alone among other European countries once one looks at the size of both these attributes together. The accumulation of these concerns to such a large extent in one single country is the factor that leads to the increased concerns of the international markets regarding the ability of the country to generate in the future the taxable income that will make

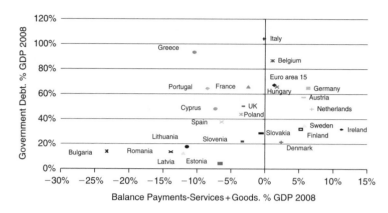

Figure 5.71   Government debt and balance of payment as a percentage of GDP. European countries

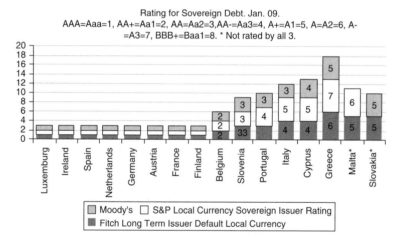

Figure 5.72   Sovereign debt ratings. January 2009. Eurozone member countries

it possible to service its public debt. The combined concerns regarding first the size of the debt stock and second the current deficits of the government budget, as well as the low competitiveness of the economy that generates the taxable income that has to service this debt, existed even before the current crisis, as was reflected by the credit rating of the Greek government debt by the three rating agencies before the emergence of the current debate regarding Greece, for example in January 2009. At the time, as Figure 5.72 shows, Greek bonds were rated lower than the bonds of all other eurozone member countries, even though this lower rating was not reflected correspondingly in the pricing of the Greek government debt as the markets were at the time pricing risk, and in particular the risk of sovereign debt, much lower that they do now.

The relatively challenging situation of the public debt and the Greek government's finances is in sharp contrast with the situation of the Greek banking system at the beginning of the current crisis, as opposed to the situation in the other major European countries. While in those countries the banks where severely challenged by significant losses that put their capital base at such a risk that the intervention of governments, with generally sound finances, was needed, in Greece the banks did not incur losses from their exposure to unwise or excessively risky investments and positions. At the same time the situation of the government finances in Greece was significantly worse than in the other European countries. Yet Greek banks were the intermediaries that financed the excessive current account deficit of the past years, as well as a significant part of the public debt, either directly of indirectly. This was the case especially during the last years, when the inflows for the purchase of stocks and government bonds that dominated after Greece's accession to the EMU gradually became less prominent. As these inflows abated, Greek banks secured the liquidity required to finance the expansion of the economy and the sustenance of the current account deficit with the tapping of the liquidity pool that was provided by the European interbank money market, as well as the European capital markets, that willingly financed Greek banks, for example with the purchase of covered bond issues. This mechanism ceased to operate once the interbank money market stopped when the current crisis hit important international banking institutions. But even as the global financial markets started to recover, increased concerns over Greece in particular, which were further enhanced by the demonstrated lack of political will to deal with the twin issues of deteriorating public finances and low competitiveness of the economy by successive Greek governments, kept the global financial markets largely shut for Greek banks, if not the Greek government. During the period that lasted from the outset of the global crisis to the beginning of 2010, Greek banks were able to avoid these problems as they had the option to use the measures installed by the European Central Bank (ECB), and which allowed them to draw at the time about 30–40 billion euros of liquidity from the ECB by offering as collateral mainly Greek government bonds, in spite of the creditworthiness rating downgrades these sustained in the meantime.

In a nutshell, even though Greek banks did not have any direct exposure to the risks that led to the current global financial crisis, they were placed in the middle of the stream of international money that financed the unsustainable growth of the uncompetitive Greek economy and the Greek government budget deficit and, as a result, of the mechanism that ensured the growth of the government tax revenue that could match the ever-increasing public expenditure. The Greek banks were simply placed in the middle of the chain of events through which the international crisis was first imported into the Greek economy. During 2009 the liquidity provided by the ECB was largely handed over to the Greek government, either through the "support measures" that were devised by the government to shore up the capital base of the banks with the issuance of about 10 billion euros of special government bonds, which the banks were strongly encouraged – by the then government – to accept, or through the direct purchase of new government bond issues. Even though according to Morgan Stanley (2010) the exposure of Greek banks to Greek government bonds has fallen in the past year, it remains at levels that are well above the European average and it can be assumed that these holdings consist mainly of Greek government bonds. So the year 2009 passed with the banks, once again, remaining at the middle of a process that financed the uncompetitive Greek economy and the (by now rapidly) faltering finances of the Greek government. During 2009 the capital base of the Greek banks, which started out healthy in 2008 and which was not harmed by the fallout of the subprime crisis (and which was further enhanced by the Greek government bonds in 2009), supported their high levels of solvency, as argued for by Hardouvelis (2008) for example. It also probably contributed significantly to the ability of the Greek banks to bypass the liquidity constraints imposed by the drying up of global money markets on the one hand and the need of the Greek economy, and the Greek government, for sizeable capital inflows on the other hand.

The year 2010 brought for the Greek banks increased challenges though, despite the fact that the challenges relating to the prospect of the retraction of the special measures taken by the ECB, which would require them to refinance the Greek government bonds that have been deposited as guarantees with the ECB at a time when the creditworthiness of these bonds is severely diminished, have been postponed now thanks to the repeated and decisive initiatives taken by the ECB. More importantly, the banks face significant losses from the Greek government bonds directly owned by them as a result of the events that have led to the agreement among the euro zone member states to ask private sector bond holders to voluntarily accept initially a 21% haircut, and then in October 2011 a 50% haircut on their holdings. Furthermore, there now is an increasing number of non-performing loans as the recession of the Greek economy starts to gather pace and proves to be deeper than the overoptimistic estimates of successive Greek governments had forecast; they also face the need to refinance a series of covered bond issues at a time that they also are sustaining downgrades of their creditworthiness. Finally, on top of these challenges, they faced for years a barrage of hostile legislative initiatives by the Greek government, that seem to abate only during late 2011, that is at a time that unavoidable events may already have been set in motion. These initiatives either seemed to blatantly ignore the advice and opinion of the ECB at a time when the ECB takes unprecedented measures to support the Greek financial system, or aimed to enhance the rights – as perceived by successive Greek governments – of the consumers of bank products during this challenging conjecture or – simply – aim to increase taxes, tax advances or other burdens that the successive governments impose on them.

It appears therefore that the Greek banks face at this point significant challenges that are largely a reflection of the weaknesses of the successive Greek governments, as well as of the policy choices that determine the competitiveness of the Greek economy. The faltering creditworthiness of the Greek government and prospects of the Greek economy seem to shut, for now, commercial banks off the money and capital markets, or at least seem to lead to an increase in the cost of money offered to them to a degree that renders it prohibitive. Furthermore, asking for a private sector involvement in the reduction of outstanding Greek government debt probably implies that, along with the Greek government, also Greek financial institutions may not be able to return to normal market financing for the foreseeable future, at least under favorable terms. The reduced creditworthiness of the Greek government bonds has thus put a significant portion of their assets at risk, implying at this point important capital losses even though their investments in Greek government bonds were, at least, traditionally actively invited by the successive Greek governments. And the low competitiveness of the economy – which follows from the insistence of the government to keep product and services markets closed to competition, to maintain such an excessive administrative burden on the economy and to actually legislate every day new laws that exacerbate these problems and that test the resistance of the financial system – puts at an ever increasing risk the incomes of the Greek households and producing companies – that is, it puts at risk the health of the loan portfolios that they are asked to service. In a nutshell, while in the other European countries the problems were largely originating from the banking system and the solutions were offered by the government, so far in Greece the problems originate from the government and the banks have provided the solutions, even though after the private sector involvement it seems that this situation will be difficult to sustain even if now decisive and well aimed corrective policy initiatives are taken by the Greek government.

The assessment of the current situation requires a realization that banks are particular organizations that redistribute funds in an economy from those that have them but do not know, or want to, put them into productive use to those that do not have them but have productive ideas or needs that need financing. The term financial intermediation thus accurately describes their role of redistributor of funds from depositors toward households and enterprises with financing needs. This process inevitably is undertaken with a relatively thin capital base. It is this ability to redistribute the funds of others with this thin capital base that is, on the one hand, the contribution of the banking system toward the enhancement of the efficiency and competitiveness of an economy, as idle funds are redirected toward productive employment. On the other hand, this also means that banks are at particular risk if their loan or investment portfolio sustains significant losses, as their capital base is relatively small when compared to the total size of their assets. Of course an excessive increase in their capital base could eliminate almost completely these risks. But then they would cease to operate as financial intermediaries, and would instead resemble private equities, something that would undermine their productivity-enhancing role of redirecting existing funds that are not owned by them toward more efficient and productive employment at a reasonable cost to the users of this flow of redirected capital. These concerns, regarding the striking of a fine balance between ensuring adequate capital to shore up the resilience of banks to shocks, on the one hand, and to sustain their efficiency-enhancing role, on the other hand, is at the core of the current debate on the reshaping of the regulation of the financial sector – exactly because of the complexity of the issues that relate not only to the quantity but also, mainly, to the qualitative aspects of supervision and the capital base that is needed to secure an adequate resilience of the financial system to severe and rare adverse shocks.

If one were to disregard for a moment the low competitiveness of the Greek economy, one would document that the Greek banks entered the crisis with an adequate, and – more importantly –highly resilient (during the unfolding of the subprime crisis), when compared to the

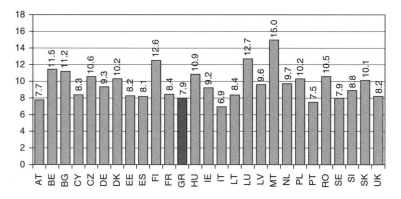

Figure 5.73 Tier 1 according to ECB. Eurozone member countries banking sector. End of 2008

banks of other countries, capital base according to Figure 5.73. Also, during the current conjecture they operated within an economy whose total indebtness, if one adds public debt to private debt, was about average compared to the other eurozone countries, as was shown in Figure 5.7. This happened as the total loans issued to Greek households and non-financial corporations, as a percentage of the GDP, was below the eurozone average, as shown better in Figure 5.8, at the same time that the respective indebtedness of the Greek government exceeded commensurately the eurozone average. It should be noted here that revised ECB data, that also includes loans to self-employed and proprietor firms, and especially the ongoing retraction of the denominator in the debt to GDP ratio, has altered this fact by late 2011.

This shows that the current concerns regarding the indebtness of the Greek government, and their implications for the whole of the economy, were not initially funded on concerns regarding the total indebtness of the economy; rather they regarded the allocation of this debt predominantly in the hands of the Greek government. This observation also suggests that if the government had decided during 2010 and 2011 the decisive deregulation of product and services markets, the reduction of the administrative burden and the exercise of economic policy that honestly and truthfully conforms with the goals of the economic and monetary union, then the increased economic activity of the private sector would have been able to take up, within a reasonable period of time, a significant portion of this public debt, as the new private sector activities would be financed with debt and, at the same time, they would have created taxable profits and personal incomes that would have led to tax revenue and demand growth that in turn would have ensured the reduction of government budget deficits and the erosion of the government debt-to-GDP ratio. Such positive prospects would, of course, have been immediately reflected in the cost of servicing the public debt, as claimed by the director of the IOBE, Professor G. Stournaras. Such a development would also have amounted, of course, to the adoption of a reform agenda that would have allowed Greece to take the next step toward the completion of its transition from developing country into a developed country, with the improvement of governance and the development of first-class institutions, besides the better regulation of markets, being the last step required. Such a development would at the same time have reduced the risks that the strength of the Greek banking system will be tested in a severe contraction of an uncompetitive economy in which the government would seek to increase its tax revenue from a fast shrinking tax base while at the same time it would probably retort increasingly to microeconomic policies that are not aligned with the goals of the economic and monetary union. Such a development, finally, might have made it possible to reduce the debt burden of the general government toward the levels foreseen by the Maastricht Treaty without the need to reduce the total debt burden on the economy and without requiring private bondholders to accept a haircut that will have unpredictable long term implications both for Greece and the euro zone as a whole. In other words, shifting the debt burden from the general government to the new activities of the private sector may have made it possible to improve the creditworthiness of the whole economy without having to severely reduce the total debt burden on the economy.

To assess the prospects of the Greek banks during the current conjecture, one has to take also into account the fact that in the existing environment of the uncompetitive but fast growing Greek economy Greek banks posted during the past decade significant increases in their profitability, which in turn allowed them both to strengthen their capital base and expand in the markets of neighboring countries. Yet with the exception of the years 1999 and 2000, during which the impact of the eurozone accession was most forcefully reflected on their balance sheets, as well as on the balance sheets of non-financial corporations as we have already seen, the increase in the absolute magnitude of banking assets, along with the rapid expansion of private credit, implied that their profitability as a percentage of their assets remained close to the average observed in other OECD countries, as shown by Figure 5.74.

Both the OECD data until 2005 and the ECB data for 2008, in Figure 5.77, show that not only the profitability of the Greek banks is

Profit after tax to yearly average of total assets.

	1993	1994	1995	1996	1997	1998	1999	2000	2001	2002	2003	2004	2005
Greece	**0.7%**	**0.9%**	**0.9%**	**0.5%**	**0.7%**	**0.8%**	**2.4%.**	**1.4%**	**1.0%**	**0.5%**	**0.6%**	**0.3%**	**0.9%**
France	0.0%	-0.1%	0.1%	0.1%	0.2%	0.3%	0.3%	0.5%	0.5%	0.5%	0.5%	0.5%	0.5%
Germany	0.3%	0.3%	0.3%	0.3%	0.2%	0.4%	0.2%	0.2%	0.2%	0.1%	-0.1%	0.0%	0.4%
Portugal	0.8%	0.6%	0.5%	0.6%	0.7%	0.7%	0.7%	0.9%	0.7%	0.6%	0.6%	0.5%	0.6%
Netherlands	0.5%	0.5%	0.5%	0.6%	0.5%	0.4%	0.6%	0.5%	0.5%	0.3%	0.5%	0.5%	0.5%
Italy	0.3%	0.1%	0.1%	0.2%	0.1%	0.5%	0.6%	0.8%	0.6%	0.5%	0.5%	0.6%	0.6%
Spain	0.1%	0.6%	0.6%	0.7%	0.7%	0.8%	0.8%	0.8%	0.8%	0.7%	0.7%	0.7%	0.7%
UK	0.5%	0.8%	0.8%	0.8%	0.8%	0.8%	0.9%	0.9%	0.7%	0.6%	0.7%	0.7%	0.6%
Belgium	0.3%	0.2%	0.2%	0.3%	0.3%	0.3%	0.4%	0.5%	0.5%	0.3%	0.5%	0.4%	0.5%
Denmark	0.4%	0.0%	1.2%	1.0%	1.0%	0.8%	0.7%	0.8%	0.8%	0.7%	0.7%	0.9%	1.0%
Finland	-1.4%	-1.2%	-0.4%	0.3%	0.6%	0.6%	0.9%	1.0%	2.8%	0.8%	1.6%	0.7%	0.9%
Poland		0.1%	2.2%	2.6%	2.0%	0.6%	0.9%	1.0%	0.9%	0.5%	0.5%	1.3%	1.6%
Sweden	0.0%	0.8%	1.1%	1.0%	0.3%	0.7%	0.4%	0.5%	0.8%	0.4%	0.5%	1.5%	0.7%
Turkey	3.2%	2.4%	4.2%	4.4%	3.4%	2.5%	-1.0%	-4.0%	-7.8%	1.3%	2.3%	2.3%	1.5%
Weighted average	0.2%	0.3%	0.4%	0.5%	0.4%	0.5%	0.5%	0.5%	0.5%	0.4%	0.4%	0.7%	0.6%
Average	0.4%	0.4%	0.9%	0.9%	0.8%	0.7%	0.6%	0.4%	0.2%	0.6%	0.7%	0.8%	0.8%

Figure 5.74 Profitability of banking sector in OECD countries

on a par with the OECD and eurozone average, when taken as a proportion of the total banking assets, but they also verify that this average profitability is a result of above average general, administrative and staff expenses paired with higher-than-average operating income, as shown in Figures 5.75 and 5.76. It emerges therefore that indeed Greek banks have been more profitable than other non-financial Greece companies, but this is only because the non-financial Greek companies, which largely operate in a legislative environment of uncompetitive product markets and high administrative burden, have posted, in a context of high growth, below-average profitability, with respect to their European peers, while the Greek banks, which operate

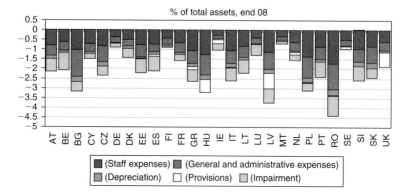

Figure 5.75 Expenditure of eurozone member countries' banking sector as a percentage of the total assets in 2008

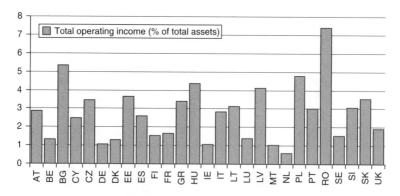

Figure 5.76 Total operating income of eurozone member countries' banking sector as a percentage of the total assets in 2008

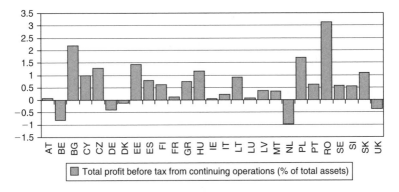

Figure 5.77   Total profits before tax of eurozone member countries' banking sector as a percentage of the total assets in 2008

in a largely competitive and deregulated financial services market, posted, in an environment of high growth, average profitability. In these circumstances, and given the current state of the conjecture of the Greek economy, government policy initiatives to tax the supposedly excessive profits of banks and to actively undermine them seem largely misplaced and untimely, especially as their profitability is set to decrease while their excess costs will most probably persist as long as the structural rigidities that are imposed by the Greek legislation keeps Greek banks from reducing their costs and from increasing their efficiency.

On the other hand, the healthy profitability of the Greek banks till the time the Greek crisis gained full speed and the potential to shift gradually the indebtness of the economy from the public sector toward the private sector, in the case that product market reforms were advanced decisively and wholeheartedly, Greek banks might well not only have contributed toward dealing with the current challenges faced by the economy, but may also have experienced a renewed period of prosperity. If this prospect seems appealing, one should not neglect the dangers of underestimating the significance of the initiatives that are required to get there. As Azariadis and de la Croix (2006) explain, when financial deregulation takes place in an economy that is not competitive enough to generate the income needed to service its debt once this has accumulated, following the expansion that comes after deregulation, the long-term growth rate of the economy can be reduced. This warning is directly related to the reality of the Greek economy as it has currently an not excessively above average level, for an advanced economy, of total indebtness, although – as we have clearly documented – its competitiveness is rather comparable to that of a developing economy. This warning is a grave and serious counterargument to those who declare that the Greek economy will return to the growth rates of the past automatically, as long as it secures access to new loans and funds, without addressing the severe structural deficiencies that still prevail today, and without risking to invite through such a strategy severe negative repercussions to the welfare and coherence of Greek society. This warning means that the argument of Anastasatos (2008) – that either the Greek economy will face a significant reduction of its welfare, as incomes adjust to the respectively lower competitiveness of the economy, or the competitiveness of the economy has to be increased to match the welfare currently enjoyed by Greek society – has to be enriched with the positive contribution and prospects of the banking sector in the latter case and the potential for a systemic meltdown in the Greek economy in the former case – that is, in the case where Greek governments keep insisting on implementing policies that are not aligned truthfully and honestly with the goals of the economic and monetary union. During 2010 and 2011 the Greek government consistently avoided to implement useful product market reforms, and in view of the wide ranging tax increases consistently pushed the country towards the first path delineated by Anastasatos. That is, the path of the so-called "internal devaluation" which implies reduced salaries, profits and income for Greek citizens. Unfortunately, that path also implies a reduced GDP, that is formed by this reduced income and consumption, and as a consequence ultimately, and in spite of repeated increases in tax rates, reduced tax income. The implications on the sustainability of, public and even private sector, debt show that this exercise is self defeating, as it directly undermines the ability of the country to service its debt. The request for the private sector to accept a large haircut on its holdings of Greek government bonds simply demonstrates the inevitability of this reality, and now adds to the cost of failing to increase in time the competitiveness of the economy to its debt level the unpredictable long-term cost of asking the private sector to pay for the policy failures of the government. Towards the end of 2011 there remained still one last option to avoid the worst scenario for the Greek economy, as proposals like the Eureka Project, and Greek variants of it, proposed to transfer as a block multiple government owned assets to a special purpose vehicle. These assets would be used as collateral to bring the government debt down to sustainable levels without an excessive punishment of private sector lenders, and privatized without the punishing constraints currently imposed by the lack of confidence in the Greek economy.

5.7 Certain basic parameters of the Greek pension system

In this section we proceed to collect basic numbers for the Greek pension system and to look at certain parameters that contribute to the significant imbalances that are projected for Greece by the European Commission (2009), as well as by organizations like the OECD. Today these projections verify the fiscal imbalances of the country that where identified a long time ago by the predictions of the so-called Spraos report (1997), but also by the projections made by the government's Actuary's Department of the United Kingdom in 2001. Furthermore, works like Boersch-Supan and Tinios (2001) give us a presentation of the complexity and opacity of the details of the design of the Greek pension system, which in turn hampers the ability to obtain a reliable oversight, on the one hand, and to estimate reliable parameters of a viable system that is able to ensure a satisfactory level of intergenerational solidarity, on the other hand.

Given the limitations regarding available data and the challenges posed by the complex details and the fragmentation of the Greek pension system, we limit our efforts to the collection of simple benchmark numbers, which may be collected with a narrower margin of error. Furthermore, we will abstain from projections (that predate the primary pension system reform implemented according to the conditionality program), taking simply as a fact existing projections that predict a gradual and severe deterioration of the finances of the system in the years to come. Therefore, we first proceed to gather data concerning the number of insured members of the labor force, as well as the number of pensioners, and then proceed to match them with the documented expenses on pensions. Regarding the number of pensioners, the Annual Social Budget for the year 2007 provides the data for all the main social security organizations, except for the payments of the basic pension and health plans of government employees. But fortunately the number of pensioners directly paid by the government, as well as the expense of the budget on pensions, is provided in the government budget, for this case for the year 2007, as shown in Figure 5.78. The data for the year 2001 presented in the same table originates from the population census for that year. It gives an overview of the insured workforce for that year and aims to somehow compensate for

	Insured 2001	Primary insured 2006–2007	Beneficiaries of insurance (family members of primary insured)2006–2007	Pensioners 2006–2007
How many pensioners are there? Number of pensioners and insured.				
Government	549,000			376,240
IKA-ETAM	2,425,000	2,016,000	5,533,625	982,216
OGA-farmers fund	661,413	715,000	2,030,000	853,179
OAEE – Main fund of self-employed	576,426	804,727		290,688
Other, mostly funds for self-employment types not covered by OAEE	398,000			156,397
Total	**4,609,839**			**2,658,720**

Figure 5.78   Number of Greek pensioners

the lack of more recent data regarding the numbers of all the insured employees and self-employed.

Our second step is to add the expense for pensions in our benchmark year of 2007. Again, the government budget provides the expense for pensions directly paid by the government to former public sector employees, while the social security budget provides the data for the remaining social security entities. Of this expenditure, we take out the payment to the EKAS, which is a supplementary pension plan that works in addition to the basic pension plan, as well as the Public Sector Political Employee Fund, which basically pays out the lump sum bonuses that public sector employees receive when they retire. These numbers are presented in Figure 5.79. Please note that the expenditure of the central government for public sector pensioners that was still 5.05 billion euros in 2007 was registered by the 2010 budget for the year 2009 at 6.5 billion euros, thus documenting the rapid increase of this expenditure item.

Having obtained an approximate number for the aggregate number of pensioners and the annual expense on pensions of the given reference year 2007, we can estimate, in Figure 5.80, that the per-capita annual expenditure, per pensioner, for the year 2007 was 12,707 euros. Divided by 14, the monthly pension handed out is estimated to be 907.7 euros.

What is spent each year on pensions? In 2007. Euros.	
Total pension payments (Source: Social Budget)	26,861,305,000
Payment for EKAS (Source: Social Budget)	976,534,152
Payment for lump sum payments to new public sector pensioners (Source: Social budget and Fund of Political Employees of Public Sector)	894,347,894
Expenditure for pensions of former government employees (Source: Government budget)	5,052,000,000
Total expenditure in 2007 for pensions and EKAS	33,784,187,046

Figure 5.79   Greek yearly expenditure on pensions

What is spent each month on each pensioner on average? In 2007. Euros.	
Average annual per pensioner expenditure, euros	12,707
Average monthly (annual/14) expenditure per pensioner	907.64
Average monthly per pensioner expenditure on main and supplementary pension	857.38
Average per all pensioners monthly expenditure on public sector new pensioner lump sum payment, with average payment per public sector new pensioner being 40.000 euros.	24.03
Average monthly payment for EKAS	26.24

Figure 5.80   Average monthly expenditure per Greek pensioner

Of these, 857.4 euros are sourced from the main and supplementary pensions. The public sector employee lump sum payment and the additional pension plan (EKAS), when allocated to all pensioners, represent about 50 euros per month per pensioner. Even though this approach is not correct for the lump sum payments of public sector pensioners, who each used to receive on average 40,000 euros as a lump payment when they retire, it shows that the majority of the per-capita expenditure on pensions originates from the payment of the main and supplementary pensions. We would like to remind here that the average declared income for the fiscal year 2007 from salaries and pensions, according to the data provided by the General Secretariat for Information Systems, was 12,500 euros, which means that the average expenditure for each pensioner is more or less equal to the average taxable income declared not only by pensioners, but also by salaried labor. This seems quite counterintuitive, unless one believes either that salaries are low or underreported, or pensions are excessively high. Of course the allocation of the bulk of salaried

Monthly income bracket, euros	Main pension distribution. All funds supervised by Ministry of Employment and Social Protection except farmers fund (OGA)	Main pension distribution *plus EKAS.* All funds supervised by Ministry of Employment and Social Protection except farmers fund (OGA)	Main pension distribution *plus EKAS and supplementary pension.* All funds supervised by Ministry of Employment and Social Protection except farmers fund (OGA)
Under 400	31.9%	17.5%	9.8%
401–600	38.2%	51.8%	41.3%
601–800	12.5%	13.2%	22.8%
801–1000	6.7%	6.8%	10.7%
Over 1001	10.7%	10.7%	15.4%

Figure 5.81   Distribution of Greek main and supplementary pensions in 2005

employees to this income bracket, as we have seen in our analysis in section 5.3.3 (which also stressed the attractiveness of self-employment for higher incomes), does contribute largely to an attempt at explaining this situation, which initially appears paradoxical. Especially if one also takes into account the fact that numerous pensioners receive more than one pension, especially if they belong to privileged special interest groups that are affiliated with the public sector.

Given that the average monthly expenditure per pensioner is at about 907 euros, for 2007, we turn to examine data provided by the Panhellenic Federation of Employees of Institutions of Social Policy. For the year 2005, the data the federation has posted shows, in Figure 5.81, that 31.9 percent of the main – basic – monthly pensions paid were below 400 euros, and 70.1 percent were below 600 euros. Please note that this data is for all pension funds except the fund for farmers. When EKAS is added, the number of low pensions (below 400 euros) falls to 17.5 percent. An even greater impact follows when the supplementary pensions are added. In this case, only 9.8 percent of all pensions are below 400 euros and half the pensions paid are below 600 euros, which means that half of them are over 600 euros. Interestingly, 15.4 percent of the pensioners received pensions in excess of 1,000 euros – assuming that they only receive one pension. This data shows that even though the benchmark main pensions of many pensioners may be low, the reality faced by most pensioners once other payments are added

Main monthly pension distribution. All funds supervised by Ministry of Employment and Social Protection except farmers fund (OGA). Euros.		Distribution of pensions paid by the farmers fund (OGA)	
Under 450	31.4%	Under 400	59.6%
451–600	29.3%	401–500	28.3%
601–750	11.7%	501–600	9.6%
751–900	7.3%	601–700	2.1%
901–1050	5.5%	701–800	0.3%
Over 1051	14.8%	Over 800	0.1%

Figure 5.82 Distribution of Greek main pensions except farmers fund and comparison with farmers fund in 2005

changes dramatically, and most pensioners appear to receive, finally, a much more decent pension. EKAS, it has to be stressed, was introduced mainly as a way to supplement the income of the poorest pensioners. The use of mean-testing for its payment explains how, in spite of being a rather small sum when compared to the main pension, it manages to significantly reduce the number of very low pensions.

We have available data for the pensions of the (numerous) pensioners of OGA – that is, the farmers fund – for the year 2008; this data is given in Figure 5.82. We can compare them to the main pension of the other funds, which – as we have seen in the previous figure – are significantly lower than the final pension that is paid once the supplementary pension and EKAS are added to the tally. Yet the available data clearly shows us that the pensions paid out by the farmers fund are much lower than the pensions paid by the other funds. Some 97.5 percent of these monthly pensions are below 600 euros, when only 60.7 percent of the main pensions of the other funds are below this level. As we have seen this percentage is drastically reduced once the additional pensions are added to the other funds, and these supplementary pensions are not added to the pensions of the farmers fund. Of course one has to stress here that, for one, farmers do not pay income taxes nor social security contributions toward their pensions during their professional lifetime. They only pay a contribution for the medical insurance provided to them and their family members. Therefore one can argue that it is reasonable to compare their pensions only with the main pensions paid out by the other funds, since the supplementary pensions are all funded by the extra contributions paid during the professional life of the pensioner. Furthermore, one can reasonably argue that given that no contributions or taxes are paid by farmers during

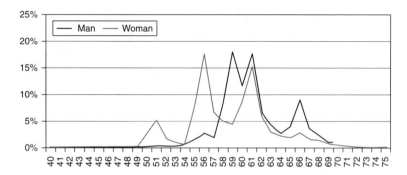

Figure 5.83   Distribution of retirement age for IKA, men and women in 2005

IKA	2002	2003	2004	2005	2006
Average old age pension retreat age	60.52	60.40	60.24	60.35	60.27
Average inability pension retreat age	51.21	51.37	50.89	49.75	51.00

Figure 5.84   Average retirement age for IKA. Old age and inability

their professional life, it is not unreasonable that the pensions they receive should be relatively modest.

Concerning the age of retirement, the median age for the IKA fund, which covers most – but not all – private sector salaried labor, was in 2006 around 58-59 years of age. As shown in Figure 5.83, for old age pensions the average age of retirement was for IKA a little over 60 years, which follows from a lower average of women and a higher one for men. For the combined population of men and women, this number has declined slowly during the past years. Since the average retirement age for those who draw disability pensions is lower, around 51 years, the average age of retirement for IKA is settling below 60 years, as shown in Figure 5.84, given that in 2006 a little over 10 percent of the new pensions paid out were disability pensions. We can also see from Figure 5.85 that on average the old age pensions that are issued correspond to 25 full years of insured work, while of course for the disability pensions these years are lower (14.4 insured years of work in 2006).

These numbers are puzzling. How is it possible for the private sector employees, who are predominantly insured with IKA, to exit the labor market on average at an age of around 60, with only 25 years of insured labor? The answer lies in the arguments made by Tinios (2003).

IKA	2002	2003	2004	2005	2006
Average full years of insured work for old age pensions	24.0	24.5	24.8	24.9	25.0
Average full years of insured work for inability pensions	14.5	14.7	14.6	14.2	14.4
Average full years of insured work for all pensions	21.4	21.8	22.0	22.2	22.4

Figure 5.85 Average full work years retirement at IKA. Old age and inability

Some insured employees enter the labor force early, and work at jobs that insure them continuously – like jobs with large private sector employers. In certain cases, like for banks – which were often previously government-controlled – or former and current publicly-owned companies, there are special laws that secure very favorable terms for the employees – terms that include a relatively low retirement age. So these employees may fulfill the requirements for retiring after 25 years of continuous salaried labor and at an age that may be a little above 50 years. On the other hand other private sector employees may work for many years uninsured. Alternatively, they may not work for part of the year – such as workers of the tourism industry, who mainly work in the summer, or construction workers. In their case they may either work for, say, 40 calendar years, but accumulate insurance months that would equal to, say, 25 years of continuous work, or they may work uninsured up the age of, say, 35, and work officially after that age up the age of 60, when they finally will fulfill the required number of workdays that will allow them to retire. This presentation shows how, apart from the average age at which workers retire, the number of full equivalent working years that are required to gain the right to retire are a significant parameter of the Greek pension system. Actually, the intricacies that regulate the fasttrack award of pensions, the exceptions from the normal rule and the number of years of work required, as claimed by Tinios (2003), may be ultimately more important than the statuary age of retirement for the Greek pension system. One last piece of evidence that has to be taken into account here is that the farmers fund only issues pensions after the age of 65. As a result of the large number of the pensioners of this fund, as seen in Figure 5.78, and as a result of their relatively high age at retirement, they increase significantly the average age at which Greeks retire. Given, though, that they do not pay any noteworthy contributions, their higher age of retirement does not lead to higher income for the social security system; it simply postpones the related expenditure and increases the average age of retirement in Greece up to near the European average. As a result, the proximity of the average age at which Greeks retire to the European average documented by Eurostat is misleading, as the details presented so far indicate that the paying members of the workforce retire, on average, at a much lower age, and this average is formed largely by the large number of pensioners from the farmers fund.

It has also to be stressed that for IKA the number of disability pensions has declined during the past decade, from an unnatural high number, documented by Tinios (2003) for previous decades, to numbers that are now around 10 percent and much more in line with what is observed in other European countries. Still the peculiarities of the nomenclature for what is labeled hard and arduous, as well as numerous other intricacies, ensure that a very large number of Greeks retire at a relatively low age, as for example Figure 5.83 shows for IKA. This has been documented by many studies, including Tinios (2003) and the "Spraos Report" of 1997, for example. Among certain small funds, which may have more generous terms, one can find small, but not negligible, pockets of employees that enjoy significantly more generous terms than the ones offered by IKA. The same is true of the distribution of pensions. Small pockets of pensioners of small and privileged funds may either benefit from high pensions, or accumulate multiple pensions that may lead to a monthly income of well over 1,500 euros. For some very privileged groups, this monthly income may reach over 3,000 euros, and sometimes these pensions are received at a relatively young age and are accompanied by surprisingly high lump sum payments, which one should note are in addition exempt from the exceptional taxes levied on high incomes since 2008. This is the case especially with early retirement schemes of publicly-owned, or previously publicly-owned, companies.

Given the average amount paid out per pensioner, and the distribution of pensions paid (except from the farmers fund), as well as the average retirement age, it seems rather plausible that the resources of the system should suffice to ensure that no pensioner faces excessively harsh terms, especially once his lifetime contributions are taken into account. In other words, it should be possible to improve the viability of the system significantly, even in face of the unfavorable and rapidly deteriorating demographic projections that all relevant studies document, without putting at risk the minimum pensions received by the poorest who have paid all their contributions during their professional life, and without increasing the statutory retirement age too much, simply by making sure that those who retire have accrued on average more years of declared work, and by removing a number of extreme privileges that seem to benefit a small, but not negligible, number of pensioners. Of course, issues – such as the equalization of the retirement age of men and women – that are also mandated by EU legislation, the elimination of motives to leave early the job market, the benefits accruing to mothers – not during the time they tend their children, but in terms of early retirement once their children are grown up – and other details of the Greek pension system that are highlighted by all research that investigates it are also parameters of the problem, and a possible solution. Still, the basic parameters presented here seem to demonstrate that the system probably offers enough room to devise a viable reform that should not be too hard on the weakest members of society, and that can at the same time significantly reduce the mounting pressures the pension system puts on the finances of the Greek government. Having come to that conclusion, one observes that the majority of the measures taken in the context of the conditionality program regarding the stabilization of the finances of the the social security system in Greece during 2010 and 2011 aimed at across the board cuts that did not target specifically the identified "islands of privilege". This is not to say that numerous measures taken were not in the right direction, but it is to point out that the resistance to reform from those that have benefited most from the lack of reform during the past decades once again succeeded to avert reforms that would affect them, at least till the end of 2011.

5.8 Main parameters of the Greek public finances

We can observe in Figure 5.86 how the primary expenses of the central government were reduced in the 1990–2 period and, after a significant increase, in 1993, which was related to the change of government following the elections at the end of the year, essentially kept under control, as a percentage of the GDP, until 2003. After 2003 the ratio of expenses to GDP, which was contained all these years with the help of the rapid growth of the GDP over that period, started to increase, as the government that won the 2004 elections did not fulfill its promise of fiscal responsibility. In the year 2009, when the GDP growth had started to falter for the first time since the mid-1990s, the ratio of central government expenditure to GDP increased rapidly. This happened as a combination of expenditures, such as an increase in salaries that

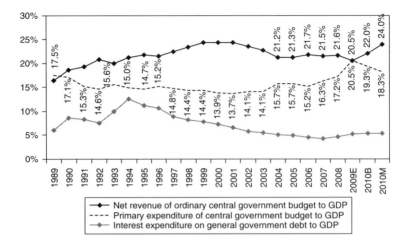

Figure 5.86   Net revenue, primary expenditure and interest expenditure of Greek central government budget

reflected the lack of restraint in government hiring the previous years, increasing needs of the social security funds for unbudgeted cash infusions and increases in the former public sector employees' pension bill. The problem of runaway expenditures, which already was of a sizeable proportion, was further aggravated by the decision of the newly elected government to proceed in the fiscal year 2009 with a "solidarity" handout, and by an initiative to incorporate in the budget of 2009 certain expenditures that where so far either kept off budget, like the procurement of hospitals, or that had not been allocated to a certain fiscal year, like the settlement with former Olympic Airways employees. These developments on the expenditure side were paired with the petering out of the falling trend of the interest payment-to-GDP ratio that, starting in 1994, had consistently contributed positively to the improvement of the general government budget bottom-line. To make matters worse, the increasing trend in the central government revenue-to-GDP ratio that had started in 1990 and that had been kept on an upward trend until 2000, with the significant assistance, toward the end of this period, of the operation of the tax authorities' integrated information system (TAXIS), which had been started at the very beginning of the 1990s, was gradually reversed. In the 2004–8 period the situation was stabilized at a lower level, but a renewed reduction in 2009 coincided with the abovementioned developments and resulted in the rapid deterioration of the budgetary net position in that year. These developments demonstrate that

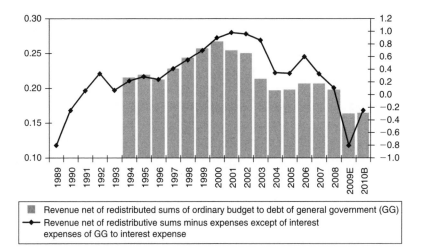

Revenue net of redistributed sums of ordinary budget to debt of general government (GG)
Revenue net of redistributive sums minus expenses except of interest
expenses of GG to interest expense

Figure 5.87   Interest cover of Greek general government

the estimated deterioration for 2009 (2009E in Figure 5.86) was built on
the foundation of a period during which the structure of the budget was
gradually weakened, as the structural gains and efforts of the early 1990s
were not followed up. The period after the year 2000, which was a period
of stable and rapid growth, was not taken advantage of in any way with
regard to the strengthening of the structural position of the budget, and
only the falling interest expense, as a percentage of the GDP, kept contributing to the improvement of public finances. Figure 5.87 presents this
reality from another point of view. The ratio of the central government
budget revenue, net of funds collected by the budget on behalf of other
beneficiaries and the redistribution of these funds, to the stock of government debt, which was increasing until 2000, then started to decline.
At the same time the "interest cover" of the government – that is, the
budget surplus available to finance interest expenses – followed a similar
trend, assisted though by the fall in the interest expense, and in 2009
even turned negative. Figure 5.86 also shows the projections of the 2010
budget (2010B) regarding the evolution of revenue and primary expenditure of the central government, as well as the measures announced after
the presentation of the 2010 budget as they had cumulated up to March
2010 (2010M). They also show – if one assumes that the GDP used in the
2010 budget, as well as all other revenue and expenditure items, remain
as foreseen in the budget – that the impact as a percentage of the GDP of
these measures amounts to roughly 3 percent of GDP, while further and

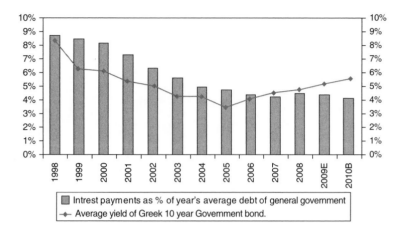

Figure 5.88 Interest payments to government debt and ten-year government bond yields. Greece

significant measures had to be taken subsequently according to the conditionality program. Figure 5.87 thus also documents the source of the concerns of financial markets regarding the Greek government bonds, and the ability of Greece to finance its public debt, which increased gradually until the announcement of the more decisive corrective measures.

These concerns are further substantiated by certain uncertainties that prevail over the parameters of the budget for the year 2010, which will in turn affect the realities of the budgets after 2010. One concerns the budgeted cost of borrowing, which according to the 2010 budget, as shown in Figure 5.88, is declining as a percentage of the year's average existing stock of debt, while so far the yield of the government ten-year bonds remains at levels that significantly exceed the average yield of 2009 and 2008. As a result the question remains open of whether, gradually, the debt that has been rolled over in 2010 will imply an increase in the cost of borrowing for 2010 and the future years until the debt issued in 2010 matures. While the 25 billion euros, less than 10 percent of the outstanding debt, that have been rolled over by the summer of 2010 may not crucially affect the average cost of servicing the total debt, the related challenge will become more pertinent during the following two years when, according to the government budget for 2010, nearly half of the outstanding general government debt will have been rolled over.

A second concern is the gradual increase in the expenditure from the central government budget to finance the social security system. During the past years the pensions for the former public employees, along with the contribution of the central government budget to the social security funds, has been one of the fastest growing expenditure items of the budget. Since the absolute magnitude of these expenditure items is also large, amounting to 31.7 percent of all central government expenditures in 2009, their impact on the net fiscal position of the government budget is one of the most crucial parameters that will determine the net position of the general government budget in the coming years. As a result a reform of the social security system to reduce these significant and increasingly mounting pressures on the fiscal position of the general government is the other important, and still unresolved by late 2011, for the supplementary pension schemes, parameter of the fiscal prospects of Greece. As shown in the previous section, it should be possible to fine tune basic parameters of the system in a way that will significantly improve its financial resilience in the face of the mounting challenges and at the same time retain a satisfactory level of social and intergenerational solidarity.

Finally, a third risk remains for the projected fiscal prospects of the country. A deep and prolonged recession in the economy will not only undermine the prospects of the economy in general but of the government revenue as well, as has been demonstrated by the experience of 2010 and 2011. And at the same time the denominator in the debt-to-GDP ratio will face an unfavorable development in that case, which can threaten the gains that result from any efforts main in relation to the previously mentioned concerns, as also documented by the events of late 2011. The latter risk, which is not insignificant at all, can of course be reduced, and possibly even eliminated, with the promotion of aggressive product market reforms, as previously outlined, and with an aggressive program to reduce the administrative burden that is today imposed on the economy. The importance of this risk is highlighted by the fact that according to the updated Stability and Growth Program submitted at the beginning of 2010 by the Greek government, the return of satisfactory growth from 2011 was expected to gradually dilute the ratio of general government expenditures to GDP without necessitating their decline in absolute size and even permitting their increase after 2010, as shown in Figure 5.89. At the same time the increase in taxable incomes and profits, along with the growth of the GDP, supposedly would have permitted an increase in the revenue of the general government – not only as a percentage of the GDP but, most significantly, by a sizeable absolute number, as shown in Figure 5.90. The success of this strategy evidently depended crucially on the ability of the economy to return to

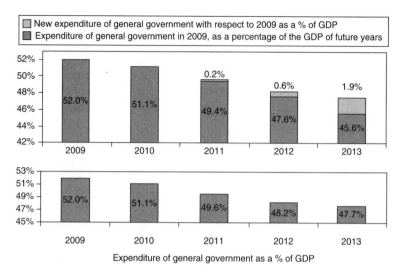

Figure 5.89   General government expenditure as a percentage of the GDP. Greek Stability and Growth Program projections. January 2010

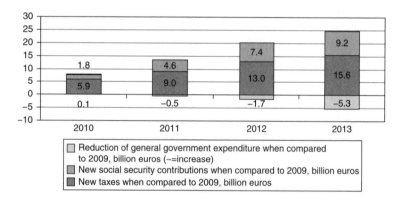

Figure 5.90   General government expenditure reduction and revenue increase as a percentage of the GDP. Greek Stability and Growth Program projections. January 2010

the positive growth rates projected in the Stability and Growth Program after 2010, a fact that did not materialise in the absence of a determined product market reform agenda.

Even though the Greek government announced a new series of measures in March 2010, when added to the measures announced since

December 2009, it emerges that most of these measures amounted once again to extraordinary tax increases, which were set to become permanent after 2011. Only a smaller part of these measures, less than one third as shown in Figure 5.91, comprised expenditure cuts or the freezing of expenditure increases. In addition, these measures simply cancel out revenue shortfalls as the recession of the Greek economy gathered pace and given the absence of a determined efforts to reform the issues analyzed in this Chapter.

The significance and size of these risks, as well as the potential suggested from the experience of other countries regarding these reforms, in combination with the currently adverse ranking of Greece on these aspects strongly suggested even at that time the appropriate way to move, swiftly and decisively, forward.

Regardless of the implications that the failure to implement the right policy mix till the end of 2011 has, and regardless of the implications that the private sector involvement will have, it will remain a reality that the Greek public sector not only has more employees than it needs, who are paid on average very generously when compared to private sector salaries. It will remain, above these realities, that the human resources management and the organizational chart of the public sector does not permit its efficient operation and the supply of quality services at low cost to society. Unfortunately this problem has no easy and fast solution. Given that a reduction in the number of public sector employees not only will adversely affect the job market, but also will probably involve the risk of expelling the better working, but less well connected, part of the staff, cuts in the average pay of public sector employees should be preferred over layoffs. The argument for pay cuts, over layoffs, is also substantiated by the high average wage bill per public employee that was revealed by the data presented in Figure 5.62. At the same time the better management of wage bills will become possible thanks to the operation of a centralized payment system that should be able to identify potential cuts in a way that will not hurt too much those who receive relatively low pay and mainly seek out those cases in which numerous handouts and wage-related payments lead to very high annual incomes that are not justified by the quality and quantity of the services provided. Tackling the issue of public sector pay is of significant importance, because after paying for public sector pensioners and social security funds, as well as covering interests on debt, the wage bill is the third largest expenditure of the budget, amounting to 28.4 percent of all central government expenditure in 2009, with all other expenditure items being less significant.

Million euros. Tax increases.	December 2009	January 2010	February 2010	March 2010	Total
One-off tax on profitable companies and large estates	1,085				1,085
Permanent VAT increase				1,400	1,400
Increase in consumption tax of fuels			934	616	1,550
Increase in consumption tax on tobacco		645		350	995
Increase in consumption tax on alcohol		70		80	150
Luxury tax and new tax on expensive cars				120	120
Abolition of tax exemption of Public Power Corporation from consumption tax on fuel				87	87
New consumption tax on electricity				180	180
One-off tax of 1% on 2009 incomes over 100,000				141	141
Reapplication of estate tax		200			200
Total new taxes payable from or in 2010	1,085	915	934	2,974	5,908
Expenditure cuts or freezing of expenditures				March 2010	
Reduction in wage bill of public sector				−1,218	
Freezing of increases in cash handouts and working group remunerations				−14	
Reduction of annual grant to the pension funds of Public Power Corporation and Hellenic Telecoms employees				−146	
Freezing of increasing pensions in 2010				−450	
Cuts in Ministry of Education programs				−100	
Non-execution of part of the public investment budget				−600	
Total expenditure reduction or freezing of expenditures				−2,528	

Figure 5.91 Extraordinary measures taken by the Greek government for the stabilization of the fiscal situation until April 2010

The reform of the social security system and the reduction of the wage bill are pressing priorities since projections to increase taxes are subject to the developments of the economy and the resilience of economic activity, while expenditure cuts will yield the budgeted savings with certainty, regardless of the developments of the economic situation. As a result the measures implemented between December 2009 and May 2010, which included increases in VAT for fuel, tobacco, alcohol and so called "luxury items," as well as a number of extraordinary taxes on profitable corporations, high personal incomes and big estates, are all subject to the development of the conjecture, and failed ultimately to yield the results anticipated by the legislators. The deepening of the recession negated the projected increase in revenue, thus undermining the effort of fiscal consolidation. On the other hand only 30 percent of the measures announced during this period refer to cuts in expenditures or the freezing of increases in expenditure. This is unfortunate as, according to Guichard et al. (2007), episodes of fiscal consolidation that are based on government revenue increases are generally less successful and long-lived than those based on expenditure cuts. The size and historic growth rates of the wage bill and social security-related items mentioned above singles these two items out as the preferred targets for such cuts, as has already been described. Such cuts will have also another implication. Today the numerous public sector employees, who receive, compared to the private sector, high pay and produce no value added, contribute to the pattern of disproportionally high consumption as a percentage of the GDP (compared to other European countries) that prevails today in Greece. A reduction in the excessive public sector wage and public sector pension bill will contribute to the rationalization of this statistic as well.

5.9   The examples of Finland and Ireland and how they can be an example for Greece

Finland experienced a serious recession at the end of the 1980s when the excesses from the financial services sector deregulation ended at a time of a serious global economic downturn that coincided, in addition, with the collapse of Finland's trade with Russia.

In the wake of these testing times Finland opened up the economy, deregulating important sectors that used to impose significant restrictions on market entry, as described by Høj and Wise (2004) and the OECD (2003a), even though the OECD structural indicators still identify a number of areas that remain relatively regulated or under government control. Following the capital markets, which where deregulated before the onset of the Finnish crisis and which fueled a boom in the runup to the crisis, the telecommunications, electricity, road transport and many other sectors were liberalized, which helped reshape the economy from one based on the principles of economic nationalism to one of open markets, which in addition had been, since 1995, a member of the European Union. Reforms were wide-ranging and included numerous measures that freed up many aspects of the economy besides these main, flagship, sectors. Along these reforms, an emphasis was put on sound macroeconomic and fiscal management, moderate wage settlements and the modernization and empowerment of competition authorities. Also a vigorous and continuous effort to improve the efficiency of the public administration, as documented by the OECD (2003a, 2003b), as well as to improve the budgeting process, as documented by Blöndal et al. (2002), the quality of regulation and a determined effort to reduce administrative burdens was observed. All that led to a strong and prolonged recovery, many aspects of which are documented by Honkapohja et al. (2009), that exceeded any positive impact of any cyclical upturns since the beginning of the 1990s.

Regarding one of the flagship sectors, the electricity sector was the subject of an early and relatively fast track liberalization in the 1990s. The process started with the 1995 Electricity Market Act, which introduced third-party access to the monopolistic grid and allowed large users to choose between different suppliers. From 1997 all consumers could choose their supplier, and from 1998 they could do this without paying for a new meter. The vertical supply chain has been disaggregated (through accounting unbundling) to separate the grid from potentially competitive distribution and supply. A regulator (now called the Energy Market Authority) was set up, which today also covers the gas market. Another positive feature is the full integration of the Nordic electricity market. But in general, with regard to product markets, Finland implemented comprehensive reforms over the period 1985–95, as documented by Høj et al. (2007), under the influence of the EU's internal market program.

A significant part of the Finnish reform efforts aimed to prepare the central administration for its new role as a facilitator, rather than direct provider, of public services. This effort included an antibureaucracy drive and reforms to increase customer orientation while at the same time the budgetary process was also significantly reformed. This process was undertaken in the context of an open and honest political dialogue that followed the crisis of the early 1990s. This dialogue focused on the role of the state in the economy, the challenge of reconciling the need to reap the benefits that open markets bring to consumers with the values of social solidarity, and the need to insist on the improvement of the efficiency of public spending in times of fiscal pressures. This dialogue led to the acceptance of the principle that the role of the state is primarily that of a guarantor of the law and order and of the supply of essential infrastructure and public services, but within the framework of open and competitive markets. It also helped to reconcile the need to cut public spending, especially social transfers – which were skyrocketing at the time – with the need to improve the efficiency of public spending. In that way Finland was able to secure the core policies that enhance social coherence, while at the same time improving public finances, whose state today guarantees the sustainability of these policies.

Regarding the modernization of the public administration, the Finnish reforms were promoted in spite of the significant challenges that arise when authority is reallocated between the competent ministries and authorities, and the difficulty of adapting a system and reeducating individuals who were accustomed to a certain way of executing their daily tasks. In particular, the increase in municipal autonomy has raised some concerns over whether it undermines central policy coherence, which started a debate on how the government can strengthen this.

Public sector reform priorities in Finland during the past decades contained the following elements:

1. Ex-ante budgetary controls have been replaced with ex-post reporting, auditing and evaluation. All ministries and agencies prepare an annual report.
2. Effective adaptation of frame budgeting that led to budget surpluses and a low public debt.
3. Result-oriented approach that focuses on targets.
4. Decentralization and empowerment of municipal authorities.
5. An evaluation program of administrative reforms.
6. A constant promotion of the quality and functioning of the public sector since the 1990s.
7. Decision-making is based on a search for consensus and the avoidance of conflict.

Of course Finland has not solved all its problems, with the performance of the job market being one good example. Still its experience in overcoming a severe downturn in which significant external adversities coincided with a financial sector crisis and deteriorating public finances thanks to a determined and wide-ranging reform effort in product markets and the public administration, together with a program of fiscal stabilization, certainly contains useful lessons on which Greece can draw today.

Ireland, where the public sector has had to provide significant support to the domestic financial system, has experienced so far a forceful contraction. Yet it is facing the prospect of a gradual recovery in a context of flexible and competitive markets and a friendly business environment, following the reforms of the 1980s, even though certain aspects of the functioning of markets relating to network industries, professional services and the retail sector are still considered relatively stringent by the OECD. Yet Ireland, according to the OECD (2009), did not proceed to sufficiently restructure the public sector during the years of fast growth, and still faces related challenges, as described by Hardiman (2010). As a result of the weakness of budgetary institutions, the in-built increase in public expenditure led to a rapid deterioration of public finances once the rapid growth in the GDP disappeared, leading to a significant shortfall in the projected revenue increases. Apart from the measures taken, initially only in Ireland but now also in Greece, to restrain the short-term increase in public expenditure – largely through the reduction of public servant pay – both countries still face the challenge of substantially restructuring their public sectors in order to increase their respective efficiency and capacity to provide quality services to citizens and businesses. In Greece, it must be noted, these challenges appear to be more significant though, as Ireland has already reaped significant benefits from the reforms it implemented in the public sector and the tax system in the late 1980s. In addition, in Ireland the deterioration of the public finances is largely related to the initiative to rescue the domestic financial system – unlike Greece, where so far the financial system has provided either directly or indirectly through the ECB, which accepted as collateral large amounts of Greek government bonds, a substantial financing cushion for the Greek government.

One should stress that in both countries government expenditure until the onset of the current crisis had risen in line with the rapid GDP growth, but the improvement of budgetary institutions, the increase in the efficiency of the public sector, the rebalancing of public expenditure and the reform of the tax systems did not proceed at the required pace. This negligence means that once the downturn occurred, it led to a fast deterioration of public finances as revenue fell but expenses kept rising in both countries. The size of the challenges posed currently by the fiscal position is larger in Greece. Yet Ireland has dealt in the past effectively with similar challenges, when it embarked on a determined effort to correct fiscal imbalances and support future growth in the late 1980s. Also a strategy to attract foreign investment, that was further assisted by a number of favorable developments summarized by Hardouvelis (2006), shows that a determined effort can deal with such challenges effectively. The legacy of the fiscal consolidation of Ireland in the 1980s should be used as a case study for Greece today, but it can also be used as an example to stress the future benefits that the current fiscal stabilization efforts promise for Ireland.

With regard to product market regulation, Ireland started out in 1998 from a favorable position relatively to other OECD countries, as a result of the reforms undertaken since the late 1980s. Since then it has made some further improvement. Greece started out from a much more unfavorable position in 1998 and, especially since 2003, it has not achieved any further noteworthy improvement, according to the OECD integrated product market regulation indexes.

The OECD data, which starts in 1998, does not capture how Ireland – before the 1980s – proceeded for many years with the establishment of state monopolies, the adoption of regulation that curtailed competition in markets, and a fiscal policy based on high government spending and increasing tax rates. In the wake of the oil crises, increasing tax evasion and social unrest, unemployment increased along with government debt in a context of economic stagnation. A determined effort to deregulate markets, sell off publicly-owned companies and reduce tax rates helped reverse this situation and turn the "sick man of Europe" of the 1980s into the "Celtic tiger" of the 1990s, and lead Ireland to the advantageous position recorded by the OECD for 1998.

One should stress that as part of this effort Ireland not only embarked on a path of fiscal responsibility, but at the same time actively championed the improvement of the business environment, and policies designed to attract FDI. As a result today Ireland faces the challenges of the current conjecture and the fallout from the excesses of its financial system with a much more favorable business environment than it had in the 1980s, which is not the case for Greece, whose situation is closer to the situation that Ireland was facing in the late 1980s.

The current debate over tax reform in Greece becomes most relevant given the experience of Ireland in the 1970s and at the beginning of the 1980s. At the time successive Irish governments tried to balance the deteriorating public finances with increasing tax rates, a strategy that yielded few tangible results and contributed to the stagnation of an uncompetitive and closed economy. After the late 1980s the reform agenda included not only reduced tax rates, as documented also by Alpha Bank (2001), but more importantly a process that meant that any changes in the tax laws were announced well in advance of their application, as described by Flinter (2006). It is now generally accepted that this strategy, which was supported by a number of favorable developments that occurred during the same period – as explained by Hardouvelis (2006) – helped the economy grow fast and attract significant investment from abroad, which in turn contributed gradually to an increase in employment. Today, even though the Irish corporate tax rates are much lower than in Greece, as shown in Figure 5.64, the revenue of the Irish government from corporate income tax as a percentage of the GDP exceeds the equivalent revenue of the Greek government. Actually, this was also true in the past years when the corporate tax rate in Greece was even higher.

Furthermore, the highly progressive personal income tax system of Greece, which essentially exempted more than half the households from any income tax and which aims to collect most personal income taxes from the relatively few families that declare high incomes, secured a revenue for the Greek government of about 2.5 percent below that of the Irish government, as can be demonstrated with the data behind Figure 5.53. As a result the Irish approach after the late 1980s provides significant lessons for Greek policymakers, including of course the commitment to implement a predictable tax system and the usefulness of a simple tax system that is enforced in a way that minimizes tax evasion.

5.10   Conclusions

In this Chapter we started out with a detailed description of the Greek economy. We were able to identify both the drivers of the recent strong growth performance and to document the reasons why, in spite of this strong performance, the competitiveness of the Greek economy remains so low. Extensive regulation of markets, high administrative costs, a business environment that is not favorable and, in the end, widespread corruption are the cause of this low competitiveness, despite the reforms in the credit market and, initially – but not lately – the telecommunications market, and the benefits accruing from the EMU accession. Greece appears therefore to have benefited from certain reforms, in the sense described by Rodrik (2007), but on a very large scale because of the nature and importance of these positive developments, while it retains other, also significant in importance and magnitude, weaknesses that undermine the long-term potential to guarantee lasting growth and social coherence for the country. These weaknesses are ultimately described as "weak institutions and governance," and their existence is deeply rooted in the equilibrium that is formed today between the interest groups that collect the rents that they secure thanks to the regulation of the markets and the inflation of the administrative costs, the politicians, the voters and the strong growth of the past years, which has made the need for further reforms less pressing, as was described in Chapter 2. This equilibrium affects the labor market, financial and non-financial corporations, the pension system and fiscal discipline – in particular on the expenditure side, as we have seen thanks to the available detailed and credible evidence that was presented. The way all these aspects of the Greek economy are affected may lead to apparent paradoxes when the evidence is looked at bit by bit, but once all available evidence is juxtaposed, then it appears that all these paradoxes and peculiarities fit well together and simply reflect the dysfunction that originates from the high regulation of the markets, the excessive administrative burden and the relevance of a two-tier private sector labor market, along with a large and inefficient public sector that operates in a context of weak institutions and governance.

The stakes are the long-term growth prospects of the Greek economy, once the rate impact of the reforms and of the EU and EMU membership peter out, as seems to be the case at this point. What is needed now is the adjustment of the country to a new equilibrium in which rents that are accrued from state intervention and high administrative costs are replaced by profits that accrue from competitive markets and that are not distributed on the basis of the ability to secure favors from the unified executive and legislature, as shown in Chapter 4, but instead from innovation-driven entrepreneurship in competitive markets. Such a shift, if achieved, could ensure many years of continuous growth and employment creation, along with enhanced social coherence as a result of this employment growth, even in view of the implications that the failure to implement growth enhancing reforms in 2010 and 2011 and in view of the potential implications of the private sector involvement. Primarily it is expected to also facilitate the establishment of the institutions that remain today underdeveloped in Greece, since, according to the argument presented in Chapter 2, the main bloodlines that are now supplied with the rents derived from the uncompetitive economy and that feed interest groups that resist both reform and the development of advanced and good institutions will have been cut.

The memorandum of understanding (MOU) that was accepted as part of the financial package offered by the European Union and the International Monetary Fund to Greece intially included measures to address all the shortcomings of the fiscal consolidation strategy mentioned so far, including, for the first time, substantial expenditure cuts, specific instructions for pension reform and a binding timetable for specific actions that should lead to a reduction in tax evasion. Furthermore the MOU, as part of the 'conditionality program', included significant structural reforms that aimed to address the major failings that are identified both in the workings of the product and services markets, and in the labor market. In a sense, therefore, the analysis of this book currently indicates the challenges the Greek society faces to enforce this MOU, rather than to formulate the necessary reforms that are now stated in this MOU.

An overview of the Chapter

A. Facts on the competitiveness of the Greek economy

1. In Greece the competitiveness of the economy is consistently ranked well below the performance of all other members of the eurozone and of most members of the OECD. This is documented by the OECD aggregate structural indicators for product market regulation (in particular, regulation of the command and control type regarding the operation of companies), and the similar indexes for selected product markets (in particular transport, retail and – until recently – energy and road freight) and professional services (in particular minimum government mandated prices, obligatory purchase of services and entry restrictions) contained in the World Bank Doing Business Reports (which include startups, licensing, collecting debts and liquidating a bankrupt company, among others). It is also documented by governance indicators (which examine the quality of governance and institutions that also go beyond the business environment) in surveys like that of the IMD and the WEF, and similar work by the European Commission, as well as numerous other similar work, that measure the quality of product market regulation and the extent of the administrative burden the economy is subjected to.

2. In Greece the wage share, which includes the wage bill of the public sector, is one of the lowest in the OECD and the European Union.

3. In Greece the ratio of self-employed to dependent labor is, by far, the highest in the European Union, a fact that contributes significantly to point 1. In particular, about 1.3 million self-employed correspond to about 1.9 million insured with IKA (which may include up to 200,000 individuals who work for publicly-owned companies or entities controlled by the general and central government), about 350,000 salaried employees insured with other professional funds and about 560,000 officially registered central government public sector employees.

4. In Greece the average private sector wage for dependent labor is about 33 percent lower than the average private sector wage in the EU-27 (35 percent for the eurozone), largely as a result of the tendency of smaller companies to pay wages close to the minimum wage. According to Eurostat, the average public sector wage, on the other hand, is about 5 percent lower than the corresponding EU-27 average (15 percent for the eurozone).

5. This relatively low average private sector pay further contributes to point 1, even though the relatively high public sector salaries, and equivalent pay, often lead to high documented average wage increases in Greece, especially in years where private sector wages also increased above the European averages.

6. The private sector wage increases coincide with the reality of an uncompetitive economy that produces relatively little, and as a result employs but few of the most productive workers, as shown by the low ratio of total employment to total population – which is one of the lowest in the EU and the OECD.

7. In Greece the higher-than-average regulation of the labor market, which is documented by similar surveys, largely follows from the regulation of temporary and part-time employment. The latter imposes a constraint that is largely overcome by the proliferation of self-employment, which is not subject to the limitations imposed by this legislation.

8. Substantial tax evasion and social security payment evasion, as well as legislation that allows relatively low social security payments by the self-employed, distorts the playing field in the labor market to the detriment of salaried labor, and especially salaried labor with above-average income. This fact is also related to the extent of self-employment in Greece.

9. Larger companies pay, on average, their salaried employees higher wages than smaller companies do. These larger companies employ

about half of the employees who are insured with IKA and who do not work in construction.

In view of the abovementioned pieces of evidence it follows that

1. The failings of the business environment, which are documented repeatedly and reliably by numerous studies and surveys, are of a magnitude and extent that can explain the significant competitiveness deficit of the Greek economy. They also primarily identify these failings to consist of (a) a very high administrative burden, (b) government legislation that prohibits competition in significant product markets and professional services, (c) vague and complex legislation that regulates the licensing and operation of companies in Greece, (d) the uncertainty and corruption all the abovementioned invite, and (e) the strong causal link between this widespread corruption and the inability of the political leadership of the country to produce good laws and promote useful reforms.

2. These failings of the business environment are reflected in the low employment ratio, which in turn renders the impact of changes in the cost of the relatively few employed less important for the aggregate macroeconomy.

3. Failings of the labor market in the private sector are relatively minor when compared to the failures, mentioned above, of the government to provide competitive product markets and quality governance, and the impact these have on the operation of the government and the public administration.

B. Facts on the public finances of Greece

1. The Greek central government in 2010 spent about 75 billion euros and had revenue of about 50 billion euros.

2. The majority of the central government spending comes from the central government wage bill (27.4 percent of the central governments ordinary budget expenditure), the central government pensions for former public servants and former publicly-owned companies employee pension funds (12.3 percent), the government contribution to social security funds – other that the pension fund for former public employees– and expenditure for "social coherence" (20.4 percent) and, finally, interest on the government debt (18.6 percent). These expenditure items add up to 79 percent of

total central government ordinary budget expenditure, which does not include public investment, and amount to 100.1 percent of the central government net income from taxes.

3. The average monthly wage for the public control, according to Eurostat, in Greece is, relatively to the average monthly wage for private control, the fourth largest in the EU-27. Correspondingly, as already mentioned, the average public sector pay is much closer to the EU-27 and eurozone average public sector pay than that of the private sector salaried employment.

4. The number of public sector employees, both permanent and in short-term contracts, in the central government, general government entities and companies owned by these is, according to all available pieces of evidence, excessive and inadequately managed.

5. A comparison with other European Union member countries reveals that the Greek government earns significantly less revenue from personal income tax than its European peers, as a percentage of the GDP. Furthermore, VAT receipts are also relatively low once the above-average contribution of consumption to GDP is taken into account. Finally, a small number of families that declare high incomes and a small number of large companies pay a disproportionately large share of the total personal and corporate income tax, when compared with the similar distributions of other countries, while the vast majority of families and small companies pays no, or insignificant, income tax.

6. The latter is further enhanced by the fact that for small companies (individual enterprises and general partnerships) profits are taxed differently. In particular, only half the profits are taxed at an advantageous rate as company income, and the other half is taxed as personal income, which in most cases – and especially if there is more than one partner – is below the threshold for tax-free personal income.

In view of the abovementioned pieces of evidence it follows that

1. Fiscal consolidation in Greece needs to follow from a combination of sizeable expenditure reduction and revenue increases.

2. More emphasis needs to be put on expenditure reductions, given the limited emphasis that has been given to them so far, the

contribution of expenditure increases during the past years to the emergence of the current challenges, and the fact that episodes of fiscal consolidation that are based on expenditure cuts have a much better track record.

3. Expenditure reduction inevitably need to include *large cuts in the government wage bill*, and this in turn needs to include both cuts in the average take-home pay (which includes salary, but also large sums for overtime, special cash handouts and numerous special payments for various professional duties in the public sector), as well as in the number of general government staff.

4. *Cuts in the non-wage take-home pay*, which is also a source of unjustified inequalities in the public sector and which is often linked with taxes on economic activity, should take priority in any effort to aggressively reduce the average take-home pay of the public sector. Such a reduction would also reduce the pressure to proceed with indiscriminate layoffs, which may have a more severe adverse social impact.

5. Expenditure reduction inevitably needs to include large cuts in the *public sector pensions and pension funds for employees of former publicly-owned companies* that are paid to former civil servants and former employees of publicly-owned companies, as well as reforms that will rein in the tendency of this expenditure item to increase rapidly over time. Cases where individuals benefit from evidently excessively beneficial terms should be aggressively tackled.

6. Expenditure reduction inevitably needs to include reforms that put a cap on the government's contribution to the private sector social security system *without leading to a commensurate increase in the contributions of private sector employees and employers*. That will imply *a significant reduction in the number of cases where private sector employees, self-employed and farmers benefit from retirement schemes that are clearly out of proportion with their lifetime contributions*.

7. *Revenue increases need to address the shortfall in personal income tax revenue* that results from the excessive progressivity of the personal income tax system, which now excludes more than half of the Greek households from the obligation to pay any personal income tax and which concentrates, more than in most major European countries, the bulk of the personal income tax on a small minority of families that report, truthfully or half-truthfully, relatively high annual income.

8. *Revenue increases need to address in particular the widespread tax evasion among numerous self-employed and smaller enterprises,* as well as the corruption of tax controllers, which is a major reason why so many Greek families declare income that is, according to the excessively progressive tax law, exempt from income tax. In particular, the contribution of the self-employed toward the government revenue from personal income tax and social security contributions should be better aligned with their dominant position in the workforce. Furthermore, the large number of small companies that operate in spite of their limited or non-existent profitability also suggests widespread tax evasion among them. As tax evasion is reduced, tax rates should become more competitive.

9. *Revenue increases need to address also the widespread tax evasion of VAT* among numerous self-employed and smaller enterprises, as well as the related corruption of tax controllers.

10. Public support for these measures could be enhanced with a reduction of the members of parliament down from 300 to 200, as is allowed by the Constitution in Article 51, the corresponding reduction in the staff of the parliament, as the support positions for the redundant members of parliament would be abolished, as allowed by the Constitution, and a substantial extra tax, or pay cut, for the members of parliament and the remaining parliament staff for as long as the country fails to meet the Maastricht criteria.

6

The Greek Economic Crisis and the Conditionality Program

6.1 How the crisis unfolded and how the Greek government initially reacted

The beginning of the current crisis in Greece is officially documented by the events of the fall of 2009 when the, then, New Democracy (ND) center-right-wing government called for a snap election citing the need to take measures to deal with an international crisis that "started to affect the Greek economy more than initially and 'reasonably' had been expected." Yet a closer observation of available facts and references, as presented in this book, quickly reveals that the causes of this crisis were deeply rooted in the way the country had been run during the past 30 years. These facts show how Greece had chosen over these past decades to gradually turn its economy into an uncompetitive impediment of excessive, rigid, and vague regulations that distributed rents to well-organized interest groups and created a fertile breeding ground for corruption and abuse of office and public money. Back in 1995 the electorate started to realize these problems, which had become commonplace during the "change" of the 80s, and supported the promises suggested by the Simitis' PASOK government to "modernize" the economy and society without reverting to the liberal choices that were attempted in the period between 1989 and 1993, and that were still deemed by the broad public to be unnecessarily excessive. Yet the electorate was to realize ten years later that these promises had been kept only superficially as, apart from successfully administering the EMU accession of the country, few reforms were passed regarding the complicated web of government interventions in the economy and the feeding lines of the rent-seeking interest groups and corruption that, according to Kaufmann and Kraay (2006), breeds in such environments. Thus, the shortcomings of the peculiar Greek economic model, which combined elements of extreme government intervention in markets that was paired with corruption and the failing of the rule of law with some token concessions to free market principles, became gradually more entrenched in the system even while the public became more alerted about its potential implications. For a while, the economy was fueled by the long-term impact of the deregulation of key markets and important infrastructure projects, which sustained a boom that emerged in the wake of EMU accession and which, conveniently, kept financing the abovementioned rents. In particular, the deregulation of the financial services sector that had been initiated by a reform-minded liberal ND government till 1993 was successfully completed by the Simitis government during the EMU accession. Also, the wide-ranging infrastructure projects financed by concessions to the private sector and by the EU structural funds, and that were mostly initiated by the same reform-minded ND government, were also successfully expanded and completed by the Simitis government. Finally, other initiatives, like the creation of the market for mobile communications by the reform-minded government and the subsequent, less aggressive, deregulation of fixed-line telecommunications by the Simitis government further added to the sense of reform and progress. Yet, at the same time, the deeper failings of the adopted economic model of unconstrained rent creation and distribution in an environment of faltering rule of law kept permeating a society whose coherence steadily deteriorated as quality employment, especially for the young, became ever more difficult to secure for most Greek families, a process that is described in OECD (2009).

Increasingly aware of the accumulating problems, the electorate handed over in 2004 a strong mandate to the ND party that promised to "reinvent" the government, battle corruption, and put public finances in order, in spite of the fact that the most reform-minded members of the party had been expelled after 1993. Once again, the hopes of the electorate were not fulfilled, as, with the notable exceptions of a handful of ministers and managers of public companies, the majority of the members of the new government quickly proved to share the same aversion to useful reforms its predecessors had demonstrated. At the same time, the engagement in corruption and mismanagement of public affairs by several members of the ND government demonstrated an incompetence that kept surprising, day after day, the increasingly gasping in disbelief electorate.

While it is the pattern of structural failings that gradually set the scene for the current crisis in Greece, and the political events marked the milestones toward this crisis, it was the evolution of public finances that ultimately acted as the catalyst to the events that led the Greek government to request financial assistance in the spring of 2010. The failures of the Simitis governments to pass useful reforms regarding the control of primary expenditure, the reduction of tax evasion and the shadow economy that easily could have built on the painful but critically useful fiscal efforts of the 1991–93 period, as well as the even worse performance of the successor ND government in the 2004–09 period, are clearly documented in Figure 5.86. There we can see how the primary expenditure of the central government was reduced, as a percentage of GDP, in the 1990–92 period, and how, after a significant increase after the election of the year 1993, they were simply kept under control, as a percentage of GDP, till 2003. Yet, we have to note that in the 1999–2003 period, growth was already increasing rapidly, which, at least partly, implies that government expenditure was not controlled sufficiently. After 2003, the ratio of expenses to GDP, which was matched all these years largely with the help of the rapid growth of GDP and the consequent growth in tax revenue, started to increase, documenting how the new government that won the 2004 elections did not fulfill at all its promise of fiscal responsibility. In the year 2009, when GDP growth had started to falter for the first time since the mid-90s, the ratio of central government expenditure to GDP increased rapidly while the tax revenue ceased to increase at the very high rate observed during the previous decade. This happened, among other reasons, as a result of unbudgeted expenses, like an increase in salaries that reflected the lack of restraint in government hiring the previous years, the increasing needs of the underfunded and completely unreformed social security funds for large unbudgeted cash infusions and the increases in the former public sector employee's pension bill. At this point the irresponsible strategy that was consistently adopted by successive Greek governments over the past 15 years to take double-digit government revenue growth rates as a permanent and unquestionable certainty that will forever finance runaway expenditure was forcefully exposed.

As 2009 started with signals about the upcoming impasse, the ND government replaced the economics and finance minister, who had guided economic policy for almost five years during which little was done to improve the revenue collecting mechanism, control, rationalize government expenditure, and reform the economy. Yet, as his successor was not granted the political mandate to proceed aggressively with reforms, given that other principal ministers who had the senior positions in the ministerial council dogmatically opposed useful reforms, no coherent reform strategy was formulated until autumn 2009. The only measures approved by the ministerial council included some consumption tax increases, an excessive increase of taxes on mobile communications, a scheme for the replacement of old cars, and a constitutionally questionable scheme to legalize buildings that had exceeded the size foreseen in their building license.

At that time the then prime minister sought what seemed like an exit strategy from what increasingly appeared as a fiscal and political impasse and called for a new electoral mandate. The snap election was announced along with a proposed reform platform that was rather haphazardly put together and that lacked both necessary detail and sufficient strategic coherence. Rationally, the electorate did not reward a government that asked for a third mandate to implement the same reforms it spectacularly failed to implement after receiving two strong mandates to do so, and gave a mandate to the only alternative. Following the 2009 elections, and while it was already clear that the deficit would largely exceed the latest officially quoted number of the outgoing government for a deficit in excess of 6 percent of GDP, the problem of runaway expenditures was further aggravated by the initially inappropriate response to the crisis of the newly elected PASOK government.

The new government proceeded in the end of the fiscal year 2009 with a "solidarity" handout and with an initiative to incorporate in the budget of 2009 as many expenditure items as it could saddle on the 2009 budget. These were either expenditure items that were so far kept off budget, like the procurement of hospitals, or that had not been allocated to a certain fiscal year, like the settlement with former Olympic Airways employees. A number of other items also included the decision to pay out an unusually high amount of tax returns in December 2009, and the reduced zeal to collect a number of taxes in 2009 and postpone their collection for 2010, like the individual real estate tax for 2009. In total, these actions and inactions added about 3 percentage points to the deficit that already was settling at an exorbitant 10 percent of GDP.

As a result of the combined effect of the weakening revenue, runaway expenditure, and rising interest expenditure, the primary government budget surplus available to finance interest expenses followed a deteriorating trend, and in 2009 even turned negative.

Figure 5.70 documents the reflection of the concerns of financial markets regarding the Greek government bonds, and the ability of Greece to finance its public debt, through the rise in the yield of the benchmark

Greek government 10-year bond. Financial markets initially observed with bewilderment the choice of the ND government to apparently run away from the problems, but decided to wait until the new government took its first initiatives. At that time, the Greek government was still able to raise cash with the practice established in early 2009, according to which the government extracted new borrowing from Greek commercial banks via the ECB, which accepted Greek government bonds as collateral for cash that was then used by Greek commercial banks to buy more Greek government bonds. But by early 2010 the ECB tried to put a stop to this process, as at that point it already was dangerously overweight on Greek government bonds. And when the new government started to act toward the end of 2009 in a way that signaled that it actually ignored the seriousness of the situation, international financial markets simply shut down for the Greek government. At that time, spreads between the ten-year Greek government bonds increased to a level that was implying approximately a 25 percent possibility that the Greek government would default on its debt. By early 2010 the Greek government gradually came to recognize publicly that a sizeable problem existed, and that demonizing international capital markets would not solve the problem. At last the government started to take measures to increase taxes and, finally, even to cut expenditure, as summarized in Table 5.91.

So, in January 2010, Law 3815/2010 was passed to reinstate estate taxes and at the same time taxes on alcohol and tobacco were increased, while in February fuel taxes were increased. Law 3833/2010, named specifically as a law to deal with the crisis, was passed in March and increased consumption taxes, reduced tax exceptions for electricity, introduced an extraordinary tax on high-declared incomes for fiscal year 2009 and introduced a luxury tax. Finally, a new tax law, Law 3842/2010 of April 2010 for "reinstating tax justice," introduced some measures to fight tax evasion by taxing assumed income according to "objective criteria," gave incentives to collect receipts from providers or professional services that traditionally did not issue receipts, and abolished the exemptions and predetermined, irrespectively of income, flat income taxes previously foreseen by the legislation for a number of politically favored professional groups and self-employed. In addition, cash handouts to government employees were set to be taxed, for most cases, like any other income. But it also made personal income taxation of Greece even more progressive and increased taxes on corporate profits and dividends to one of the highest rates of the OECD and EU. Flat taxes on real estate transactions were reintroduced, abolishing a badly designed scheme to tax capital gains on such transactions by the previous government. But once again, the tax rate was set to be among the highest in the OECD. The annual tax on property, which was already administered in 2008 by a new electronic database and which was set by the previous government at a very low rate that encompassed almost all property, was now limited to "large" holdings of properties. But for those the tax rate was put to one of the highest levels in the OECD. Finally, favorable terms to import large sums of money within a deadline with a flat tax and with no background check regarding to the legitimacy of the imported sums were included in the new tax law, in an effort to repatriate undeclared and untaxed funds that had fled the country.

The law "to deal with the crisis" (Law 3833/2010) of March 15, 2010, also included, for the first time, serious measures to cut government expenditure. An upper limit on paid overtime and travel expenses was introduced, one of the many cash handouts that have been granted to government employees during the past decades was cut by a certain percentage, even though a substantial number was exempt from the reduction, and government committees were ordered to convene in working hours and not to ask for extra payments. Also, Christmas, Easter, and summer gifts to government employees and pensioners were cut, a hiring freeze was announced and the public investment budget was slashed by half a billion euros.

While, starting in January 2010, the government had initially attempted to solve the impasse solely through tax increases, it had taken in March the step to actually target government expenditure and especially the wage and pension bill of the public sector. The mustering of this "political courage" can be explained by the fact that at this point, with money markets shut, the Greek government had no alternative but to demonstrate at least the existence of a will to slash some expenditure. Yet the measures announced by March were perceived by the markets to be "too little and too late," and in addition the targeted fiscal correction of these measures still amounted to only a small fraction of the government deficit of well over 25 billion euros. The same can be said of a new tax law that indeed tried to abolish some of the tax exemptions that made, so far, so many professionals and self-employed pay so little personal income tax and that made the everyday circulation of undeclared income so easy. By now, financial markets had become completely aware of the cobweb of the intervening problems of the uncompetitive Greek economy. And they wanted to see a fiscal consolidation effort commensurate to the deficit as well as a coherent reform strategy. Yet, by April they had not received that, and they remained firmly shut for the Greek government, leaving the government with only two options: Disorderly default or seeking financial assistance. Contemplating the fallout from a disorderly default, the government rationally chose to seek financial assistance, by sending in late April 2010 a letter in which it requested the initiation of a process that had been formulated and offered to it by the European Commission, ECB, and IMF in anticipation of the unfolding events. This offer required the signing of a Memorandum of Understanding (henceforth: the Memorandum), which was ratified by the Greek parliament with Law 3845/2010 of May 6, 2010, and in which the Memorandum of Understanding on Specific Economic Policy Conditionality described the measures the Greek government had to implement in order for the 110-billion loan facility agreement to be activated.

6.2 What the Memorandum initially provided

The Memorandum, as presented by European Commission (2010), constituted a brand-new approach toward the implementation of a reform program in a country whose government seeks financial assistance in an environment of fiscal and macroeconomic pressures that it cannot manage any more by itself. This approach was different from the one adopted by the IMF so far in countries that had sought such assistance in the sense that, once the political agreement was stuck, the euro-zone membership of Greece called for an active involvement of the European Commission and the ECB, together with the representatives of the IMF, to draft the conditions set and then to supervise the implementation of the commitments made by the Greek government.

This collaboration between the European Commission and the ECB, on the one side, and the IMF, on the other side, brought together an unprecedented combination of expertise and capacity to formulate a detailed plan to stabilize the finances of the Greek government and the macroeconomic fundamentals of the Greek economy. A crucial ingredient has been the increasingly more advanced benchmarking exercises that are undertaken especially by the European Commission. The coming together of the know-how at the level of the European Commission to formulate the precise details of the gravest failings of Greece that followed from these benchmarking exercises and the experience accumulated from the "Lisbon Agenda" allowed the European Commission to pinpoint the exact contours of the conditions that had to be set in the case of Greece before the financial support package could be activated. At the same time the IMF had the necessary experience to oversee and implement such a program. Furthermore, it had tried in the past years to improve the design of the measures that countries seeking its help are asked to implement in a way that addresses the demonstrated weaknesses of these countries without any prejudice toward the measures that have to be taken. Hence the program designed for Greece did set a useful precedent, regarding the use of detailed knowledge of the understanding of the challenges posed by a country with a political system that demonstrates a consistent and deeply rooted aversion to useful reforms. All this was combined with the accumulated expertise required to implement such a custom-made program.

As a result the Memorandum provided measures that (a) aimed to deal with the acute fiscal imbalances of the Greek government; (b) tried to propose long-term solutions to the underlying reasons that have allowed these imbalances to emerge over many decades, and that relate to the inability of the general government to supervise the use of public funds, control widespread tax fraud, and abolish tax exceptions by privileged professional groups; (c) tried to deal with general government entities, from social security to the public electricity company and public railroads, that have traditionally operated in complete disregard toward the realities of fiscal constraints; (d) tried to remove the most important of the binding constraints that suppress competition and productivity in product markets; and (e) tried to introduce some flexibility in a better supervised labor market. As such the Memorandum was wide-ranging. In all, it contained, in its original version, over 200 separate actions that were planned to be taken until 2014, either as small individual actions or as groups of separate actions that in the end aim to secure the successful achievement of some goals, the most important of which are presented in Table 6.1.

For example, the Memorandum provided for the complete deregulation of road freight transport. The knowledge of the lack of political will from the side of successive Greek governments meant that the wording included in the Memorandum was very specific and that it allowed practically no wriggle room. Greece was asked to deregulate this network industry and to include no constraints beyond those that are foreseen by the EU directives regarding road freight. Such a strong wording is not binding for the other EU member countries and was a result of the additional obligations Greece had accepted, beyond EU membership, as a result of the extraordinary – and unforeseen by the Treaty for the European Union – financial assistance the Greek government had asked for, and received. The inclusion of road freight transport in the Memorandum follows as a result of the unprecedented for the OECD, as

Table 6.1 Selection of most important actions included in the initial Memorandum, with the implementation dates initially foreseen

1	Reduce government wage bill through reduction of Easter, Christmas, and summer gifts as well as cash handouts to government employees. By 6/10.
2	Reducing pension bill through reduction of Easter, Christmas, and summer gifts but with protection of weakest pensioners. By 6/10.
3	Reduction of highest pensions. By 6/10.
4	Unique tax bracket for all incomes. By 6/10.
5	Abolishing of privileged tax treatment for cash handouts to government employees. By 6/10.
6	Publication of monthly data on the finances of social security organizations. By 6/10.
7	Publication of monthly data on the finances of hospitals. By 6/10.
8	Publication of monthly data on the finances of municipalities. By 6/10.
9	Creation of fund for the stability of the financial system. By 6/10.
10	Stress tests for banks and insurance companies. By 6/10.
11	Legislation for the reform of local government and the reduction of their operational expenses and wage bill. By 6/10.
12	Publication on the internet of all decisions on government expenditure. By 6/10.
13	Law to simplify start-ups. By 6/10.
14	Preparation of business plan to rationalize public railroads, shut down loss-making lines, comply with EU directives, and rationalize holdings of property and other assets. By 6/10.
15	Equalize retirement ages for man and women. By 6/10.
16	Link contributions with benefits of the pension plans. By 6/10.
17	Draft budget that includes detailed financial data for the publicly owned enterprises. By 9/10.
18	Replace one in five retirees of the public sector. By 9/10.
19	Freeze in pensions. By 9/10.
20	Extraordinary crisis tax on profitable companies till 2013. By 9/10.
21	Scheme to pay for violations of building permits. By 9/10.
22	Objective criteria to determine the income of professionals. By 9/10.
23	Expand VAT base. By 9/10.
24	Introduce green tax gradually. By 9/10.
25	Increase official values of property to increase revenue from property taxes. By 9/10.
26	Luxury tax. By 9/10.
27	Setting of upper limits of expenditure to entities financed by the budget. By 9/10.
28	Law to improve efficiency of tax audits. By 9/10.
29	Working group to improve tax compliance through (a) supporting collection mechanism, (b) collect verified debts in cooperation with social security funds, (c) creation of special division that deals with large tax payers, (d) creation of special division to deal with high-risk groups, (e) penal prosecution for large tax evaders, (f) enhance control of filed returns. By 9/10.

(*continued*)

Table 6.1 Continued

30	Adoption of new pension law with numerous precisely specified details. By 9/10.
31	Frequent publication of data regarding the wage bill and employment at publicly owned enterprises. By 9/10.
32	Initiate simplified mechanism to pay all wages and cash payments to government employees and link pay with performance. By 9/10.
33	Supervision by independent auditors of the use of human resources at the level of central government, entities supervised by the central government, assessment of initiatives to reduce expenditure through this supervision, evaluation of social programs and termination of the least effective ones and estimation of expected savings. By 9/10.
34	Operation of companies register. By 9/10.
35	Deregulation of road freight transport with abolishing of all requirements not foreseen in directive 96/26/EU and the abolition of all unnecessary obstacles to entry in the profession of road freight including minimum set fares. By 9/10.
36	Deregulate wholesale electricity market and rationalize consumers' electricity bills. By 9/10.
37	Empower the finance minister with respect to the ability to control the budget of other ministries, by giving him the power to veto expenditure decisions. By 12/10.
38	Ensure that the parliament focuses on the composition of the expenditure side of the annual draft budget and that the included expenditure and revenue projections are reliable. By 12/10.
39	Introduce stronger controls with respect to the fiscal responsibilities accruing to the central government that may derail the budgeted commitments via other entities of the general government, the local government, social security funds, and hospitals. By 12/10.
40	Creation of special budget division in the parliament. By 12/10.
41	Law regarding the wage policy of the public sector. By 12/10.
42	Application of new law for local government, and transfer of responsibilities and funds to them. By 12/10.
43	Full operation of single-payment authority. By 12/10.
44	Completion of first phase to rationalize public procurement, with creation of supervising authority, activation of electronic platform and e-auctions and introduction of ex ante and ex post checks. By 12/10.
45	Adoption of better regulation agenda. By 12/10.
46	Completion of reform of procurement in public health sector, with encouragement of use of generics, computerized supervision of prescriptions, reform, and audits in hospital finances. By 12/10.
47	Adoption of new legislation regarding the wage bargaining process, overtime pay, flexibility in work time allocation, connection of pay with productivity, and change of the meditation process. By 12/10.
48	Reduce minimum wage for weak social groups that are at high risk of long-term unemployment. By 12/10.

(*continued*)

Table 6.1 Continued

49	Freeze of minimum wages for three years. By 12/10.
50	Reduction of severance pay and unique treatment for white- and blue-collar workers. By 12/10.
51	Increase of the level for group layoffs. By 12/10.
52	Facilitate use of part-time and partial employment. By 12/10.
53	Adoption of directive 2005/05/EU. By 12/10.
54	Compliance with European Court of Justice decisions regarding professional skill recognition. By 12/10.
55	Law to simplify business licensing and creation of business areas and spatial plan to be operationally activated. By 12/10.
56	Changes in competition law to harmonize it with EU directives and make its operation more streamlined and efficient by focusing on important cases and by enhancing its independence. By 12/10.
57	Adoption of directive 2007/66/EC regarding appeals in public contract cases. By 3/11.
58	Adoption of plan to rationalize public railroads. By 3/11.
59	Legislation to separate activities of electric energy and gas market deregulation, including liberalizing use of the grid and gas supply infrastructure. By 3/11.
60	Measures to enhance Energy Regulatory authority. By 3/11.
61	New remuneration scheme in public sector to link productivity and responsibility with pay as part of better human resource management in the public sector. By 6/11.
62	Following the independent report, legislation to rationalize use of resources and improve organization of social programs in public sector. By 6/11.
63	Complete reform of employment inspection authority and ensure it is sufficiently staffed with adequately trained employees. By 6/11.
64	Shore up legislation to declare new employees. By 6/11.
65	Reform social programs to enhance support of those who are most in need. By 6/11.
66	In addition to the full implementation of the services directive, legislation to allow competition in professional services, including abolition of minimum mandated fees and other profession specific constraints. By 6/11.
67	Reduction of government staff beyond attrition from the 1 to 5 rule. By 9/11.
68	Unemployment benefits to adapt to minimum living standards. By 9/11.
69	Report on the better regulation agenda application. By 9/11.
70	Measures to reduce administrative burden by 20% with respect to 2008. By 9/11.
71	Change tax law to reduce disincentives in company mergers and sale of companies. By 9/11.
72	Decision to allow certified companies to clear customs procedures. By 9/11.
73	Abolish requirement to register in exporters' register of chambers of commerce in order to proceed with exports. By 9/11.

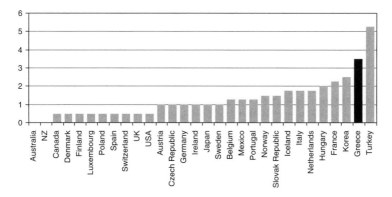

Figure 6.1   OECD indicator. Regulation of road transport, 2007

shown in Figure 6.1, extent of government regulation in Greece of this market before the implementation of this deregulation.

Another similar example is the deregulation of professional services. The past experience of the European Commission regarding the lack of will from successive Greek governments to usefully implement significant reforms had already put the European Commission on increased alert as the deadline for the implementation of the services directive was closing in. As expected, successive Greek governments did not adopt on time a detailed and convincing legislative and infrastructure package that would lead to an honest implementation of the services directive, in spite of the fact that professional services appear, according to the OECD indicators and for the most important of them, at least, to be very stringently regulated in Greece. Legal services, for which Figure 5.22 shows the OECD regulatory indicator, are only one example. Again, very specific terms were included in the Memorandum that foresaw the implementation of the services directive and, in addition, the abolition of administratively set minimum fees, regional constraints on professional activity, and other constraints that are particular to each profession.

The Memorandum also included measures to deregulate the wholesale electricity market and to simplify company start-ups. More crucially, it asked for the simplification of the licensing process, which has as a prerequisite the ironing out of the details of the incomplete laws for spatial planning as well as the laws for the establishment of areas for business activity, and for a reduction in the daily administrative burden that businesses face. While these crucial requirements were sometimes initially spelled out in a more general and less precise way than other measures, these areas have since been repeatedly revised and spelled out in greater detail, according to the procedure foreseen in council decision 2010/320/EU, Article 4(3).

It seems surprising, given the extent that the structural reforms dictated by the Memorandum are so wide-ranging, detailed, and strategically important, that the Greek government initially put all the emphasis on the fiscal measures included. Even in cases such as the initial draft law for road freight, it seemed to blatantly ignore the goals and conditions set in the Memorandum. This fact becomes even more surprising once one realizes that the Memorandum is less of a contract dictated by lenders to make sure that they get their money back and more of a consistent and well-orchestrated package of measures that aims to ensure long-term prosperity for the majority of the Greek society. This is not to say that fiscal measures are not included in the Memorandum. On the contrary, a large number of measures aim to further increase government revenue, reduce tax and social security payment evasion and avoidance, and put, at last, a break on runaway and unsustainable public expenditure. But while it is true that there are measures that dictate a fast increase of taxes or cut in expenditure, there is also an extensive list of administrative and structural measures that strategically aim at almost all of the documented weak points in the way the Greek economy operates.

6.3   The implementation of the Memorandum till July 2011

The implementation of the Memorandum started with a further confirmation of the adopted government strategy to base the fiscal consolidation mainly on tax increases rather than expenditure cuts, in spite of widespread evidence that episodes of fiscal consolidation that are based on tax increases, rather than expenditure cuts, are far less likely to succeed and have a much shorter expected duration.

So, the act of the parliament that accepted the Memorandum included measures to further increase consumption taxes as well as an extension of the extraordinary tax on corporate profits. Also, the reduction in the Christmas, Easter, and summer gifts to government employees presented in the previous law was replaced by a new, more complicated and less effective, scheme. At the same time, some of the other cash handouts to government employees received a second, additional, reduction. In the end, the cumulative fiscal measures taken by the Greek government before, and with, the Memorandum aimed at tax increases that should lead to tax revenue increases that were projected to be significantly higher than the revenue increases prescribed in the initial draft of the Memorandum. On the other hand, the concrete measures to cut expenditure that had been taken till the summer of 2010, were significantly lower than the measures prescribed by the Memorandum, as shown in Table 6.2. For the year 2014, and according to the government projections that were included in the text of the laws that were passed by the summer of 2010, the tax revenue increase should exceed by 60 percent the tax revenue increase asked for by the Memorandum, while, till the summer of 2010, the concrete and quantifiable cost-cutting measures met significantly less than half the target set by the Memorandum.

During, and after, the first half of 2010 the large increase in consumption taxes, that occurred mainly from the March and May 2010 increases, had compensated for the fall in private consumption as the Greek economy slipped in a deep recession, as shown in Figure 6.2. The price paid for maintaining this tax revenue on a track that seems relatively stable was a significant increase in consumer price inflation, which had increased – during a strong recession – to over 5 percent during the first half of 2010, as a result of these consumption tax increases as shown in Figure 6.3.

The apparent government strategy to bridge with extraordinary taxes the time interval till the implementation of the new tax law for 2011, which would make most extraordinary taxes permanent, and the full activation of measures to fight tax evasion and to abolish tax exemptions, stabilized the tax revenue in a contracting economy during the first six months of 2010 and till the end of the year. The extraordinary tax on corporate profits of December 2010, which was collected in January 2010, significantly supported revenue during the first six months as shown in Figure 6.4. The question of the future impact these high taxes would have on generated income and profits apparently remained a concern to everyone besides the Greek government, as underlined by the weakening revenue during the first six months of 2011. The fall in the revenue collected from the extraordinary tax on profitable companies in 2011, for example, exemplifies the shrinking base of these taxes as the recession deepened in Greece during 2010 and 2011.

On the other hand, the cuts in expenditure, that is salaries and cash handouts to public servants, may have managed to stop their annual

Table 6.2 Comparison of cost-cutting and tax increase measures foreseen by Memorandum (MOU) and the tax revenue increase and cost reduction estimated in the laws passed by the Greek government from December 2009 till May 2010

		2010	2011	2012	2013	2014
Accumulated impact of measures taken since 12/20/09						
A. Increase in public revenue						
Prescribed by MoU	**Total, million euros**	1.250	7.150	7.975	8.050	7.000
Prescribed by MoU	*% of estimated GDP*	*0,5%*	*3,2%*	*3,5%*	*3,5%*	*3,0%*
Specific measures taken	**Total, million euros**	5.886	11.763	11.713	11.833	11.033
Specific measures taken	*% of estimated GDP*	*2,6%*	*5,3%*	*5,2%*	*5,1%*	*4,7%*
B. Decrease in Government Expenditure						
Prescribed by MOU	**Total, million euros**	-4.550	-6.600	-10.850	-11.150	-11.150
Prescribed by MOU	*% of estimated GDP*	*-2,0%*	*-3,0%*	*-4,8%*	*-4,8%*	*-4,7%*
Specific measures taken	**Total, million euros**	-4.567	-4.754	-4.754	-4.754	-4.943
Specific measures taken	*% of estimated GDP*	*-2,0%*	*-2,1%*	*-2,1%*	*-2,1%*	*-2,1%*
C. Remaining non-specified measures						
Prescribed by MoU	**Total, million euros**				4.200	9.950
Prescribed by MoU	*% of estimated GDP*				*1,82%*	*4,23%*
Measures announced in principle but not specified	**Total, million euros**	6.017	4.617	3.117	3.117	3.117
Measures announced in principle but not specified	*% of estimated GDP*	*2,64%*	*2,08%*	*1,38%*	*1,35%*	*1,32%*
% of expenditure reduction prescribed by MoU for which specific measures have been legislated in a way that will lead to almost certain realization of projections		100,4%	72,0%	43,8%	42,6%	44,3%
Tax increased that have been legislated in a way that will lead to certain tax increases and, given baseline projections for economic activity, to a relatively certain increase in tax revenue. For 2010 only tax increases that have been legislated after the signing of the MOU are included in the estimate of this row.		101,0%	164,5%	146,9%	147,0%	157,6%

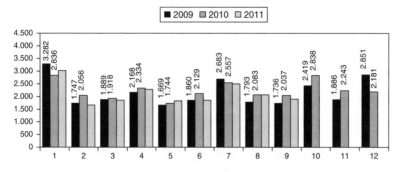

Figure 6.2 Monthly revenue in million euros from VAT and special consumption taxes, as gas, alcohol, and tobacco

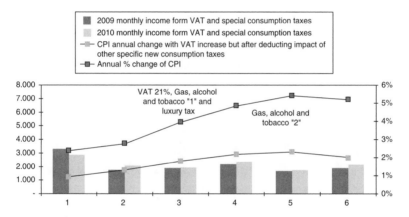

Figure 6.3 Monthly revenue in million euros from VAT and special consumption taxes, as gas, alcohol, and tobacco and inflation

increase after March 2010, but till June 2010 the monthly saving had been rather modest, with the exception of April where some cuts were computed retrospectively from January, as shown in Figure 6.5. A larger fall was observed in July, where the summer gift was paid, and an even clearer indication of the impact of these cuts appeared in the data for December 2010, when the reduced Christmas gifts were paid. But the final impact of these measures was not expected, even at the time, to

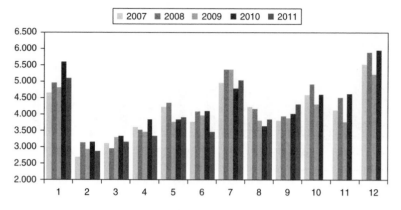

Figure 6.4   Ordinary budget of central government monthly revenue net of tax returns in million euros

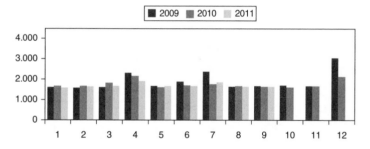

Figure 6.5   Central government payments for salaries and public employee pensions in million euros

exceed significantly the sums projected in the respective laws, which as said aimed at expenditure cuts that cover less than the half of the expenditure cuts foreseen by the initial Memorandum and that were a small percentage of the government's high deficit.

The supervising lenders had identified these problems and urged the Greek government to take expenditure cuts more seriously. Supervision regarding a plan to rationalize the debt-laden (10 billion euros) and loss-making (up to one billion annually, of which 450 million is the wage bill and up to 450 million interest on accumulated debt) publicly owned railroads rapidly become tighter, as resistance by interest groups within the railroad staff indicated a possible faltering of the government's willingness to deal with the issue. Supervision of hospital and medical expenditure bills should also become gradually tighter, along with supervision of the social security system and contribution collection mechanism. At the same time, more detail on the implementation of measures to control runaway expenditure items was constantly asked for and the mechanism that prepared and audited the implementation of the central and general government budgets has to be enhanced, always with initiatives included in the Memorandum. By the early summer of 2011, the debt of the railroads had been transferred to the government debt, the measures to reduce medical expenditure still were in various stages of progress, but had failed to yield tangible results, and a plan to restructure the public railroads apparently had demonstrated some significant initial successes regarding cost reduction.

Finally, the government, under the intense pressure of its lenders, was faced with a far-reaching agenda of structural reforms in product and labor markets. Regarding labor markets, Law 3863/2010 included measures to abolish a number of constraints to the operation of private-sector labor markets that were not even considered by past governments, and was passed under the pressure of the representatives of the lenders. A clause to balance the mediation process was postponed at the last minute, and announced before the deadline included in the Memorandum. These measures aimed to have an important impact, as together with the increase of the effective taxation of self-employment they can make salaried labor more attractive.

Regarding the core of the important reforms, as social security, opening of crucial network industries and professional services to competition, as well as the cost-cutting side of fiscal consolidation, one can identify during the first year of the implementation of the Memorandum an initial unwillingness of the responsible ministers to fully conform with the spirit of the Memorandum, subsequent and increasing pressure from the lenders, and a tendency to finally, with great delay, present initiatives that seemed to conform with the basic guidelines of the Memorandum. Yet, often these were subsequently undermined by the ministers responsible. Road freight was deregulated, with a three-year adaptation period, only after repeated oscillations by the responsible ministers and after the exercise of intense pressure from the lenders. An initial effort to deregulate professional services with Law 3919/2011 ultimately succumbed, at least partly, to the pressures of the legal profession and, especially, engineering representatives. This is clearly documented by the opinion

11/VI/2011 of the Competition Authority, which was mandated by the Memorandum. Further uncertainties regarding the truthful deregulation of sectors that are significant for the competitiveness of the economy as well as professional services emerged, as with the postponement of the deadline for the deregulation of medical professions till the end of 2011 and with the half-hearted deregulation of the pharmacist's profession. Regarding the latter, constraints like the mandatory ownership by a licensed pharmacist and the regulated, albeit reduced, administratively set profit margins were defended effectively by the responsible minister. Regarding the reduction of red tape, a one-stop shop for company start-ups was created, even though the underlying procedure was not significantly simplified and its effectiveness seems to be questioned by various observers. Furthermore, an action plan to identify 30 obstacles to doing business still had not been implemented by winter 2011, even though it was mandated for December 2010 and in spite of the fact that unofficially it has been rumored that working groups are making progress in the drafting of the law. A draft law presented in November 2011 includes some minor improvements that nevertheless fall short of an coherent effort to make substantial progress. Finally, regarding the energy market, all the main challenges still remained by the winter 2011, even though initiatives have again been repeatedly announced and discussed. On other fronts though, some substantial progress was gradually accumulating regarding the important issue relating licensing and spatial planning, which is especially important to production and manufacturing. By the summer of 2011, key pieces of legislation had been put in place, as, for example, Law 3982/2011, that significantly simplified the process for smaller establishments. By the late summer of 2011, the new process for environmental licensing, which was the crucial remaining obstacle for larger establishments, was legislated with law 4014/2011 and the required supplementary decrees were in a, reportedly, very advanced state of preparation by winter 2011. Drafts for the at last two were announced soon after a cabinet reshuffling in early 2011 and were probably marked to be legislated by late winter 2011. Also, a new law to issue building permits was legislated in late 2011, and is expected to become operational later during 2012.

Since product market reforms usually take some time to bear fruit, the insistence to allocate them mostly toward the end of the implementation agenda, as was already manifest in the initial draft of the Memorandum, and then to further procrastinate their truthful and aggressive implementation evidently risked exposing the economy to a longer, and possibly unnecessary deep, slowdown. This procrastination regarding especially reforms related to product markets, professional services, and the improvement of the business environment, has been repeatedly documented by reports like European Commission/ECB/IMF (2010), International Monetary Fund (2010), European Commission (2010), and almost all the subsequent progress reports. The extent of this procrastination may in the end undermine even the fact that markets might price in the anticipated impact of these reforms immediately, as Professor J. Stournaras of the Greek think-tank IOBE has correctly pointed out. The torpor with which structural reforms that can create a substantial upside to the Greek economy have been promoted, has created the risk that these reforms will be implemented at a time during which the domestic financial institutions and the productive fabric of the economy will be weakened to such an extent by a deep and prolonged recession, that they will be unable to take quick advantage of the opportunities that the reforms will create.

On the other hand, regarding the ministry of finance especially, there was, as mentioned, an initial reluctance to publicly admit the severity of the situation and a failure to present for over a year the parameters of a coherent and adequate exit strategy. But, finally, the additional measures described in the Medium Term Fiscal Strategy (MTFS), announced in the context of the European Semester by May 2011, appeared to have a magnitude that seems proportionate to the problem at hand, regardless, if one can argue, of the policy mix and the details of the suggested measures. Furthermore, press reports and announcements from officials of the ministry of finance and the tax authorities indicate at least a truthful effort to end the days of unchecked tax evasion, tax avoidance, and tax fraud by private individuals. A similarly determined approach regarding abuse of public office and corruption in the public sector is still missing, though. On the positive side, a census of public servants was completed, a census for employees of public companies is planned, and the single-payment authority for public employees is moving toward completion during the last months of 2011, more than two years after its initial announcement.

Remaining on the positive side, a number of initiatives included in the Memorandum, some of which were already on the agenda, appeared to receive increasing attention and to make firmer progress under the supervision of the lenders. Especially regarding the two laws on social security reform, Law 3863/2010 and 3865/2010, their speedy implementation, following the pressure of the lenders to do so, seemed to alleviate the forecasts of crippling future fiscal imbalances that till now significantly burdened the long-term creditworthiness of the

Greek government. This significance follows from the fact that pensions for former public employees and contributions to social security funds are, together with government wages, among the largest, and fastest-growing, single expenditure items. These laws will contribute much to the reestablishment of the creditworthiness of the Greek government as they remove some of the major uncertainties regarding the future ability of the Greek government to honor its obligations, even before the full impact of these laws is felt and before the actuarial studies, which are currently being prepared, are finished and published. Crucially, this social security reform introduces, for those who are first insured after 2011, a link between lifetime contributions and the pensions received. For older workers it makes marginal adjustments, but this is less important for the long-term projections that are largely stabilized as a result of the new system.

In the meantime, these laws include important measures like increased contributions by pensioners, an increase in average retirement ages and disincentives for early retirement, reforms regarding the employment of pensioners and pensions inherited by spouses and unmarried daughters, measures to make social security contributions evasion and fraud more difficult, the equal treatment in the future of private sector and public sector employees as far as their pensions are concerned, and changes in the way prescriptions are supervised. In addition, a number of administrative measures are expected to enhance the administrative capacity of the system to operate more efficiently, even though some other measures still leave some questions open.

6.4   July 2011 and the implementation of the Medium Term Fiscal Strategy (MTFS)

The new structure for economic governance in Europe, as represented by the European Semester, asked for an intensified and coordinated effort on the fiscal and structural front from the member states starting from 2011. For Greece, the comments of the European Commission regarding the National Reform Program amounted, simply, to the requirement to fully implement the Memorandum, thus demonstrating effectively how the Memorandum now incorporates in Greece the National Reform Program. Regarding the fiscal consolidation process, the European Semester asked for the MTFS to incorporate recommendations made by the Commission in the case in which the submitted national five-year fiscal plan is not based on measures that are realistic or appropriate to the challenges the country faces. Thus, the MTFS of

Greece at the end of the first semester of 2011 had to be adjusted with sizeable new fiscal measures in order to present, for the first time, a bundle of measures that promised, at least on paper, a prospect of fiscal sustainability by 2015.

As can be seen in Figure 6.6, in the absence of new measures, Greece would have been on a baseline path of increasing general government deficits that would have led to an accumulated general government debt of 500 billion euros (200% of GDP) by 2015. The reality presented in the baseline scenario can be identified as the main reason markets were so far reluctant to accept the reform progress of Greece as sufficient, as neither the fiscal consolidation strategy matched the size of the problem at hand nor was the reform strategy aggressive enough to generate a sufficiently large upside. As a result of this reality, which was identified on paper due to the requirements of the European Semester and, in particular, through the exercise of the MTFS, measures were proposed to put the country on a baseline path of almost zero general government budget deficits by 2015 and to aim for a debt of 350 billion euros by 2015. To achieve this, a plan that included an extensive list of fiscal measures that amount to an additional, to the baseline scenario, fiscal adjustment of 28 billion euros from 2011 till 2015 was presented, and approved both by the EU bodies as part of the process that constitutes the European Semester and the lenders. Also, and in spite of the initially stern opposition of the government to such a plan, an ambitious privatization program was announced to

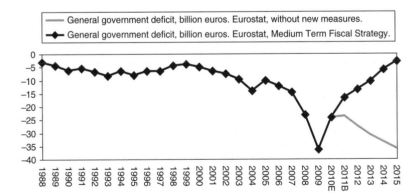

Figure 6.6 General government deficit, in billion euros, according to revised Eurostat data and according to the projections of the Medium Term Fiscal Strategy (MTFS) 2011–2015 with, and without, additional measures

reduce the stock of debt by about 50 billion euros, and the tools to implement it were outlined.

Law 3986/2011 implemented immediately measures amounting to about half of the total size of the fiscal adjustment program. Essentially, these measures attempted to make up for the inability of the fiscal consolidation strategy initiated in 2010 to achieve its targets and, in addition, provided a credible path that aimed for a sustainable fiscal situation within a tractable time frame. It is important to point out that it did so within the standard mechanisms set up to form the European Semester, and thus also formed the groundwork for the 2012 budget of the Greek government and the Stability and Growth Program. The same law created the fund responsible to administer the public property and shares that are set to be sold, or leased out. Crucially, this fund was empowered to overcome the obstacles regarding licensing and ownership disputes that have often dwarfed similar efforts in the past.

One, credible, point of criticism against the composition of the fiscal measures immediately implemented as part of the MTFS for 2011–2015 is that while in principle it introduced measures that are equally split among revenue increases and expenditure cuts, it once again proceeded with the aggressive and front-loaded implementation of the revenue increasing side of the measures, rather than the expenditure cut side of the measures. Increases of taxes and levies on the existing revenue and tax base amounted to over half of the revenue increasing measures, and all of them were implemented immediately, as can be seen in Table 6.3. That is, out of all the tax increasing measures listed, which amount to more than 50 percent of the revenue increasing measures, 94 percent was implemented immediately, implying that 54 percent of the revenue increasing measures were implemented immediately. Sizeable measures to reduce tax evasion and social security payment evasion, that amount to the other half of the revenue increasing measures, were postponed essentially after 2013, even though progress appears in the meantime regarding the collection of taxes from individuals that owe large amounts of verified taxes. Furthermore, specific expenditure cuts that were implemented immediately amounted to less than 27 percent of the total amount of the listed expenditure cuts. In late October 2011, the measures of Law 4024/2011 were legislated. These included the implementation of a schedule to move public employees in a redundancy pool, measures to implement a new uniform pay structure and provisions to slash benefits from supplementary pension schemes. Thus, finally, the legislated cost-cutting measures reached about 50 percent of the measures foreseen in the MTFS before the end of 2011. Yet,

Table 6.3 Measures described in the Medium Term Fiscal Strategy (MTFS) for 2011–15 and implemented by Law 3986/2011

Measures, mil. Euros.	2011	2012	2013	2014	2015	Sum
Wage bill	770	600	448	306	71	2.195
Operational expenditure	140	92	161	323	370	1.086
Mergers among public entities	490	150	200	200	150	1.190
Restructuring of public enterprises		414	329	298	274	1.315
Defense spending		200	333	333	333	1.199
Improvement in medical care finances	60	204	149	203	363	979
Medical expenditure	250	493	200	100	100	1.143
Social security expenditure reduction	1.088	1.280	1.025	1.010	700	5.013
Social security revenue increase	629	259	714	1.139	504	3.245
Tax evasion reduction			878	975	1.147	3.000
Tax exemption reductions and tax increases	2.318	3.380	152	69		6.549
Improvement of regional and municipal authority finances	150	355	345	350	305	1.505
Investment budget	850	–346				504
Sum	6.745	7.081	4.934	5.936	4.317	28.923
Measures, mil. Euros.	2011	2012	2013	2014	2015	Sum
Revenue increase	3.095	3877	2069	3153	1896	14.090
Instantly legislated revenue increase	2.882	3.691	154	809	4	7.540
Expenditure cuts	3.650	3.004	2.664	2.783	2.222	14.323
Instantly legislated expenditure cuts	1.553	1.260	440	415	130	3.798
Sum	6.745	6.881	4.733	5.936	4.118	28.413
Sum	4.435	4.951	594	1.224	134	11.338
Postponed measures		200	201		199	600

overall, the MTFS still seemed to initially repeat the fundamental mistake of the strategy of fiscal consolidation initiated in 2010, that is, to put almost all the weight on tax increases rather than expenditure cuts. Only after strong pressure from the lenders was this partially rectified before the end of 2011. While this criticism definitely is true, one has to acknowledge that for the first time Greece – after almost 2 years of crisis – presented a multi-annual budget that includes credible and reliable numbers for the central government and the general government entities, and that in addition presents a baseline scenario that aims toward fiscal sustainability. Furthermore, the cautious approach regarding tax and social security payment evasion is also related with the request of the European Union and the IMF that that numbers included are not overly optimistic, thus leading to the inclusion of conservative estimates regardless of the gradual, but probably substantial, progress observed in the activities of the responsible working groups. Finally, the increased aggressiveness of the supervision of the implementation of the Memorandum, which follows from the slow progress observed in many areas during the first year of its implementation, suggests that a rebalancing of the measures toward more aggressive expenditure cuts can be expected every time that the expected revenue increases fail to materialize. The introduction of a new property tax to be collected through electricity bills, and that aimed to replace the revenue that was not collected because of the inability to send out the notes for the collection of the existing, much increased, property tax, demonstrated in late 2011 the limits to the introduction of new, and increased, taxes. Besides the provisions of the Memorandum, the framework of the European Semester as well as the emerging details of the legislative packages that will support the permanent support mechanism of the euro area also hint toward a more aggressive and determined implementation of measures that aim to achieve fiscal sustainability with greater predictability in the future.

Regardless of this accelerated, and better scrutinized, implementation process, and the size of the new fiscal consolidation program, the misjudged mix of the fiscal measures taken in 2010 that put so little weight on expenditure cuts, in addition to the delay and procrastination in the implementation of the structural measures listed in the Memorandum, implied that during the summer of 2011 the Greek government faced a continuing loss of confidence in the markets. This was reflected not only by the continuing downgrades of the rating of its sovereign debt that remains in private hands well below investment grade. It was also reflected by the apparent unwillingness of private lenders to further finance the needs of the Greek government even at very high interest rates, besides from the contribution of Greek banks, which purchased increasing amounts of government bonds and notes offered in the past years, thus providing the Greek government with much needed liquidity that was often provided at the expense of the funds available to the private sector. As a predictable result, the time frame envisioned by the initial draft of the Memorandum regarding a gradual return of the Greek government to market-based financing ceased to be realistic, and a financing gap became apparent starting early 2012. Amid fears of contagion to other European countries, it became inevitable that Greece would need an extension of the size of the fiscal support it received even before the activation of the permanent support mechanism of the euro zone. A European Council decision on July 21, 2011, offered the Greek government an additional 109 billion euro financial assistance program, under the condition that private financial institutions that held Greek Government Bonds would choose among a number of alternative options that effectively meant that they would voluntarily accept a haircut of about 20 percent, thus avoiding an official default of the Greek government. While the private sector involvement (PSI) did not have at the time a punishing haircut for the financial institutions that had financed the Greek government through the purchase of its bonds, it altered the maturities of the outstanding private debt in a way that significantly contributed toward the resolution of the looming financing gap of the Greek government. The other parts of the new program, which also included further cash for the Greek government and secondary market bond repurchases, further contributed toward securing for the Greek government a much longer period of time during which it would not depend on markets to finance its current deficits or refinance its maturing debt. Finally, this second package also reduced the interest on outstanding debt held by the European Bodies and the IMF, further improving the sustainability profile of Greek debt.

The additional fiscal measures needed to present, with the MTFS, a fiscal plan that aimed, at least on paper, at sustainability, was effectively set as a prerequisite for the adoption of this second assistance program, that once again protected the Greek government from an unorderly default. At the same time, the elaboration of the structural reform agenda in the fourth review of the Memorandum of July 2011 (IMF, 2011b), suggests the increase of the pressures of the lenders on the Greek government to proceed, at last, more aggressively and truthfully with reforms that can remove the binding constraints on the prospects of the Greek economy.

Apart from the insistence to finally truthfully implement labor market reforms that had been fudged previously, an elaborate list of reforms asked the government to specifically and very speedily address key issues regarding professional services. Also, the long overdue deregulation of the energy sector now was laid out in great technical detail, in order to limit any opportunity to avoid proper implementation of the needed legislative action. Even the unorthodox design of the one-stop shop for company start-ups was requested to become immediately subject to an impact assessment. Furthermore, an almost immediate reduction in start-up costs was mandated as was a provision to abolish the requirement to publish corporate acts in daily newspapers.

The revisions of the Memorandum had in the meantime also touched issues that were missing from the initial draft, like education reform, which was included in the third review of March 2011 (IMF, 2011a). An important initiative on that front built on the, less determined, previous reform attempts. It finally dealt with the structure that made higher education institutions fall prey to interest groups, abolishing the influence political parties have through student unions on the governance of these institutions. Furthermore, academic evaluation was made an integral part of the workings of these institutions, their administrative independence was increased and at the same time accountability was enhanced. Finally, a law that made it impossible to hinder and punish criminal acts on the premises of these institutions was abolished. Regarding another important topic, details regarding the reform in the judiciary and reform regarding issues of governance were also included after the fourth review of July 2011 (IMF, 2011b).

After its fourth review, the Memorandum included a long list of clearly specified immediate measures, some of which are selected in Table 6.4. They meticulously describe a removal of key legislative realities that for many decades have been the core of the mechanism that allocated rents to Greek vested interests.

6.5 After October 2011: Greece and the new structure for economic governance in Europe

As already mentioned, the events of early summer 2011 included the new tax measures of the MTFS in spite of the strong evidence that the tax-paying capacity of the economy was being pushed beyond its limits, the second support program for the Greek government that alleviated the immediate concerns regarding the imminent financing gap, and the agreement of the Greek government to proceed with a

Table 6.4 Selected key reforms that are spelled out in great detail in the fourth review of the Memorandum and that confront vested interests deeply rooted in the Greek society

1	A medium-term reform of the judicial system (without prejudice to the constitutional principles and the independence of justice).
2	Implement the announced anti-tax evasion action plan
3	Medium-term staffing program of government, including cancelation of vacant job posts
4	Legislation for a simplified remuneration system introduced in July 2011, and phased in three years
5	Align wages in state-owned enterprises with wage grid of public sector
6	Launch of e-procurement platform by July 2012, and make it fully operational by Q2 2012
7	Include supplementary pension schemes in the reform of the pension system, and the related forecasts. In-depth revision of these funds with an aim to ensure their sustainability.
8	Adjustment of lump-sum retirement payments that are out of line with contributions
9	Government freezes nominal supplementary pensions and reduces the replacement rates for accrued rights in funds with deficits, based on the actuarial study prepared by the National Actuarial Authority. In case the actuarial study is not ready, replacement rates are reduced, starting from January 1, 2012, to avoid deficits.
10	The Health Committees set up by Law 3863/2010 will start operating the planned revision of disability status and produce a first quarterly report of its activities by the end of December 2011.
11	Initiation of joint purchase of medical services and goods to achieve substantial expenditure reduction of at least 25 percent compared to 2010 through price – volume agreements.
12	The Bank of Greece commits not to grant pension privileges to its staff and to revise the main parameters of its pension scheme to align them with those of IKA.
13	Government revokes market regulation 40 (17.12.1990) to abolish the 0.4 percent contribution of wholesale sales prices in favor of the Panhellenic Pharmaceutical Association.
14	Starting from 2012, pharmacies' profit margins are calculated as a flat amount or flat fee combined with a small profit margin with the aim of reducing the overall profit margin to no more than 15 percent, including on the most expensive drugs as defined in Law 3816/2010.
15	Calculation of stocks and flows of medical supplies in all the hospitals using the uniform coding system for medical supplies developed by the Health Procurement Commission and the National Centre for Medical Technology for the purpose of procuring medical supplies.
16	The program of hospital computerisation allows for the setting up of a basic system of patient electronic medical records
17	The Ministerial Decision also lowers fees for company creation, for copies and for additional pages

(continued)

Table 6.4   Continued

18	An audit is launched to assess to what extent the contributions of lawyers and engineers to cover the operating costs of their professional associations are reasonable, proportionate, and justified.
19	Government identifies measures to reinforce transparency in the functioning of professional bodies by requiring them to publish an annual report on their webpage regarding their financial performance and statistics on disciplinary actions in defense of consumers' interests.
20	All Presidential Decrees needed for the implementation of the law on fast-track licensing procedure for technical professions are adopted.
21	Abolish provisions of the regulations of the professional chambers on access to, and exercise of, the profession and on pricing, that are against Law 3919/2011 and EU law including competition rules.
22	Set up contributions of lawyers and engineers to their professional associations that reflect the operating costs of the services provided by those associations.
23	Legislation amending Law 3328/2005 is adopted to ensure that holders of franchised diplomas from other Member States have the right to work in Greece, accordingly, under the same conditions as holders of Greek degrees.
24	Facilitate establishment by abolishing or amending unjustified and disproportionate requirements, including those relating to quantitative and territorial restrictions, legal form requirements, shareholding requirements, fixed minimum and/or maximum tariffs, and restrictions to multidisciplinary activities.
25	Simplify and reduce costs linked to company publication requirements
26	Address restrictions in the transport sector, including the transport of empty containers and of nonhazardous waste;
27	Reduce the complexity of the Code of Books and Records and provide clarity on all categories of nondeducted expenses.
28	Government starts screening Ministerial Decision A2-3391/2009 on market regulations as well as any other related regulations. The screening is carried out, in cooperation with the Hellenic Competition Commission, with a view to identifying administrative burdens and unnecessary barriers to competition for elimination.
29	A comprehensive list of nonreciprocating charges in favor of third parties is presented, identifying beneficiaries and quantifies contributions paid by consumers in favour of those beneficiaries.
30	Legislation is adopted to simplify and shorten procedures to complete studies on environmental impact and to get the approval of environmental terms with a view to reducing the number of projects subject to environmental licensing and the duration of approval procedures to EU average levels. The acceleration of the environmental licensing is assured by committing the authorizing authority to proceed with the approval procedure after a specified time period.

(continued)

Table 6.4 Continued

31	Government reviews and codifies the legislative framework of exports (i.e., Law 936/79 and Law Order 3999/59), simplifies the process to clear customs for exports and imports, and gives larger companies or industrial areas the possibility to be certified to clear cargo for the customs themselves.
32	The obligation of registration with the exporters' registry of the Chamber of Commerce is abolished; such a registration is simplified and becomes voluntary.
33	The Decrees necessary for the implementation of the law on fast-track licensing procedure for manufacturing activities and business parks are implemented.
34	An impact assessment is presented to evaluate Law 3853/2010 on simplification of procedures for the establishment of companies in terms of the savings in time and cost to set up a business.
35	Government finalizes the remedies to ensure the access of third-parties to lignite-fired electricity generation.
36	Government adopts legislation to improve regulatory governance.

substantial privatization program. Regarding the latter, proposals like the EUREKA project of Roland Berger outlined potential schemes to address concerns that the Greek government would not be able to execute an ambitious privatization program, especially under the market conditions Greece was facing, even though official response to such proposals has been so far limited.

Thus, in a nutshell, while Greece was still facing the bulk of the challenges it faced in early 2010 regarding the deregulation of the economy and the rationalization of public expenditures, it was offered a renewed window of opportunity to deal with these issues and was able to roll over much of the cost of the delay to deal with these problems within the initially agreed time frame to the financial institutions that had bought Greek government bonds.

Unfortunately, during the remaining summer of 2011 and till October 2011, the Greek government did not grasp this opportunity. Little was done to promote structural reforms and cost-cutting measures, and by winter 2011 the deficit of the government budget was once again off track, jeopardizing the payout of the sixth tranche of the initial Memorandum.

Under severe pressure to implement the measures agreed in the MTFS, and to cover the emerging deviation of the budget, the Greek government introduced another real estate tax to be collected through electricity bills and, at last, legislated some of the more serious cost-cutting measures promised in the MTFS, like the activation of the common payment authority in the public sector and the implementation of a uniform pay structure throughout the public sector. Also, for the first time, serious cuts were foreseen in the supplementary pension schemes as well as the retirement cash bonuses they offered, especially to pensioners of the broad public sector. Given the absence of the actuarial studies, probably these measures implied injustices, nevertheless they addressed a significant cost item of the social security system that touches on opaque privileges and that had not been addressed at all since the implementation of the Memorandum had begun.

Furthermore, the policy mix of the past years had contributed, at least partially, to the deepening of the recession in Greece, with immediate implications on the outlook of the public finances. As a result, the IMF raised concerns regarding the extent to which the agreement of July 21 was sufficient to ensure the sustainability of the debt of the Greek government. Given the fact that technically the Memorandum and the second assistance program of July 21 are loans to a solvent government, and thus respect the no-bail-out clause of the Treaty of the European Union as well as IMF requirements, the sustainability of the debt of the Greek government is more than a mere technicality, and actually is the cornerstone according to which this program is legalized on an European level, as well as for the IMF.

To address these concerns, the European Council decision of October 26/27, 2011 reaffirmed the second assistance program to cover the financing gap of the Greek government. In return it increased the haircut on private holders of Greek government bonds to 50 percent, foresaw the activation of the European Financial Stability Facility (EFSF) to recapitalize the Greek financial system that faced probably the obliteration of most, or even all, of its core capital, mainly as a result of the losses they stand to occur because of their increased lending to the Greek government since the onset of the Greek crisis. A scheme to collateralize government property in exchange for the funds of the EFSF probably was introduced in order to facilitate the nationalization of the Greek banks by the Greek government, in spite of the fact that the latter would not be able to provide the funds needed to recapitalize it.

At the same time, the dispatch to Greece of a Technical Assistance Task Force, by the request of the Greek government, aimed to address the problems in the implementation of the measures foreseen by the Memorandum besides the increase of taxes. In some cases the task force will build on substantial groundwork that has already been put in place, like in the case of battling tax evasion. In other cases, like the inability of the administration to produce legislation that will form a business-friendly environment, the task force will have to assist the Greek government in overcoming traditions and practices that are deeply entrenched in the administration and the political system. The latter will also be one of the main challenges of the new coalition government, which has as prime minister a technocrat with impeccable credentials. This is even more true, as the 2012 budget presented in November once again appears to base its projections on very high revenue increases. While now these are to be realized through property taxes, after income and consumption taxes failed to yield the projected results in the previous two years, once again the budget carries the risk of a consolidation strategy that is largely based on tax increases, rather than expenditure cuts.

In the wake of the persistent inability of Greece to address with determination the concerns of the markets regarding its ability to control public sector expenditure and to deregulate its economy, Europe has been forced to face a simmering crisis that has started to gradually put into question the solvency of other, larger, members of the euro zone that appear to have vulnerable public finances and uncompetitive product and services markets. Actually, the markets have been even questioning the ability of the euro zone to hold together.

An exit of Greece from the euro zone would have wide-ranging implications on the confidence of markets in the future of the common currency. Even if one country appears now to be more vulnerable than others, nobody will be able to predict when in the future other countries that today appear solvent may face a financial or political problem that will push them to exit the common currency. The experience of Quebec indicates the very real implications such a looming uncertainty can have. On the other hand, respecting the "no-bail-out clause" means that neither can the ECB act as a lender of last resort for the governments of the member countries, nor can the "conditionality programs" of the EFSF and its successor, the European Stability Mechanism (ESM) be used to take over the public debt of member countries whose governments are not solvent. It also means that "eurobonds," which can be issued given either commitments from the existing national budgets or from European taxes, cannot be issued as long as the fiscal realities of the member states are as divergent as they are currently.

This leaves as the only remaining short-term alternative the possibility of an orderly default, as is effectively the 50 percent haircut on private holders of Greek government bonds, along with measures to contain the systemic fallout such events can have on the financial institutions of euro-zone member countries. In the long term, the national authority to implement structural and fiscal policies cannot be questioned unless Europe is to become an explicit federation, which will not only require strong democratic legitimacy but also the establishment of a federal bureaucracy that actually will replace many parts of the national administrations. The hurdles that such an undertaking would face are of such magnitude that probably attempting it would increase the current concerns of the markets, rather than to alleviate them.

In the end, the only viable solution appears to be a closer integration along the path already suggested by the European Semester and the attempts to improve economic governance in Europe. This implies an increase in the coordination of fiscal and structural policies among national governments through the existing European structure, that will not appear as a spectacular change but that will imply ever closer links with the European structure and the daily operation of the national administrations. Some increase in the precedence European legislation takes over contradicting national legislation may also enhance the integration among the union members. Even if these issues mainly appear as technicalities, the national implementation of European legislation is crucial for the success of the internal market and for Europe's growth prospects, and has not received so far the attention fiscal consolidation has received. Additional provisions, beyond the fines foreseen in the six legislative texts, and that aim to strengthen economic governance in the EU, can be built into the system for countries that voluntarily appeal for activation of the EFSF/ESM. Thus, a structure of incentives will exist for national governments to improve the coordination of the fiscal and structural policies that are implemented at the national level, with the European guidelines, but without the requirement of a wide-ranging transfer of national competencies to European bodies.

In such an environment, the main challenge for Greece will pertain to the extent to which the administration and the political establishment will be able to accept the accountability and transparency such an integration will imply. On the other hand, the deeper implications of the October 26/27 decisions regarding, essentially, the transfer of the cost caused by the unwillingness of the Greek government to implement crucial reforms during 2010 and 2011 to the private sector, that financed the Greek government generously since the onset of the crisis, remain an unknown quantity. They may yet prove to be small for Greece and Europe. On the other hand, they may turn out not to be small.

References

European Commission (2010), "The Economic Adjustment Programme for Greece. Interim Review (Athens, 14–17 June 2010)." European Commission Directorate-General for Economic and Financial Affairs.

European Commission/ECB/IMF (2010), "Statement by the EC, ECB and IMF on the first review mission to Greece." ECB, 5 August.

International Monetary Fund (2010), "Greece Stand-By Arrangement – Review under the Emergency Financing Mechanism." Washington D.C., IMF.

International Monetary Fund (2011a), "Third Review Under the Stand-By Arrangement." Washington D.C., IMF.

International Monetary Fund (2011b), "Fourth Review Under the Stand-By Arrangement and Request for Modification and Waiver of Applicability of Performance Criteria." Washington D.C., IMF.

Kaufmann, D., and A. Kraay (2006), "Measuring Governance Using Cross-Country Perceptions Data," in Susan Rose-Ackerman (ed.) *International Handbook of the Economics of Corruption*, Cheltenham, UK: Edward Elgar.

OECD (2009), *Employment Outlook Tackling the Job Crisis*. Paris: OECD.

Appendix 1
Road Transport in Greece and Government Intervention

A1.1   An example of how the reform debate in Greece does not focus on issues that are crucially related to the low competitiveness of the country

Greece is one of the last countries to maintain a regulation, introduced in most other countries around the 1930s that restricts competition in transport services. In addition the country has introduced a number of important obstacles that actively prevent the creation of an efficient supply chain. These obstacles range from the organization of customs to a legislative environment that effectively prohibits the creation of logistics centers as documented by Alexopoulos (2009). Yet, along with rail transport, the road transport market remains one of the main areas where government intervention is harmful to competition, as recorded by the OECD regulation indexes for non-manufacturing sectors. For example, the Greek government still issues permits for trucks that can transport cargo for a fee (public trucks). At the same time it issues permits for companies to obtain trucks that are specified only for their own use (private trucks). Furthermore, as documented by Alpha Bank (2008), these permits are split into three categories – national, international and regional. Regional permits allow only transport in given prefectures and prefectures that share a border with the prefecture for which the permit was issued. As a result the Greek economy has not enjoyed the significant productivity-enhancing developments that took place in the countries that deregulated their road and rail transport services after the 1970s, even though Greece's geomorphology makes road transport in particular, whose importance is stressed by Boylaud (2000) for all economies, even more important in the supply chain. These benefits are documented in works like OECD (2001a); they include a significant reduction in fares for full truckload cargo, a smaller reduction in fares for less than full truckload cargo, but also the development of all the logistics and on time delivery industry that has supported much of the productivity growth of the 1990s. The total impact of all these benefits is documented by certain pieces of evidence. For example, in the US total inventories dropped from 9 percent of the GDP to 3,9 percent of the GDP in the 18 years that followed the deregulation of road and rail transport. A comparable drop in the storage and distribution costs, from 16.6 percent of the GDP to 10.6 percent of the GDP, occurred over the same time period. Maintaining these restrictions also means that the value of the existing permits for public trucks constantly increases, as was also the case, for example, in France toward the end of the 1970s. Then, according to the OECD (2001b), market circumstances resembled those that still prevail today in Greece. The OECD (2001b) also documents the implications of market deregulation in a number of countries. So, in countries like France and Mexico, small transport companies struggled after the deregulation to adapt to the new competitive environment and take advantage of the increased opportunities in the way that larger companies managed to do. This happened in spite of the increase in the number of smaller companies in France, as the fares fell rapidly in the new competitive environment in which the value of the existing permits was wiped out. In France, which like Greece traditionally is suspicious of free markets, the reaction was to introduce legislation that supposedly would guarantee "fair prices" for the smaller companies. These legislative initiatives proved to be completely ineffective, as they did not help the small companies to adapt to the new environment and improve their organizational skills. The importance of the ability of small companies to adapt to the new environment is highlighted by the case of other countries, like the Netherlands, where the problems that appeared in France did not arise. In addition Boylaud (2000) documents how deregulation has not led to excessive consolidation in any country, and how small companies still are predominant in deregulated markets like Finland, for example. This conclusion is corroborated by Coopers and Lybrand (1996). They find that in the new, deregulated, environment larger companies concentrate on the adoption of innovations that increase competitiveness and reduce cost, but at the same time they outsource the physical work of delivering goods to small companies. They also illustrate how middle-sized companies find it hard to compete with either innovative large companies or competitive small companies. Boylaud (2000) describes how competition among small companies in this environment focuses mainly on the height of the fees, as there is apparently little room for other types of product differentiation. The deregulation of the road transport market has one more aspect that needs to be taken into account. As Morrison and Winston (1999) describe in the case of the US, in a regulated market the high price and low quality of the licensed public trucks encourages many companies to invest in the maintenance of a private truck, or a fleet of private trucks, even though this truck (or fleet) may not be used efficiently. After deregulation, these companies tend to abandon their own fleets and choose to outsource transport and storage management. Thus they create a significant volume of new business for truckers and logistics companies, not only because demand for such services responds positively to price decreases, efficiency increases and, as the European Commission (1997) shows, the economic activity grows, but also because a significant volume of existing business is no longer handled internally but placed on the market instead. Finally, the OECD (1997) documents how the parallel deregulation of rail transport led to an increase in volume for combined transport. This evidence has to be paired of course with concerns expressed by the Institute for Economic and Industrial Research (IOBE) (2006). These concerns are verified by the German experience documented by the OECD (2001b): in deregulated markets harsh competition often leads to the violation of labor laws in the trucking business, especially by small trucking companies.

This evidence suggests that the deregulation of the road transport market poses a threat for existing truckers – mainly with regard to their protection from extreme competition. The high value of truck permits on the secondary market therefore accurately reflected, till 2010, the present value of expected monopoly rents that accrue to the permit holder. These rents are likely to face a credible threat from a deregulation, as the example of France demonstrates. In addition to the elimination of monopoly rents, deregulation also threatens to put high competitive pressure on working conditions for small companies, as the example of Germany shows. On the other hand, deregulation will not threaten the existence of small companies, as their workload will increase – not only because the demand for such services is elastic, but also because the inefficient fleet of private trucks will be reduced in size in a competitive environment, ensuring that this business is handed over to truckers, as also argued by Alpha Bank (2008). This will be true even if the removal of obstacles to the development of combined rail and road transport, like the completion of a rail link to the container terminal in the port of Piraeus, a twin rail track between Athens and Thessaloniki, and a useful rail link to the container terminal of Thessaloniki, for example, is finally achieved, because the total increase in business volume will absorb the shift of some cargo from road to rail.

It should be noted that recent decisions (2536/2009 and 3537/2009) by the Symvoulio Epikratias (the tertiary level court) have ruled that the existing restrictions that the legislation introduces to the transport market in Greece are unconstitutional because they limit the freedom of companies to enhance their efficiency. Yet in spite of these decisions, Law 803/1978 still applied till 2010. This law not only provided that the government issues new permits only after a report proves they are needed. (An impressively succinct research report published in the Government Gazette B1607/2005 showed that there is no such need, while Alpha Bank (2008) describes how usually the trucker's unions advise the government that there is no need for new permits or for such studies) but the law also mandated that the government should set fare prices. Actually, in the past five years the increases in the fares that were legislated by the government were much higher than the annual inflation – even in 2009, when many businesses dropped their prices as economic activity slowed down in Greece, these fares, which were not supposed to be increased further, were indirectly pushed up when an additional charge was reaffirmed to the fares of fuel trucks, pursuant to the ministerial decision published in the Government Gazette B1183/2009. Furthermore, government decisions like the ministerial decision published in the Government Gazette B1491/2005 introduced limitations on the size of the parcels delivered by courier companies and on other aspects of their operation, which have been found to violate the Postal Services Directive according Opinion IP/09/157 of the European Commission. In addition, a notice by the Minister of Transportation (Γ5/19419/1676/15/4/2008) considers empty containers to be cargo that is not owned by individual companies, thus precluding their transport by the private trucks of these companies since they are allowed to be filled only with cargo they own. As a result of these government decisions and pieces of legislation, whose constitutionality and conformity with EU law and case law is highly questionable, the Greek economy still cannot enjoy the efficiency gains that other economies have achieved in the past decades. Furthermore, the ongoing denial of the need to deregulate this market means that policy initiatives are so far restricted to the defense of the existing state-sponsored monopolies and restrictions to competition – in spite of the significant contribution these have toward the increase of the cost of supply chain management in Greece and, as a result, the degradation of the competitiveness of the economy. At the same time, the debate regarding the potential adverse implications of deregulation on the smaller trucking companies, and the development of effective measures to counter these (or to adequately compensate for them) is lacking. This implies that when, or if, deregulation happens it most probably will not take place in a well organized fashion. This in turn implies that the legitimate concerns of smaller trucking companies will probably not be addressed effectively at that time. In order to fulfill the terms of the conditionality program accepted by the Greek government as part of the financial support package offered by the European Commission, European Central Bank and International Monetary Fund, the market for road freight licences and fares was deregulated in winter 2010 albeit with a three year derogation period that seemed to be questioned towards the end of 2011. Also certain, but not all, restrictions private courier companies were removed under the threat of European Commission actions. Yet numerous other constraints, that range from limitations regarding the licencing and use of trucks that are used by individual companies to limitations on courier businesses remain.

Appendix 2
Shop Trading Hours in Greece

A2.1 An example of how consumer interests are not a consideration in reform debates when one has to deregulate, rather than regulate

The regulation of shop trading hours has been an issue in Greece mainly in relation to the increase in employment and the support of small and medium-sized shops, which are the arguments usually used to justify the need to restrict shop trading hours. In addition, an observed increase in non-permanent or part-time employment is also often cited as a reason why the government has to regulate shop trading hours and restrict the ability of shop owners to choose themselves their trading hours.

Recently Law 3377/2005 introduced unified shop trading hours across the country, setting as the only limits the opening of shops after 05:00 hours, and ending them at 21:00 hours on weekdays and 20:00 on Saturdays. This revived the debate on shop trading hours. The arguments that are usually cited to postpone reforms were reiterated, and as such they offer an interesting case study of the ability of Greek society to accept and promote reforms. An important part of the usefulness of this example is the fact that shop trading hours in Greece had been deregulated in 1992, only to be re-regulated in 1994 and again, more stringently, after 1997. Furthermore, the international experience with shop trading hours and the real benefit that extended shop trading hours can offer to society are persistently absent from the related debate. The issue of permitting shops to open on Sundays is also consistently avoided, as rumors have it that the Orthodox church always persuades politicians who contemplate such changes to abandon the thought.

In particular, the available data and literature suggest that extending shop trading hours leads to both an increase in employment, which is not necessarily limited to temporary or part-time employment, and to increased convenience for consumers – especially working parents and women. The data and literature also show that the ability to use extended opening hours is predominantly used by larger shops – and in particular groceries – which serve during these extended opening hours small households. Furthermore, extended shop trading hours are erroneously accused of enhancing the expansion rate of larger shops to the detriment of smaller shops. This trend is documented irrespectively of the existence of measures that limit shop trading hours; such expansion seems to be related to the fact that larger shops offer lower prices as a result of their increased productivity as well as of their ability to better meet the needs of consumers. On the other hand, the expansion of larger stores seems to be constrained more effectively by imposing limitations on their licensing. Such limitations seem to be able to protect smaller shops, but at the same time they tend to deny consumers the advantages that may follow from the reorganization of retail trade and the increased productivity of larger stores.

A report commissioned by the government of New South Wales (2003) that preceded the deregulation of shop trading hours in 2003 concluded that a disproportionate increase in part-time employment was not expected to take place to the detriment of full-time employment. This conclusion was based on the study of data from areas of Australia that had already deregulated shop trading hours, and it was paired with an expectation that employment and sales should increase. The study of the Melbourne area is particularly important because after the deregulation of 1996 90 percent of the small and medium shops of the area had not laid off staff. In addition the "way of life" of the families that operated these shops did not change. The same study found widespread support for extended shop trading hours, even on Sundays, among consumers. As a matter of fact, in Victoria 77 percent of the voters opted for the opening of shops on Sundays by referendum.

In the US the issue can be studied better given the wider availability of data. Burda and Weil (1998) document that in the states that adopted Sundays opening hours there were positive results both regarding employment and the satisfaction of consumers – especially among working consumers that are part of small households. This study also uses international data for countries in which severe restrictions exist on shop trading hours. In these countries, the study finds, the contribution of the retail sector to the total employment levels is smaller than in the countries that have not adopted such restrictions. The study also draws the (important) conclusion that sales turnover tends to migrate from sectors in which such constraints are maintained to sectors from which such constraints have been removed or in which they never existed. Similar conclusions are reached by Goos (2004). This study also uses data for different states in the US and finds that restrictions on shop trading hours limit employment, increase salaries and, when the restrictions are severe, limit the productivity of the shops. The study also finds that restrictions on the opening of shops on Sundays limit the growth in employment – in particular in large stores.

A study by Skuterud (2005) regarding the impact of lifting restrictions on the opening of stores on Sundays in Canada after 1998 documents an increase in employment and hours worked in stores, as well as the positive reception of the measure by the vast majority of consumers.

In Finland it is been shown that after a deregulation in 1997, according to Kajalo (2001), the shop trading hours were extended by shops with the exception of very small shops, and that the increase in opening hours occurred in particular in food stores. With regard to the Netherlands and their deregulation of 1996, and especially the increase in employment in the services sector documented by Burda (2000), the study of Breedveld et al. (2002) finds that 24 percent of small shops extended their opening hours while 43 percent of large stores, shopping centers and especially large food stores extended their opening hours in the evenings. In any case the study does not find any support for the establishment of a "24 hours a day economy"; it argues that the changes where rather limited if one takes into consideration the whole retail sector. Jacobsen and Kooreman (2005) report a significant shift in the shopping times toward evening hours, especially among unmarried women and mothers, following the deregulation of shop trading hours in the Netherlands. Also an increase in the time allocated to shopping is documented among all men and women. Other studies, like Burda and Weil (1998) and Goos (2004), even argue that restrictions on shop trading hours amount to a discrimination against households that cannot shop during their own working hours.

For Sweden Gradus (1996) argued for the deregulation of opening hours ahead of its implementation, citing the positive results observed in the Netherlands in particular. The experience of Sweden in also considered by Pilat (1997), along with the experience of other countries like Germany and the Netherlands. The study concludes that extending shop trading hours increases consumer welfare, boosts employment and leads to a small increase in sales. It also documents a shift of market share from smaller shops toward larger shops, especially among food stores; there is also evidence that in Sweden large food stores extended their opening hours significantly – unlike apparel stores, which more or less maintained the same opening hours as before deregulation. It should be added here that larger stores depend usually more on salaried labor, which justifies the resistance to an extension of trading hours of the owners of smaller shops, who tend to depend on self-employment rather than salaried labor. The same study finally concludes that limitations on the establishment of larger stores limit the reconstructuring of the retail sector, that they favor existing stores and, to the extent that existing stores are small, these limitations favor mainly small stores with a corresponding cost, of course, mainly for the consumer surplus and the limitation of innovation and productivity increases in the retail sector.

In Germany Kosefeld (2002) studies the period after the relaxation of restrictions on the opening hours in 1996 and shows that 61 percent of all shops maintained the opening hours that they had before the relaxation of the restrictions, and that only supermarkets and shopping centers adopted – with a large majority of almost 100 percent – new, extended, opening hours.

For Italy, Portugal, Spain, the Netherlands, Finland, Sweden and Greece Mitsopoulos (2007) used employment data for the retail sector and showed that in the wake of the relaxation of the restrictions on shop trading hours employment increased, and – after making some adjustment to reflect the negative conjecture in the case of Germany – part-time employment rose in both Germany and, in particular, the Netherlands as a result of a change in labor laws that affected the whole economy and not just the retail sector.

Finally, a report by the European Observatory for Small and Medium Enterprises (2000) illustrates how in rural areas, and when local habits are taken into account, shops tend not to extend opening hours if restrictions are only limited. It also finds that small shops use the ability to open on Sundays when this is given.

It should be added that in Greece small food stores (called "pantopoleia" that sell some food and that have often been transformed in mini-markets using loopholes in the existing legislation and a blurring of the legislation between these small shops and the kiosks (called "periptera") that face no limits on their shop trading hours as well as the lax enforcement of laws) operate late at night and on Sundays, without restrictions on their opening hours, while small stores in areas which attract tourists already stay open mainly during the peak season, as the law allows them to do so. Furthermore kiosks in prime locations often expand beyond the size that is foreseen by the relevant legislation, even if this means that they will fully block the pedestrian walkways, turning themselves effectively into small mini-markets. This proves that in Greece, as in the rest of the world, small shops will also stay open when it is profitable for them to do so. It also shows the tendency of the market to find ways to cater to the needs of consumers, including the need to have some access to food stores even late at night or on Sundays, even if it is in a rudimentary way that does not offer consumers the best value for money.

An issue that emerges from these studies is that larger stores, and especially food stores, use the ability to extend their opening hours, and that market share tends to shift to those sectors whose opening hours are not restricted. This shows that not all shops extend their opening hours after restrictions are lifted; rather, this decision is taken by individual stores after weighing their particular attributes. Also, according to works like Boylaud and Nicoletti (2001), but also by the European Observatory of Small and Medium Enterprises (2000), the fall in the market share of smaller shops is documented in all countries, irrespectively of the existence of limitations on opening hours. The main reason why consumers prefer larger stores seems to be the fact that the latter offer lower prices, especially for food, as is documented by Asplund and Friberg (2002), Aalto-Setala (2001), Cotterill (1993), Boylaud and Nicoletti (2001), as well as Pilat (1997). It must be noted here that often the investigation of the question of whether the expansion of larger stores leads to higher prices for consumers is based on a comparison of profit margins between larger and smaller stores, as the researchers do not have access to retail prices. But the conclusions drawn from such studies can be misleading. For example, Cotterill and Harper (1994), who use price data collected through direct surveys of product prices in US stores, find a negative relationship between prices and store size. Even though this result is not always significant, it persists in suggesting that larger stores often manage to offer consumers lower prices as a result of their increased productivity and efficiency, and at the same time manage to secure higher profit margins for themselves, when compared to smaller stores. According to the authors, this phenomenon may exist only up to a certain store size, as it seems that above a large store size this effect is reversed. Pricing, according to their analysis, seems to be related to market concentration and the existence, or not, or warehouse supermarket competition. Asplund and Friberg (2002) use a similar approach, based on retail prices, for Sweden. They also find that increasing the store size reduces consumer prices, and they reaffirm the finding that monopoly power tends to lead to increased prices. The available evidence therefore seems to suggest that ensuring that there is competition among larger stores is probably the most effective way of reducing retail prices.

The existing research provides also suggestions for the protection of the interests of small shops, if such protection were to be the goal of a government, especially in urban centers. Small shops' interests can, for example, be well served by a reduction in administrative costs. Scarpetta et al. (2002) find that increased administrative costs and burdens affect negatively the rate of starting new companies, especially small and medium ones. Also facilitations regarding access to finance and, in particular, more stringent barriers to the establishment of new and large shops in urban centers, under the condition of course that these barriers do not favor existing larger stores, seem to be more effective in protecting the ability of small shops to fend off the competition and allocation of market share to larger stores. According to the study of the European Observatory for Small and Medium Enterprises, access to finance is the second most important barrier faced by small and medium enterprises, and the importance of this barrier falls as the size of the company increases. The same study also accepts that a high administrative burden is proportionally more onerous for smaller companies. Boylaud and Nicoletti (2001) also argue that restrictions on the creation of new shops benefit existing shops, and that when these restrictions are aimed against larger stores, they limit the expansion rate of these stores. The authors also mention that this avenue is used by multiple countries that want to support smaller shops. Pilat (1997) makes a similar argument, using the example of numerous countries. It should be reiterated of course that these limitations come at the cost of slowing down the restructuring of the retail sector and the introduction of innovations that benefit the consumer and increase the consumer surplus – usually through the reduction of prices, but also in other ways. Such measures, it has to be stressed, are unrelated to shop trading hours, as the examples of Norway and Denmark, which allow only small stores to open on Sundays, clearly show.

To conclude, these studies show that extended shop trading hours are adopted mainly by larger stores, especially food stores, and that these extended hours are used by consumers, and especially women and working mothers for food purchases. The impact on employment is shown to be predominantly positive and no excessive shift toward part-time employment, to the detriment of full-time employment, is recorded. It also follows that if policy makers decide to hinder the expansion of larger stores in order to secure benefits for the owners of small stores, at a cost to consumers of course, other measures like limitations on the creation of large stores – especially in urban areas – may be more effective to secure this result. This is an interesting finding, as the debate on extended shop trading hours is settled in Greece because politicians, who usually are against larger stores, heed to the calls of small shop owners, who during these debates appear as a coherent and well organized interest and voter group, and who argue that extended shop trading hours will favor larger stores. At the same time, the benefits to consumers, and especially working parents, are conspicuously absent from these debates and, interestingly, are never highlighted by Greek consumer organizations, which also tend to take the position of small shop owners on this subject. This observation remains accurate even towards the end of 2011, and in spite of the fact that the conditionality program includes specific reform requirements for the retail sector.

Appendix 3
Basic Examples of Details that Degrade the Greek Business Environment

A3.1 Tax on raised capital

A3.1.1 The situation in Greece

Today Greece is one of only seven European Union countries that still levy a tax on raised capital,[1] which is 1 percent in the case of Greece.[2] Apart from the distortions that such a tax introduces even before an entrepreneurial undertaking is started, the way in which this tax has to be paid in Greece leads to an unnecessary increase of the administrative cost faced by Greek companies. In particular, the declaration for this tax has to be submitted ahead of the publication of the act that announces to the foundation, or change in, the capital of the company in the Government Gazette.[3] As a result the entrepreneur is forced to go to the tax authorities twice, for example during a company start up: Once to pay the tax on raised capital and once to obtain his tax number, after the related act has been submitted for publication in the Government Gazette.

A3.1.2 European trends

In 2006 the European Commission recommended[4] that member states reduce the tax on raised capital to 0.5 percent by 2008 and abolish it completely by 2010. This is because, according to the evidence available to the European Commission, this tax is among those that significantly distort the efficient allocation of resources in the economy and that reduce the competitiveness of the European economy.

It has to be mentioned that the related revenue was, until now, about 80 million euros a year, which is rather insignificant when compared to the annual corporate income tax paid. Recently the creation of a one-stop shop for start-ups implies that in their case the administration executes these procedures.

A3.2 Publications in the Government Gazette

A3.2.1 The situation in Greece

Making corporate information publicly available in Greece is done through the publication of the relevant information in the Government Gazette, as provided by the law on public and private limited companies.[5] The publication fees and the subscriptions to access these publications are set by a separate ministerial decree.[6] So far these prices have been relatively high, even though access fees have recently been abolished. This has contributed to the unfavorable ranking of Greece as far as the cost of starting a new company is concerned in the World Bank

Doing Business index,[7] as well as the European Commission documentation on company start-ups.[8] This cost is disproportionately high, especially for smaller companies.

For example:

1. Publication of the start-up establishment of a public limited company costs 470 euros, as does the publication of the annual profit and loss statement and balance sheet.
2. The interested third party that wants to gain access to the published information of private and public limited companies needed, until recently, to pay an annual subscription of 645 euros for electronic access.
3. To these charges the Greek government has added the obligation to notify the Company Register,[9] and to pay the related fee,[10] without abolishing so far the obligation to publish the information in the Government Gazette. In addition the obligatory subscription to the Chamber of Commerce has been burdened with a fee that effectively finances the new Company Register, even though this is not yet operational.[11]

The fee to publish information in the Government Gazette is burdened with significant payments to third parties (in particular, the employees of certain agencies in a process that seems to validate the predictions of Chapter 2)[12] and the obligation to annually publish the profit and loss statement and balance sheet in daily newspapers in spite of their publication in the Government Gazette.[13] In addition, companies carry an excessive and unnecessary administrative burden. In particular, for start-ups, the law specifically foresaw, before the recent creation of a one-stop shop, that the company has to take the form that is to be published itself from the current Company Register, that is the prefecture for public limited companies and the courthouse for private limited companies, and hand it in to the Government Gazette office located in Athens. In addition a public limited company has then go on to separately inform the tax authorities and then inform once more the register that it has completed this process.[14] Now a one-stop shop supposedly replicates these procedures.

A3.2.2 European trends

The European Commission proposes, as a good practice,[15] to avoid the requirement to publish information in the Government Gazette when this information has already been submitted to an electronic public register. In spite of pressure from the side of the EC/ECB/IMF to abolish these excessive burden on operating companies in Greece as part of a plan to create a 'Business friendly Greece' through the conditionality program, Greek authorities resisted the implementation of such measures at least till late 2011.

A3.3   Multiple notifications of a new hiring

A3.3.1 The situation in Greece

A company that has been registered as an employer with the private sector social security fund (IKA)[16] must still, when it hires a new employee, hand in separate forms to the Organization for the Employment of the Labour Force (OAED)[17] and the Force of Labour Supervisors (SEPE).[18] The hiring of the new employee is announced a third time to IKA once the quarterly form that is foreseen by the law[19] is submitted, even though this form is now being submitted electronically.[20] Law 3655/2008 foresees a single form and electronic submission, but the mandate of the law is not practised by the authorities yet.

A3.3.2 European trends

The European Commission has recommended the reduction of administrative burden that follows from the obligation of companies to provide information.[21] The Commission further recommends the electronic submission of information, rather than the submission of paper forms as is still the case with the OAED and SEPE. In addition it sternly discourages the repeated submission of the same information, as happens in Greece. It should be added at this point that the World Bank[22] and the European Commission clearly include the process of hiring a first employee to the benchmark according to which the cost of setting up a new company is computed. The European Council recommended[23] in 2006 that member states complete by the end of 2007 the setup of one-stop shops for the establishment of start-ups. It also clearly stated that the hiring of the first employee should require informing only one administrative body, while in Greece this process still requires informing three agencies (IKA, OAED and SEPE). The implementation of relevant reforms is included in the conditionality program, but had not been implemented till late 2011.

A3.4 Taxing the transfer of private limited companies

A3.4.1 The situation in Greece

In 2006 Greece introduced "objective" procedures to compute the "excessive profit," to use the wording of the related law, of private limited companies (EPE). On the "excessive profit" of these companies a tax of 5 percent is levied when these companies are transferred.[24] Furthermore, the "excessive profit" is computed on the basis of a complicated formula that takes account of the companies' profit and balance sheet items for the five years that precede the transfer. Providing the data needed for the calculation of the tax in turn creates a significant administrative burden on the transfer of a, usually medium or small, company. In addition, this backward-looking formula cannot incorporate anticipated developments that may substantially affect the value of the company. The new tax law, it should be noted, further increases and expands taxes on the transfer of companies, therefore further aggravating this situation instead of improving it.

A3.4.2 European trends

Since 2005 the European Commission has been clearly recommending[25] the facilitation of the transfer of ownership of small and medium companies, aiming to create in this way an environment that is more favorable to their development. The implementation of relevant reforms is included in the conditionality program, but had not been implemented till late 2011.

A3.5   Regulatory impact assessment

A3.5.1 The situation in Greece

The ongoing adoption of regulations and acts that increase bureaucracy and the administrative burden on Greek companies (as, for example, the ones previously mentioned) could be limited, at least partly, if these acts had to go through an open consultation and if an evaluation of the results of such consultation had to be carried out, along with the completion of a regulatory impact assessment.

Even though the government that was elected in 2009 has committed itself to have public consultations for all new laws, this declaration is not binding and only applies to laws, not to ministerial decrees. Also, it is not clear how the comments collected during these consultations are processed and evaluated. The prime minister of the previous government had issued a memo[26] to all ministries regarding the completion of regulatory impact assessments. However, even though these assessments were allegedly completed for most new laws (but not presidential decrees and ministerial decisions), they were never made public and the new government has not made any reference to this practice.

A3.5.2 European trends

Regulatory impact assessments are good practice. They are recommended to the EU member states by the European Commission,[27] which specifically refers to the evaluation of the impact regulations have on the economy, society and the environment. The implementation of relevant reforms is explicitly included in the conditionality program, but had not been implemented till late 2011.

A3.6   Certificate of origin for exports

A3.6.1 The situation in Greece

For exporters a certificate of origin is very important as it determines how the export good will be taxed in the import country. In most countries this certificate is obtained in rather straightforward ways. In Greece the certificate of origin for export goods is issued by the Chamber of Commerce that the export company is registered with. Ministerial decree 623/1993 (YA 6234/E3/9429, Government Gazette B818) reaffirms the process and states again that the exporter must register with the Special Registry for Exporters that is kept at the Chamber of Commerce that he is registered with. This obligation is specified in paragraph A for exports toward the then European Community, now Union, and in paragraph B for exports outside the European Union. It is further specified that the Chamber of Commerce certifies the bill of sale of the exporter after the exporter presents the required documents that have been previously certified by the customs service or at least after copies are presented that have to be subsequently certified by the customs authorities.

Registering with the Register of Exporters of course entails a significant administrative burden. A written request and certified documents have to be submitted along with the related, administratively set, fee that is foreseen by

Article 9, paragraph 2 of Law 936/1979 (Government Gazette A144). Following to the law, decree E4/1628/1988 set the fee for the initial registration at 5,000 drachmas (now rounded at 15 euros) while the renewal fee has been set at 3,000 drachmas. The required certificates include the certificate that the exporter is not bankrupt and copies of the criminal record of the representatives of the exporting company as foreseen by Article 25, paragraph 1 of Law 3229/2004 (Government Gazette A38)). The certificates have to be renewed every three months. The registration with the Register of Exporters has to be renewed every three years according to Article 25, paragraph 2 of Law 3229/2004. At this time the exporter has to submit a certified declaration that states that he has realized some exports during the previous three years. Of course, the related fee must also be paid. It has to be stressed that in March 2009 the Athens Chamber of Commerce called the Greek government to set up the chambers of commerce as one-stop shops for business start-ups, stressing the importance of such a measure for the Greek business environment. At the same time the Athens Chamber of Commerce publicly called all exporters that were on its register of exporters but that had not renewed their registration on time to do so within two months and, of course, pay the related fee.

A3.6.2 European trends

According to the World Bank index Doing Business in 2009 in the eurozone countries a standardized export procedure requires on average five documents. In Greece one extra document is needed and obtained in a separate procedure. This extra certificate can be identified as the certificate of origin. For example, in Germany it is issued after an initial registration electronically by most chambers of commerce, even though membership to the chamber is not a prerequisite. Also in many countries, but not in Greece it should be stressed, certified companies may also conduct the customs procedures on site. This means that in these countries no separate trip of a company employee or of the cargo to the customs is required. Finally it should also be noted that the requirement to obtain the certificate of origin through a separate procedure pushed down the ranking of Greece in the Doing Business report by one position, according to the "simulate reforms" option provided on the report's web page. The implementation of relevant reforms is included in the conditionality program, but had not been implemented till late 2011, even though a draft law has been presented and promises to abolish the Registry of Exporters, create a new registry at the Ministry of Development and create in 2012 a electronic single window to issue all documents exporters need. Details that would demonstrate real gains to doing business were not available by late 2011 though.

References for Chapter 5 and Appendices

Aalto-Setala, V. (2001), "The Effect of Concentration and Market Power on Food Prices: Evidence form Finland." National Consumer Research Centre, Helsinki, Finland.

Alexopoulos, K. (2009), "Master Plan of the Freight Transport and Logistics Market of Greece." Presentation at the 13th Panhellenic Logistics Conference, Athens.

Alpha Bank (2001), "The Irish Economy in the Euro Zone: Drawing Experiences for Greece." *Quarterly Economic Bulletin* 77: 12–18.

Alpha Bank (2008), "Trucks: Anachronistic Operational Framework and Inefficiencies of the Freight Transport Market." *Quarterly Economic Bulletin* 107: 46–63.

Alpha Bank (2010), "*Reestablishing the State. The Fifth Labor of Hercules.*" Quarterly Economic Bulletin 111: 19–32.

Anastasatos, T. (2008), "The Deterioration of the Greek Current Account Balance: Causes, Implications and Adjustment Scenarios." *Economy and Markets III* (6), Division of Economic Research and Forecasts, EFG Eurobank.

Arnold, J., G. Nicoletti and S. Scarpetta (2008), "Regulation, Allocative Efficiency and Productivity in OECD Countries: Industry and Firm-Level Evidence." OECD Economics Department WP 616.

Asplund M. and R. Friberg (2002), "Food Prices and Market Structure in Sweden." *Scandinavian Journal of Economics*, 104(4): 547–66.

D'Auria, F., A. Pegano, M. Ratto and J. Varga (2009), "A Comparison of Structural Reform Scenarios across the EU Member States – Simulation Based Analysis Using the QUEST Model with Endogenous Growth." European Economy, Economic Papers. December no. 392. European Commission, Brussels.

Azariadis, C and D. de la Croix (2006), "Financial Institution Reform, Growth and Equality," in Theo S. Eicher and Cecilia García-Peñalosa (eds.), *Institutions, Development and Economic Growth*. CESifo Seminar Series. Cambridge, MA: MIT Press.

Bassanini, A., S. Scarpetta and I. Visco (2000), "Knowledge, Technology and Economic Growth: Recent Evidence from OECD Countries." OECD Economics Department Working Paper no. 259.

Bassanini A. and S. Scarpetta (2001), "Does Human Capital Matter for Growth in OECD Countries?" OECD Economics Department Working Paper no. 282.

Blöndal J., J. K. Kristensen and M. Ruffner (2002), "Budgeting in Finland." *OECD Journal on Budgeting* 2(2): 119–52.

Boersch-Supan, A. and P. Tinios (2001), "The Greek Pension System: Strategic Framework for Reform," in R. Bryant, N. Garganas and G. Tavlas (eds.) *Greece's Economic Performance and Prospects*. Bank of Greece and The Brookings Institution.

Boylaud, O. (2000), "Regulatory Reform in Road Freight and Retail Distribution." OECD Economics Department Working Paper no. 255.

Boylaud, O. and G. Nicoletti (2001), "Regulatory Reform in Retail Distribution." OECD Economic Studies no. 32: 99–142.

Breedveld, K., M. Cloin and A. van den Brook (2002), "Shop Opening Hours: The Persistence of Time-Structures." The Annual Iatur Congress, Lisbon.

Bryant, R., N. Garganas and G. Tavlas (2001), "Introduction," in R. Bryant, N. Garganas and G. Tavlas (eds.) *Greece's Economic Performance and Prospects*. Bank of Greece and The Brookings Institution.

Burda, M. (2000), "Product Market Regulation and Labour Market Outcomes: How Can Deregulation Create Jobs?" CESifo Working Paper no. 230.

Burda, M. and P. Weil (1998), *Blue Laws*. Berlin: Humboldt University.

Burtless, G. (2001), "The Greek Labour Market," in R. C. Bryant, N. Garganas and G. Tavlas (eds.), *Greece's Economic Performance and Prospects*. Bank of Greece and The Brookings Institution.

Carey, D. and J. Rabesona (2004), "Tax Rations on Labour and Capital Income and on Consumptio," in P. Sorensen (ed.), *Measuring the Tax Burden on Capital and Labour*. Cambridge, MA: MIT Press.

Conway, P., D. de Rosa, G. Nicoletti and F. Steiner (2006), "Regulation, Competition and Productivity Convergence." OECD Economics Department Working Paper no. 509.

Conway, P. and G. Nicoletti (2006), "Product Market Regulation in the Non-Manufacturing Sectors of OECD Countries: Measurement and Highlights." OECD ECO WP 530.

Coopers and Lybrand (1996), "Road Freight Transport," *The Single Market Review Series*.

Cotterill, R. (1993), "Food Retailing: Mergers, Leveraged Buyouts and Performance," in L. L. Duetsch (ed.), *Industry Studies*. Enflewood Cliffs: Prentice Hall, 157–81.

Cotterill, R. and D. Harper (1995), "Market Power and the Demsetz Quality Critique: An Evaluation for Food Retailing." Food Marketing Policy Center Research Report no. 29, Department of Agricultural and Resource Economics, University of Connecticut.

Djankov, S., La Porta de-Silanes and A. Shleifer (2002), "The Practice of Justice." World Bank Development Report.

European Commission (1997), *Panorama of EC Industry*. Brussels: EC.

European Commission (2006), "Measuring Administrative Costs and Reducing Administrative Burdens in the European Union." Commission Working Document COM(2006) 691 final, 14.11.2006; EU (2002), *Benchmarking the Administration of Business Start-ups*, European Commission Final Report.

European Commission (2009), Sustainability Report 2009. European Economy 9(2009). European Commission Directorate-General for Economic and Financial Affairs.

European Observatory for SME's (2000), Sixth Report. European Commission.

Flinter, D. (2006) "The Transformation of the Irish Economy – The Role of Public Policy," in Hardouvels G. (ed.), *Growth Sources: Can Greece Follow the Irish Example?* Greece and Eurobank EFG: Kerkyra Publishing House.

Gibson, H. and J. Malley (2007), "The Contribution of Sectoral Productivity Differentials to Inflation in Greece." Bank of Greece Working Paper no.63.

Goos M. (2004), "Sinking the Blues: The Impact of Shop Closing Hours on Labour and Product Markets." Center for Economic Performance, London School of Economics.

Government of South Wales, Western Australia (2003), Review of Retail Trading Hours-Public Consultation Paper, Department of Premier and Cabinet.

Gradus, R. (1996), "The Economic Effects of Extended Shop Opening Hours." *Journal of Economics*, 64(3): 247–63.

Guichard S., M. Kennedy, E. Wurzel and C. André (2007), "What Promotes Fiscal Consolidation: OECD Country Experiences." OECD Economics Department Working Paper no. 553. OECD, Paris.

Hajkova, D., G. Nicoletti, L. Vartia and K-Y. Yoo (2007), "Taxation, Business Environment and FDI Location in OECD Countries." OECD Economic Studies No. 43(1).

Hardiman N. (2010), "Economic Crisis and Public Sector Reform: Lessons from Ireland." UCD Geary Institute Discussion Paper Series.

Hardouvelis G. (2006), "The Irish Experience and Lessons for Greece: Conclusions of Conference," in G. Hardouvelis (ed.), *Growth Sources: Can Greece Follow the Irish Example?* Greece and EFG Eurobank: Kerkyra Publishing House.

Hardouvelis G. (2008), Presentation for EFG Eurobank, Athens, GR.

Harlaftis, G. (1995), *A History of Greek-Owned Shipping: The Making of an International Tramp Fleet, 1830 to the Present Day.* London: Routledge.

Haugh, D., P. Ollivaud and D. Turner (2009), "What Drives Sovereign Risk Premiums?: An Analysis of Recent Evidence from the Euro Area." OECD Economics Department Working Paper no. 718.

Honkapohja S., E. Koskela, W. Leibfritz and R. Uusitalo (2009), *Economic Prosperity Recaptured: The Finnish Path from Crisis to Rapid Growth.* CESifo Book series. MA: MIT Press.

Høj J. and Wise M. (2004), "Product Market Competition and Economic Performance in Finland." OECD Economics Department Working Paper no. 413.

Høj J., V. Galasso, G. Nicoletti and T. Dang (2007), "The Political Economy of Structural Reform: Empirical Evidence from OECD Countries." OECD Economic Studies No. 43(1).

Jacobsen J. and P. Kooreman (2005), "Timing Constraints and the Allocation of Time: The Effects of Changing Shopping Hours Regulation in The Netherlands." *The European Economic Review* 49(1): 9–27.

IOBE (2006), *The Closed Market for Trucks of Public Use: Problems and Prospects,* Institute for Economic and Industrial Research, Athens, GR.

Kajalo, S. (2001), "Use of More Flexible Opening Hours in Finland after the Deregulation of 1997." 11th Conference on research in distributive Trades, Tilburg, the Netherlands.

Kaufmann, D. and A. Kraay (2002), "Growth Without Governance." World Bank Policy Research Working Paper no. 2928, November.

Kaufmann, D. and A. Kraay (2006), "Measuring Governance Using Cross-Country Perceptions Data," in Rose-Ackerman (ed.), *International Handbook of the Economics of Corruption.* Chelternharn, UK: Edward Elgar Publishing Limited.

Kaufmann, D., A. Kraay and M. Mastruzzi (2005),"Governance Matters IV." The World Bank.

Keizer, K., L. Lindenberg and L. Steg (2008), "The Spreading of Disorder."*Science.* OI: 10.1126/science.1161405.

Kelling, G. L. and C. M. Coles (1997), *Fixing Broken Windows: Restoring Order And Reducing Crime in Our Communities.* New York: Touchstone.

Koyama, T. and S. Golub (2006), "OECD's FDI Regulatory Restrictiveness Index: Revision and Extension to More Countries." OECD Economics Department Working Papers no. 525.

Kosfeld, M. (2002), "Why Shops Close Again: An Evolutionary Perspective on the Deregulation of Shopping Hours." *The European Economic Review* 46: 51–72.

Lambsdorf, Graf J. (2006), "Causes and Consequences of Corruption: What do We Know from a Cross-Section of Countries?," in Rose-Ackerman (ed.), *International Handbook of the Economics of Corruption.* Chelternharn, UK: Edward Elgar Publishing Limited.

Lamoreux, N. and K. Sokoloff (eds.) (2007), *Financing Innovation in the United States 1870 to the Present.* Cambridge, MA: MIT Press.

Leung, D., C. Meh and Y. Terajima (2008), "Firm Size and Productivity." Bank of Canada Working Paper no. 45.

Mitsopoulos, M. and T. Pelagidis (2007), "Does Staffing Affect the Time to Serve Justice in Greek Courts?" *International Review of Law and Economics* 27(2): 219–44.

Mitsopoulos, M. (2007), "Economic Implications of Regulation Regarding Shop Opening Hours," in S. Theodoropoulos (ed.), *Topics of Regulation Policy.* Athens: Gutenberg Publishing House.

Mitsopoulos, M. and T. Pelagidis (2009), "Economic and Social Turbulence in Greece: The Product Market are a No-Brainer, the Labour Market is Not." *InterEconomics. Review of European Economic Policy,* 44(4): 246–54.

Mitsopoulos, M. and T. Pelagidis (2010), "Greek Appeals Courts' Quality Analysis and Performance." *European Journal of Law and Economics,* 30(1): 17–39.

Mylonas, P and G. Papaconstantinou (2001), "Product Market Reforms in Greece: Policy Priorities and Prospects," in R. C. Bryant, N. Garganas and G. Tavlas (eds.) (2002), *Greece's Economic Performance and Prospects.* Bank of Greece and The Brookings Institution.

Morgan Stanley (2010). "European Economics – Whither Greece?" Morgan Stanley Research Europe, January 25.

Morrison, S. A. and C. Winston (1999), "Regulatory Reform of U.S. Intercity Transportation," in J. A. Gómez-Ibáñez, W. B. Tye, C. Winston (eds.), *Essays in Transportation Economics and Policy: A Handbook in Honor of John R. Meyer.* Washington, DC: Brookings Institution Press.

Neumark, D. and W. Wascher (2008), *Minimum Wages.* Cambridge, MA: The MIT Press.

Nicoletti, G. and S. Scarpetta (2005), "Product Market Reforms and Employment in OECD Countries." OECD Economics Department Working Paper no. 472.

Nicoletti, G. and S. Scarpetta (2006), "Regulation and Economic Performance: Product Market Reforms and Productivity in the OECD," in T. S. Eicher and C. García-Peñalosa (eds.), *Institutions, Development, and Economic Growth.* Cambridge, MA: MIT Press.

OECD (1997), *Liberalisation in the Transportation Sector in North America.* Paris, OECD.

OECD (2001a), *Competition Issues in Road Transport.* CLP (2001)10. Directorate for Financial, Fiscal and Enterprise Affairs Committee on Competition Law and Policy.

OECD (2001b), *European Conference of Ministers of Transport. Regulatory Reform in Road Freight Transport.* Proceedings of the International Seminar.

OECD (2003a), *Review of Regulatory Reform in Finland.* Paris: OECD.

OECD (2003b), "E-Government in Finland: An Assessment." OECD Policy Brief, September.

OECD (2007), *Economic Survey of Greece.* Paris: OECD.

OECD (2009), *Economic Survey of Ireland*. Paris: OECD.

OECD (2007, 2008, 2009), Employment Outlook. Paris: OECD.

Paterson, I., M. Fink and A. Ogus (2003), "Economic Impact of Regulation in the Field of Liberal Professions in Different Member States, Regulation of Professional Services." Final Report-Part3, January 2003, Study by the Institut fuer Hoere Studien, Wien for the European Commission, DG Competition.

Pelagidis, T. and T. Toay (2007), "Expensive Living: The Greek Experience Under the Euro." *InterEconomics. Review of European Economic Policy*, 42(3): 167–76.

Pilat, D. (1997), "Regulation and Performance in the Distribution Sector." OECD Economics Department Working Paper no. 180.

Rodrik, D. (2007), *One Economics, Many Recipes: Globalization, Institutions, and Economic Growth*. Princeton, NJ: Princeton University Press.

Scarpetta, S., P. HemmingsT. Tressel and J. Woo (2002), "The Role of Policy and Institutions for Productivity and Firm Dynamics: Evidence from Micro and Industry Data." OECD Economics Department Working Paper no. 329.

Skuterud, M. (2005), "The Impact of Sunday Shopping Deregulation on Employment and Hours of Work in the Retail Industry: Evidence from Canada." *The European Economic Review*, 49: 1953–78.

Spraos, G. (1997), "Committee for the Examination of the Macroeconomic Policy and Pensions: Contribution to the Public Debate." Submitted by the Commission for Pension Reform.

Sutherland, D. and R. Price (2008), "Linkages Between Performance and Institutions in the Primary and Secondary Education Sector." OECD Economics Department Working Paper no. 558.

Terrovitis, T. (2005), *Production and Use of ICT in Greece: Importance and Implications*. Study No. 60, Athens, KEPE.

Tinios, P. (2003), *Growth with Solidarity: A Framework for the Pensions of the New Century*. Athens: Papazisis Publishing House.

Notes

4 Efficiency and Quality of Justice in Greece

1. Taking into consideration only new cases introduced instead of all cases introduced, including those carried over from previous years, may be misleading because congestion may discourage the filing of new cases. Also it does not measure the complete workload facing a court at any period in time – a workload that includes also the cases pending from previous years. Finally, taking the sum of all cases remaining allows us to avoid the problem that arises when one has to distinguish between cases judged and cases withdrawn.

5 Strong Growth and Weak Institutions: The Greek Paradox Reconsidered

1. An indicative selection of related OECD publications is: (1) OECD (2007), "Going for Growth." Paris: OECD. (2) P. Conway, D. de Rosa, G. Nicoletti and F. Steiner (2006), "Regulation, Competition and Productivity Convergence." OECD ECO WP 509. (3) A. Bassanini and R. Duval (2006), "Employment Patterns in OECD Countries: Reassessing the Role of Policies and Institutions." ECO WP 486. (4) G. Nicoletti and S. Scarpetta (2005), "Product Market Reforms and Employment in OECD Countries." OECD ECO WP 472. (5) G. Nicoletti and S. Scarpetta (2006), "Regulation and Economic Performance: Product Market Reforms and Productivity in the OECD." OECD ECO WP 460. (6) P. Conway, V. Janod and G. Nicoletti (2005), "Product Market Regulation in OECD Countries: 1998 to 2003." OECD ECO WP 419. (7) A. Bassanini and E. Ernst (2002), "Labour Market Institutions, Product Market Regulation and Innovation: Cross Country Evidence." ECO WP 316. (8) S. Scarpetta, P. Hemmings, T. Tressel and J. Woo (2002), "The Role of Policy and Institutions for Productivity and Firm Dynamics: Evidence from Micro and Industry Data." OECD ECO WP 329. (9) S. Scarpetta and T. Tressel (2002), "Productivity and Convergence in a Panel of OECD Industries: Do Regulations and Institutions Matter?" OECD ECO WP 342. (10) G. Nicoletti and S. Scarpetta (2003), "Regulation, Productivity and Growth. OECD Evidence." OECD ECO WP 347. (11) OECD (2003) *The Sources of Economic Growth in OECD Countries*. Paris: OECD (12) A. Alesina, S. Ardagna, G. Nicoletti and F. Schiantarelli (2003), "Regulation and Investment." OECD ECO WP 352. (13) G. Nicoletti, A. Bassanini, E. Ernst, S. Jean, P. Santiago and P. Swaim (2001), "Product and Labour Markets Interactions in OECD Countries." OECD ECO WP 312. (14) P. Conway and G. Nicoletti (2006), "Product Market Regulation in the Non-Manufacturing Sectors of OECD Countries: Measurement and Highlights." OECD ECO WP 530.

Appendix 3 Basic Examples of Details that Degrade the Greek Business Environment

1. As foreseen by Article 23 of Law 1676/1986 (Government Gazette A204).
2. The way this tax is implemented in Greece is in violation of Directive 69/335/EEC of July 17, 1969 according the European Court of Justice (Case c-178/05, decision 2007/C 170/04).
3. This obligation had been abolished by Article 1, phrase 1 of Law 2941/2001. However this abolition "confused" the employees of the Ministry of Finance and Economy who recommended the return to the old law, which they were granted through Article 37 of Law 3220/2004.
4. The recommendation was made through Proposal IP/06/1673 of December 4, 2006 named "Indirect taxation: The European Commission proposes to abolish capital duty on the raising of capital."
5. For public limited companies the information that has to be published in the Government Gazette is determined by Law 2190/1920, as amended, and for private limited companies by Law 3190/1955.
6. They were last raised by Decision 184821/2006 (Government Gazette B1589).
7. www.doingbusiness.org.
8. Benchmarking the Administration of Business Start-ups. European Commission final report, 2002.
9. According to Article 1 of Law 3419/2005.
10. Law 3419/2005 clearly states that the obligation to publish in the Government Gazette remains. It also sets the fees for the Company Register.
11. The decree published in Government Gazette B198 of 2009 under number k1-141 sets a fee of 4 percent on the subscriptions to the Chambers of Commerce on behalf of the Central Union of Chambers.
12. Under Article 15ε, paragraph 2 of Law 187/1943: 3percent; under Article 11, paragraph 1Γ of Farmers Fund Law 4169/1961: 20 percent; under 'ΤΑΠΕΤ' Law 1878/1944: 5 percent; under Article 10, paragraph 1 of Law 187/1943: 2 percent; under Article 29 of Law 2339/1995 "Fee for the employees of the Ministry of Commerce (now General Secretariat)": 7 percent. These fees finance cash handouts to the employees of the General Secretariat for the Commerce. Respectively, the surplus income of the Government Gazette finances, according to the decision ΔΙΔΚ/Φ .1/2/29851/1995 (published in Government Gazette B992), monthly cash handouts to the employees of the Government Gazette as well as the employees of the central services of the former Ministry of the Presidency of the Government.
13. For public limited companies as foreseen by Article 26, paragraph 2 and Article 43β, paragraph 5 of Law 2190/1920, as amended. For private limited companies as foreseen in Article 8, paragraph 2 of Law 3190/1955.
14. These obligations are foreseen by Article 1, phrase 13 of Law 2941/2001, which added the phrase "γ" to Article 7β of Law 2190/1920, as amended.
15. This is already a recommendation in COM(2007)394 of July 10, 2007.
16. Article 6, paragraph 1, phrase α of Law 2972/2001.
17. Article 2, paragraph 2, phrase γ of Law 763/1970 (Government Gazette A283).
18. Article 16, paragraph 5 of Law 2874/2000 (Government Gazette A286).
19. Article 6, paragraph 1, phrases γ and ε of Law 2972/2001.

20. Decree Φ.2//2002 (Government Gazette B87).
21. Measuring administrative costs and reducing administrative burdens in the European Union, Commission Working Document COM(2006)691 final, November 14, 2006.
22. www.doingbusiness.org.
23. Council of the European Union, Presidency Conclusions, 7775/06, March 24, 2006, point 30.
24. Article 11 of Law 3522/2006 (Government Gazette A276).
25. Recommendation of the Commission and Proposal for a Council Decision (number 10), Integrated Guidelines for Jobs and Growth (2005–8), European Commission, COM(2005)141 final.
26. Letter (protocol number Y190) of July 18, 2006 from the Prime Minister's Office.
27. Proposal of the Council to Member Countries, COM/2005/0141 final.

Index

Note: Page numbers in *italics* refer to figures and tables.